"To Be an Author"

"To Be an Author"

∾

Letters of
Charles W. Chesnutt

1889–1905

∾

Edited by

Joseph R. McElrath, Jr., and

Robert C. Leitz, III

PRINCETON UNIVERSITY PRESS

PRINCETON, NEW JERSEY

Frontispiece courtesy of the Western Reserve
Historical Society, Cleveland, Ohio.

Library of Congress Cataloging-in-Publication Data

Chesnutt, Charles Waddell, 1858–1932.
"To be an author" : letters of Charles W. Chesnutt, 1889–1905 /
edited by Joseph R. McElrath, Jr., and Robert C. Leitz, III.
p.   cm.
Includes index
ISBN 0-691-03668-3 (cl : alk. paper)
1. Chesnutt, Charles Waddell, 1858–1932—Correspondence.
2. Afro-American novelists—19th century—Correspondence.
3. Afro-American novelists—20th century—Correspondence.
4. Afro-Americans—Social conditions.   I. McElrath, Joseph R.
II. Leitz, Robert C., 1944–   .   III. Title.
PS1292.C6Z48   1996
813'.4—dc20
[B]   96-32656

CONTENTS

⁖

PREFACE

༚

*Every time I read a good novel, I want to write
one. It is the dream of my life—to be an author!*

Chesnutt's journal, 26 March 1881

THE redefinition of American literary history in process since the 1960s has been guided by two goals. The first is the inclusion of numerous female writers who, despite the high visibility of many in their own time, were marginalized and even dismissed from serious consideration earlier in this century. Kate Chopin ably represents the former group of no longer "minor" authors whose considerable accomplishments are now acclaimed; the prolific and once quite popular nineteenth-century novelist Mary Jane Holmes still awaits her redeemer. The second goal is twofold in nature: the rediscovery of "minority" authors whose works once enjoyed some celebrity, and the identification of less successful ones doomed to obscurity from the start because handled by small presses outside the American publishing mainstream. This volume of letters is devoted to an already rediscovered African-American author, whose prose fictions began to receive widespread attention in the late 1960s and who now enjoys a much greater degree of fame than he did in the 1890s and early 1900s, when his works were both praised and vigorously criticized—even attacked—in the national press.

Short-story writer and novelist Charles Waddell Chesnutt (1858–1932) may, however, still prove to be a fresh discovery for many contemporary readers who are familiar mainly with his successors during and after the Harlem Renaissance, and who have not yet given sustained attention to the pioneers in African-American literary history. He is particularly important in that he was among the most visible figures of the group testing the commercial viability of African-American authorship at the turn of the century. Like Paul Laurence Dunbar and Booker T. Washington, Chesnutt was one of the first to succeed in "crossing the color line" into the Anglo-American publishing industry of the Jim Crow era, when his six books were manufactured, advertised, and distributed to a national readership by three distinguished firms from 1899 to 1905.

By 1905, though, Chesnutt had already reached the zenith of his brief career as a professional author. He had impressed his publishers and many liberal, reform-minded book reviewers interested in his original treatments of African-American experience. But novelty of subject matter, the artfully droll tone in many of his short stories collected in book form, and Chesnutt's fiery zeal in novels exposing the chicanery of Southern racists did not interest book buyers enough to advance his long-dreamed-of career as a professional author. The Cleveland attorney and head of a very profitable stenography business continued to write in free hours, but his lapse into relative obscurity in the literary world was, through his death in 1932, interrupted only by a brief flurry of attention when the NAACP awarded him the Spingarn Medal in 1928 for literary contributions to the African-American cause.

What it meant to be an African American attempting what Chesnutt did at the turn of the century, and how he both won a place in the limelight and then precipitated his own demise by writing exposés of racism for an unappreciative white readership—these matters are dramatically documented in this collection of his letters.

Chesnutt maintained files of drafts and carbon copies of his letters of 1889–1905 that dealt with his short stories, novels, and essays; many of the delivered versions were preserved by distinguished authors and social reformers such as George Washington Cable, Albion W. Tourgée, William Dean Howells, Booker T. Washington, and W. E. B. Du Bois. Those most important, in the editors' judgment, have been brought together here and, with annotations explaining what transpired in the ones not selected for publication, they tell the story of the extraordinary achievements of an individual determined to realize his version of the American Dream. Lamentably, they also chronicle the frustration of a lifelong quest to transcend the limitations faced initially by a man of color born free in the antebellum North, then by a largely self-educated provincial who came to maturity in North Carolina, and next by a sophisticated belletrist whose workaholic habits once promised a literary success at least equal to that which he enjoyed in the Cleveland business world. It would take almost a century before the recognition that he hoped for would occur—that is, before his 1901 novel, *The Marrow of Tradition*, would be viewed the way he saw it: as the equal of Harriet Beecher Stowe's *Uncle Tom's Cabin* and the now almost-forgotten *A Fool's Errand* of Albion W. Tourgée.

That is now a fait accompli. Chesnutt has at last arrived, and thus the need for this record of how an outsider did what was necessary to find a place in the pantheon of American literati.

ACKNOWLEDGMENTS

Of the many individuals who made this volume possible, Charles W. Chesnutt himself merits the premier position. Had he not been so businesslike an individual with a proper sense of how his papers documented history in the making, cultural historians would not enjoy the wealth of data that the editors of this volume have had the privilege of making available. Next in order of importance is his daughter Helen, who preserved the greater part of what her father bequeathed us in his files. The largest collection of these papers has been organized for the scholar in the Charles W. Chesnutt Collection at Fisk University; we are indebted to Ann Allen Shockley for permission to transcribe the letters therein and to Beth Howse for her kind assistance and especially her good cheer when performing "one last favor" several times. John J. Grabowski at the Western Reserve Historical Society's Library was also a major ally; we thank him and the Society not only for permission to use the many letters in their keeping but for easy access to their periodicals collection, which proved an indispensable resource when we were researching the explanatory notes.

For permission to transcribe other letters in collections, we thank the Beinecke Rare Book and Manuscript Library, Yale University; the Manuscripts Division, Library of Congress; the Howard-Tilton Memorial Library, Tulane University; the Houghton Library, Harvard University; the Archives and Manuscript Collection, University of Massachusetts, Amherst; the Berg Collection, New York Public Library; the Schomburg Center for Research in Black Culture, New York Public Library; the Chautauqua County Historical Society; the Rutherford B. Hayes Library; and the Fred Lewis Pattee Library, Pennsylvania State University.

Chris Suggs, who was the 1994–1995 Schomburg Fellow when we were conducting our research at the Schomburg Center, repeatedly made available to us his research expertise, kindly answering for us over the following months an inordinate number of queries; he never turned away a request and always found exactly what we needed. Leon Cahill Miller's guidance was invaluable as we analyzed the extensive George Washington Cable Collection at Tulane University. Louis R. Harlan generously gave his time and energy when we called upon him to display his comprehensive knowledge of Booker T. Washington's papers. Lawrence I. Berkove shared with us his knowledge of Midwestern history and geography. We are also indebted to Charles Hackenberry, whose unpublished "Guide to the Letters of Charles W. Chesnutt in the Fisk Manuscript Collection" facilitated our analysis of that collection. Lisa Cooper's meticulous transcriptions and her kind assistance with the verification of the same are gratefully acknowledged. Joel Myerson, Juanita Hayes, Genevieve West, Amy Johnson, Charles Duncan, Ann Leitz, and Sharon M. McElrath contributed much in various ways to the completion of this edition.

For financial support of this project, we are indebted to the National Endowment for the Humanities, Louisiana State University in Shreveport, and Florida State University. The Library Company of Philadelphia not only advanced the research by awarding the project an Andrew W. Mellon Fellowship but accelerated our progress by unstintingly making available the expert assistance of its staff. Phil Lapsansky, whose command of the Library Company's distinguished Afro-American Collection was constantly startling, was the apotheosis of the professional research librarian.

We hope that Chesnutt's literary executor, John C. Slade, without whose consent this volume would not have been possible, is pleased with what we have made of the materials in his charge.

EDITORIAL NOTE

❧

THE preparation of Charles W. Chesnutt's letters for publication—in a manner consistent with what surviving evidence indicates about his epistolary intentions and behavior—has proven a relatively simple matter. The forms sent, revised drafts, and corrected carbon copies reveal a meticulous wordsmith sedulously projecting the image of a learned individual, a man of letters of the old school who had read his Addison and Steele and demonstrated not only clarity of thought and expression but the sophistication requisite for fashioning complex, balanced sentence structures including multiple clausal qualifications and even qualifications of qualifications. The prose styles of Oliver Wendell Holmes and William Makepeace Thackeray come to mind; happily, the elaborations fashioned by Chesnutt are not so convoluted as to recall Henry James'. Chesnutt was in every sense of the term a Victorian gentleman who approached the writing of letters with an earnest desire to make each of his missives as stylish as it was substantive.

On remarkably few occasions he did slip, however. In each case, editorial emendation of the version mailed, or—if it does not survive—the carbon copy or draft most proximate to it, has been as conservative as possible. Noted below are the regularizations uniformly imposed upon the letters as they were styled for book publication; in the main our interpretation on a case-by-case basis of what Chesnutt intended to write, or have a typist transcribe, determined the ways in which we altered the source-texts. These silent emendations conveniently fall into the following categories, and the examples cited are representative:

Spelling errors. Corrected, for example, is the misspelling of "advice" when Chesnutt asked "on which of those two grounds your advise was based?" (Variant British spellings at the turn of the century do not include "advise" as a noun.)

Omitted words. The word "not" was omitted in "I do not know why I should undertake to write a Labor Day story" as Chesnutt actually *agreed* to write such a story; the sentence is emended accordingly.

Inappropriate word choices. The adjective "adequate" appeared where the adverb "adequately" was required in "It is my sincere desire to honor the memory [of Frederick Douglass], as adequate as the scope of this little work will permit." Also, in another letter a reading clearly not intended as a neologism—"disconcernment"—demanded emendation since "discernment" was as clearly required by the context.

Omissions of essential punctuation. When expressing thanks for counsel and the motivation to continue improving a manuscript, Chesnutt acknowledged "the incentive thereto your kindly advice and criticism, . . ."

The "thereto" may appear an inappropriate word choice or create the impression of a problem in sentence structure unless a comma follows it, making clear that "your kindly advice and criticism" refers to the "incentive" in question. There are many instances, however, in which Chesnutt either uses "light" punctuation or punctuates in the "rhetorical"—rather than grammar-based—manner, employing the comma to indicate only an emphatic pause in the rhythm of a sentence. When meaning is judged not to be threatened, such readings are allowed to stand.

Apparent Mistranscriptions. That Chesnutt's typists originated authorially unintended readings is clear and made even more apparent by his hand corrections of both the versions sent and carbon copies. But Chesnutt was not an infallible proofreader, and some carbon copies were not perfected. In this edition one reads "I think the book may serve a very useful purpose, beyond the pecuniary returns which it will bring to author or publisher. Fortunately the two things, in the case of a book are very nearly co-terminous, and there is every inducement from either point of view, to push a good thing along." In the uncorrected carbon-copy source text the second sentence differs dramatically: "Fortunately the two things, in the case of a book are very nearly co-terminous, is that there is every inducement from either point of view, to push a good thing along."

Normalizations of the letters' texts are minimal. A few of the letters close with "Sincerely yours" and like formulaic expressions, but the comma is lacking after "yours"; since Chesnutt does include a comma in the vast majority of cases, the editors have emended accordingly. The other normalization has to do with the titles of separate publications—for example, novels and musical compositions. When underlined, they are italicized in this edition. Chesnutt, however, most often puts such titles within double quotation marks, as one would works appearing in periodicals and collected along with other writings in books. All separate publications have been italicized here, as is customary in our time and was as well in Chesnutt's when previously unpublished texts were translated into print.

The letters have been styled for presentation. Unless otherwise indicated, they originated in Cleveland, Ohio, and the return addresses have not been included. The addresses of the recipients, too, are excluded; when they are significant, that information is given in the explanatory notes. Otherwise, the letters in their edited forms are complete or, as will be seen in some cases, as complete as the fragmentary source texts were.

Immediately following the texts of the majority of letters, the formal closing and the form of Chesnutt's signature in the source-texts appear. Many of the most authoritative forms of the letters, however, are not the documents actually sent; and, in this edition, the absence of a closing or a signature, or both, indicates the omission of the same in the draft or carbon copy employed by the editors.

Below each letter appears the identification of the nature of the source-text and its location. To the left of the colon is described the nature of the source-text:

ALS, autograph letter, signed
ADS, autograph draft, signed
ADU, autograph draft, unsigned
TLS, typed letter, signed
TDU, typed draft, unsigned
TCS, carbon copy, signed
TCU, carbon copy unsigned

To the right of the colon is the Library of Congress symbol for the location. The symbols used here and in the explanatory notes are:

CtY, Beinecke Rare Book and Manuscript Library, Yale University
DLC, Manuscripts Division, Library of Congress
LNHT, Howard-Tilton Memorial Library, Tulane University
MH, Houghton Library, Harvard University
MU-Ar, Archives and Manuscript Collection, University of Massachu-
 setts, Amherst
NN-B, Berg Collection, New York Public Library
NN-Sc, Schomburg Center for Research in Black Culture, New York Pub-
 lic Library
NWefHi, Chautauqua County Historical Society
OClWHi, Western Reserve Historical Society
OFH, Rutherford B. Hayes Library
PSt, Fred Lewis Pattee Library, Pennsylvania State University
TNF, Fisk University Library

MH:P, indicating the collection of the business records and correspondence of Houghton, Mifflin & Co. at the Houghton Library, appears only in the explanatory notes. If a source-text is incomplete, that is indicated in parentheses; if a typed letter, not the one sent, was kept by Chesnutt as a file copy, that too is indicated thus.

When, in the explanatory notes, one encounters quotations of or references to letters written by Chesnutt that are not presented in this volume, or letters received by Chesnutt, or nonepistolary documents, one should assume that they will be found at Fisk University in the Charles W. Chesnutt Collection, unless otherwise indicated by the location symbols identified above.

"To Be an Author"

INTRODUCTION

◆

In 1928, Charles W. Chesnutt was the recipient of the Spingarn Medal, awarded to him by the National Association for the Advancement of Colored People in recognition of his literary contributions to the welfare of the African-American community. That he had been selected for this honor was undoubtedly a surprise for many. It had been almost a quarter-century since his last book appeared. *The Colonel's Dream* (1905) had followed upon the heels of two other novels, *The Marrow of Tradition* (1901) and *The House Behind the Cedars* (1900). Behind them stood three more volumes. In 1899, his first and banner year as an author of books, he saw the publication of two collections of previously published and new short stories, *The Conjure Woman* and *The Wife of His Youth and Other Stories of the Color Line*; the third work to appear before the year's end was a biography, *Frederick Douglass*. His was an extraordinary achievement. But he had not become a widely celebrated or best-selling writer; and the announcement of the honor to be given him in 1928 could not have been expected in the Chesnutt household.

True, Carl Van Vechten had made much of his fiction two years earlier in his novel *Nigger Heaven*. The character Byron Kasson, a literary aspirant, feels a profound sense of obligation to the Cleveland author of an earlier generation who demonstrated what was possible for an African-American author determined to excel:

> He lifted *The Wife of His Youth* . . . and opened the pages for the hundredth time. How much he admired the cool deliberation of its style, the sense of form, but more than all the civilized mind of this man who had surveyed the problems of his race from an Olympian height and had turned them into living and artistic drama. Nothing seemed to have escaped his attention, from the lowly life of the worker on the Southern plantation to the snobbery of the near whites of the North.[1]

Chesnutt had changed his life. But, although encomiums almost as laudatory had appeared in periodicals at the turn of the century (and particularly those published in the one-time cauldron of abolitionist fervor, still-liberal and reform-minded Boston), such praise was more than rare by 1926.[2] Outside of the network of social reformers and intellectuals in which Chesnutt remained a participant until his death in 1932, and until the rediscovery of his writings that began in the wake of the 1960s Civil Rights movement, he remained at most a bit player on the national stage.

[1] (New York and London: Alfred A. Knopf, 1926), 176.

[2] For succinct summaries of commentaries on Chesnutt and reviews of his publications, see Curtis W. Ellison and E. W. Metcalf, Jr., *Charles W. Chesnutt: A Reference Guide* (Boston: G. K. Hall, 1977).

His prose fiction is now no longer excluded from the canon of national scriptures. Since the 1960s his major short stories have appeared in the American literature anthologies used on college and university campuses, and four of his six books are available in paperback. Along with the works of contemporaries Booker T. Washington and W. E. B. Du Bois, his books are more often than not "required reading"; as Paul Laurence Dunbar unfortunately shows signs of waning, Chesnutt is waxing. And yet, both within and without the academic world, he is still very much overshadowed by numerous authors; and there is no consensus on how he stands in relation to the larger and most significant trends in the history of American letters. Historians have yet to move beyond broad generalities about his being a protest writer related to the "local color" school of late nineteenth-century American fiction. Even though he has been more specifically described as a turn-of-the-century champion of the African-American cause, his identity has not assumed so precise a definition as those of Dunbar and Washington.

Chesnutt himself unwittingly came close to glossing his present, relatively nebulous status among the reading public as he ruminated over his particular predicament in his journal on 3 January 1881. He was a sophisticated, fair-skinned mulatto with Native American ancestry who could pass for white but lived on the other side of the color line. When twenty-two years old and residing in North Carolina, he was continuing to experience an identity crisis; he did not then feel as though he fit in socially any more neatly than he does now vis-à-vis the main categories in which our memorable literary artists have been situated:

> I occupy here a position similar to that of the Mahomet's Coffin. I am neither fish, flesh, nor fowl—neither "nigger," poor white, nor "buckrah." Too "stuck-up" for colored folks, and, of course, not recognized by the whites. Now these things I would imagine I would escape from, in some degree, if I lived in the North. The Colored people would be more intelligent, and the white people less prejudiced; so that if I did not reach *terra firma*, I would at least be in sight of land on either side.[3]

Chesnutt did move to the North, in 1883, and to some degree mollified his persistent problem of dual identity—African-American but at least seven-eighths white—as he chose to associate with other middle class "blue vein" mulattoes in Cleveland.[4] Over a century later, though, the literary historian can still legitimately pose the question he did: what was Charles W. Chesnutt? How should we construct a frame of reference appropriate for him?

[3] *The Journals of Charles W. Chesnutt*, edited by Richard H. Brodhead (Durham and London: Duke University Press, 1993), 157–58. Subsequent quotations of and references to Chesnutt's journal are documented according to entry dates.

[4] That is, "blue veins" were visible if one's skin color was light enough. In two stories collected in *The Wife of His Youth and Other Stories of the Color Line* (Boston: Houghton, Mifflin, 1899) Chesnutt described members of this caste within African-American society: "The Wife of His Youth" and "A Matter of Principle."

The first step toward the end of understanding what Chesnutt accomplished over the next decade involves recognition of the state of African-American literary achievement by 1893 and the unique role Chesnutt was playing as a representative of a minority group whose potential for belletristic performance was not yet recognized at large.[5] It was a time during which a white novelist and near-monomaniacal champion of the African American, Albion W. Tourgée, could, without risking offense, declare in a book review, "Aside from newspaper articles, some controversial pamphlets, volumes of sermons and speeches, the colored people of the United States can scarcely be said to have produced any literature." To Tourgée it was a lamentable but undeniable fact that he had so bluntly stated—one that now serves as a means of appreciating how extraordinary Chesnutt appeared to him. He continued,

> This is not surprising nor at all discreditable to them. . . . [A] race by law barred from the fields of literature for two centuries, needs at least the lifetime of a generation in which to produce good literary work. The wonder is not that it came so late but that it came so soon, and is of such simple, genuine quality. Except Mr. Chesnutt, [whose] brief [short stories] were something marvelous in their unpretentious realism, of which there are no more because prosperity in other fields has smothered his rare gift, hardly any colored writer has made a serious attempt in the realm of fiction, and not one has ventured upon good-tempered, keen, yet kindly, discussion of present conditions with any specific attempt at literary excellence.[6]

In 1893, then, there was articulated a point of view on the period that is still current outside the relatively small circle of literary historians who have recently drawn attention to black writers such as the two whose works Tourgée was reviewing when he made his typically magisterial pronouncement on the state of things in racist America. His praise was not fulsome but he did appreciate William E. Easton's *Dessalines, A Dramatic Tale: A Single Character from Haiti's History* (1893) and Anna J. Cooper's *A Voice from the South: By a Black Woman of the South* (1892). Had he waited one year more, he might as well have complimented William H. Anderson and Walter H. Stowers, whose *Appointed: An American Novel* was published under the pseudonym Sanda in 1894, though it is unlikely that he would have advanced a different thesis about the state of black letters.

In one sense, Tourgée was wrong. That year Dunbar's *Oak and Ivy* appeared;

[5] In 1931, Chesnutt described the situation thus: "At the time when I first broke into print seriously, no American colored writer had ever secured critical recognition except Paul Laurence Dunbar, who had won his laurels as a poet. Phillis Wheatley, a Colonial poet, had gained recognition largely because she was a slave and born in Africa, but the short story, or the novel of life and manners, had not been attempted by any one of that group" ("Post-Bellum—Pre-Harlem," *Colophon* 2, Part Five [February 1931], n.p.).

[6] "A Bystander's Notes," Chicago *Inter Ocean*, 8 April 1893, 4.

and, although Tourgée did not mention her, Frances Watkins Harper was far from a literary neophyte when her novel, *Iola Leroy*, was published in 1892. Further, those articles in "white" periodicals to which Tourgée referred were often first rate: the artfully fashioned essays of William S. Scarborough and Bishop Benjamin T. Tanner, for example, met any standard for evaluation of formal expository prose that one might apply. In fact, what one finds, when focusing upon black writing at and immediately after the turn of the century for the purpose of fashioning the explanatory notes in a collection of letters such as this one, is that a large sea of ink was being expended by blacks in books, pamphlets, and periodicals for black readers and the relatively few white ones who chose to pay attention to what was transpiring on the other side of the great divide in a segregated society. African-American culture had long since passed an oral stage of development by the 1920s; the Harlem Renaissance generation was reared in a densely verbal, print-suffused environment generated by blacks, though Chesnutt in his correspondence makes it clear that long after 1893 he shared Tourgée's estimation of its lack of "literary excellence."

Chesnutt was singled out for special praise by Tourgée in 1893 for two reasons. The first was that he was, as Van Vechten later indicated, a remarkably sophisticated stylist in the short stories that Tourgée had read. He wrote as a Victorian gentleman, careful to distinguish between the high formality of his own narrative voice and the rural Southern dialect of the black characters he described. Chesnutt, in short, fashioned prose fiction very much in the style of Tourgée's best-selling polemical novels *A Fool's Errand* (1879) and *Bricks Without Straw* (1880); although Chesnutt most often dealt with black subject matter, his aesthetic values were Tourgée's, from the 1880s through 1905, when his last novel was published. When he related in a letter to Van Vechten on 7 September 1926, "I suspect I write like a white man," he was deliberately understating the fact of the matter. With regard to tone, Mary Love, the black heroine of *Nigger Heaven*, put it best as she, without sarcastic intent, related to another character, " 'He's written several novels from a white point of view.' "[7] This was almost as frequently the case in his nonfiction works as well. The white social reformer who served as Chesnutt's mentor in the late 1880s and early 1890s, George Washington Cable, modeled the manner Chesnutt employed when directly addressing racism in the United States; and in many of Chesnutt's quite angry essays on the "Negro Problem" one finds little or nothing indicating his African-American identity.[8]

[7] *Nigger Heaven*, 104; the letter to Van Vechten is in the Schomburg Center, New York Public Library.

[8] For example, see "The White and the Black," *Boston Evening Transcript*, 20 March 1901, 13, wherein the description of racial discrimination in the South appears to have been offered by an especially literate and reform-minded Bostonian who had recently spent a month "in the South, mainly among colored people." Although a number of Boston readers would have been aware of Chesnutt's identity as an African American, the majority undoubtedly assumed that his article was only one of many written by New Englanders interested in the need for egalitarian reform in the South; the *Transcript* regularly focused upon the "Negro Problem" in the 1890s and early 1900s.

The other reason that Tourgée distinguished him from William Easton and Anna Cooper is that Chesnutt, although he was not yet a book author like them in 1893, had "arrived" in a way that they never would during their lifetimes. As did Anderson and Stowers, so did Cooper, Easton, Harper, and Dunbar (before 1896) find themselves compelled to publish their works in a way that guaranteed low visibility. Washington was a successful author not simply because of his omnipresence in periodicals as the "Wizard of Tuskegee" and his frenetic pace as a public speaker who displayed considerable charm. That would not have been enough, nor would his evident talent as a writer have sufficed. He achieved the stature he had as an author because a major firm, Doubleday, Page & Co., published and conducted a massive advertising campaign in behalf of *Up From Slavery* in 1901. He thus obtained what, for an African-American writer, was the sine qua non in the world of professional authorship: integration. As Paul Laurence Dunbar did shortly before, he succeeded in crossing the color line into the Anglo-American publishing industry. Cooper, Easton, Stowers, and Anderson were not able to leave their backwaters to plunge into the mainstream; rather, they quickly disappeared from sight because their books were printed by small presses with neither national distribution capabilities nor the financial means of attracting the attention of reviewers and book buyers.

Chesnutt in 1899, on the other hand, would do the same as Washington when the prestigious Boston firm, Houghton, Mifflin & Co., handled the first of the four books by him that it published. But, as Tourgée well knew, Chesnutt had accomplished over five years earlier a feat just as great. He had, beginning in 1885, successfully submitted his work to the S. S. McClure newspaper syndicate; and pieces by him were published in the magazines *Puck* and *Tid-Bits*. Then the transcending event occurred; the special connection ensuring access to the predominantly white national readership was fashioned. When his short story "The Goophered Grapevine" appeared in August 1887 in the magazine owned by Houghton, Mifflin, the non plus ultra that then was *Atlantic Monthly*, he established his claim to fame as the first African-American prose fiction writer to penetrate the sanctum sanctorum of Bostonian, and thus American, high culture. To his and the collective American mind, he thereby "counted." "Po' Sandy" confirmed his promise when it was included in the May 1888 issue; and it was followed by "Dave's Neckliss" in October 1889. Further, the magazine that Bret Harte made famous, *Overland Monthly*, had printed "The Conjurer's Revenge" in June 1889; and the liberal political weekly, *Independent*, published "The Sheriff's Children" in its 7 November 1889 number.[9] Tourgée had every reason to be impressed by such credentials

---

[9] The index of this edition directs the reader to the publication specifics of the works by Chesnutt cited in this introduction; see the page numbers in italics for such bibliographical citations. A convenient list of Chesnutt's publications is provided by William L. Andrews, *The Literary Career of Charles W. Chesnutt* (Baton Rouge and London: Louisiana State University Press, 1980), 279–86.

and to celebrate Chesnutt as an unique representative of his race, its most stellar performer.

Tourgée had misstated the case in one respect, though. As will be seen below, Chesnutt was quick to inform him in 1893 that he had not "smothered his rare gift" because of "prosperity in other fields." As convinced of his talents as a writer as he was of the business acumen that elevated him to Cleveland's black bourgeoisie by means of the very profitable stenography firm he started in the late 1880s, he was determined to thrive someday in a superior career, as a self-supporting, professional man of letters, a velvet-jacketed gentleman who lived by the more dignified labor of words.

A theme that runs through the letters presented here is that Chesnutt meant to secure his place in history by making good—so far as it was possible—the claim he enunciated as he unsuccessfully submitted a collection of short stories entitled "Rena Walden and Other Stories" to Houghton, Mifflin on 8 September 1891: his book, he proclaimed to its editors, would be "the first contribution by an American with acknowledged African descent to purely imaginative literature." He appears to have been sincere with regard to this actually unsupportable notion, an idée fixe implying that he, like most of his contemporaries, was unaware of the writings of William Wells Brown, Harriet E. Wilson, and Martin R. Delany. He was forever deprived of the right to make this claim by Dunbar when *Oak and Ivy* (1893) and *Majors and Minors* (1895) were followed by the book of poems to which William Dean Howells drew everyone's attention, *Lyrics of Lowly Life* (1896). In his introduction to this volume published by Dodd, Mead and Company, Howells, who had positively reviewed his second book, cited Dunbar as providing "the first instance of an American negro who had evinced innate distinction in literature."[10] And yet, despite the failure of Chesnutt's manuscript in 1891 and the subsequent diminishment of his literary efforts as he gave an increased amount of attention to stenography through the mid-1890s, he finally did establish a claim to special attention as a pioneer in 1899.

If not literally the first contributor to imaginative literature, he was at least the second African-American short-story writer to practice his craft in the context of mainstream publishing. While Chesnutt was attending to his business and giving his evening hours to literature, Dunbar had beaten him on two counts: Dodd, Mead marketed his collection of short stories, *Folks from Dixie* (1898), the year before Houghton, Mifflin printed *The Conjure Woman*; then Dunbar's novel *The Uncalled* (1899) appeared the year before Chesnutt's first, *The House Behind the Cedars*. These may have been disturbing developments for Chesnutt, who had missed his chance to assume precedence over all other African-American fiction writers, but we will never know whether they were: despite Dunbar's high visibility and Chesnutt's association with African Amer-

---

[10] "Introduction," *Lyrics of Lowly Life* (New York: Dodd, Mead, 1896), xiii–xx.

icans in the District of Columbia, where Dunbar was as well known an artist as musical composer Samuel Coleridge-Taylor, the only time he is even briefly mentioned in Chesnutt's letters through 1905 is in 1896. What could not be taken away from Chesnutt, though, was that he had finally prevailed as an author, unlike the majority of black writers, who could do no better than Pauline Hopkins when she placed her 1900 novel *Contending Forces* with Boston's Colored Co-operative Publishing Company. And if he privately brooded over Dunbar's alacrity and accalim, he could still console himself with the thought that his publisher was the superior one. The panache Chesnutt displays in his letters when referring to Houghton, Mifflin & Co. was warranted; one could locate himself in no better venue, since this Boston firm was at that time the publisher of the classic American writers Hawthorne, Emerson, Thoreau, Whittier, and Longfellow—and major nineteenth-century British authors as well.

One wonders how Chesnutt could have fared differently, given his pronouncedly competitive achievement orientation, his near-obsessional commitment to the goal of becoming a novelist who would equal Tourgée and Harriet Beecher Stowe, his native intelligence honed by decades of self-directed study, and his unshakable conviction that he possessed not just the artistic afflatus but oracular powers of insight into the "Negro Problem." As will be seen in these letters spanning the years 1889–1905, during which he energetically carved his niche in American literary history, Chesnutt was as doggedly persistent a pursuer of literary fame and fortune as he was an indefatigable advocate for those victimized by racism. Disappointments and rebuffs that would have crippled most men and women were regularly neutralized by an ego that was as resilient as it was distended by confidence in himself and a conviction of the rightness of the moral crusade in which he enlisted; on the several occasions that it seems to have been deflated, it was only a matter of time before it assumed its previous proportions and verve. Even at the close of the fifth act of the tragical drama witnessed in his letters, when the curtain made its final descent and the metier of publishing novelist was to be his no more, Chesnutt was ready for a sixth act and more, proceeding to develop new novels that would never be published in his lifetime. When his art was at its best, it was never quite as spectacular as the driven personality that generated it. The story that the letters collected here tell is as compelling as his best-wrought fictions, though readers familiar with Benjamin Franklin, Ralph Waldo Emerson, and Horatio Alger, Jr., will find the find the narrative that they comprise far from foreign.

CHARLES WADDELL CHESNUTT, who later enjoyed an upper-middle-class lifestyle, with daughters at Smith College, a son at Harvard, and a wife used to the assistance of domestics and to summering away from home, was born in more modest economic circumstances in Cleveland on 20 June 1858. Although the economic condition of his family remained working-class despite his father's entrepreneurial ventures, the Chesnutts still enjoyed a social standing higher than most African Americans' in that, as he took pains to explain a 1908 letter to a Dr. Park, neither of his parents was "shot free." It was a distinction that carried weight in black society.[11] The son of free, self-respecting mulattoes who had emigrated in 1856 from Fayetteville, North Carolina, and married in Cleveland in 1857, he was personally fortunate in another way that promised upward mobility. From his earliest years, he had access to formal education, which would, while he was still in his teens, enable him to rise above Andrew Jackson Chesnutt's station in life: his father drove a horse car in Cleveland and, according to family lore, served as a teamster in the Union Army during the Civil War. After the war, the parents and their three sons returned to Fayetteville, where Andrew's apparent father, white Waddell Cade, enabled him to establish a grocery store, followed by an equally unsuccessful transfer business; then he resorted to farming his own land to support his wife and, by 1871, six children. When Chesnutt's mother died that year, Andrew remarried within a short time, and his obligations continued to increase with each new birth.

Although his father served as a county commissioner and a justice of the peace before North Carolina was "redeemed" by the Democrats, Chesnutt found his first role model not in the expanding family circle but at school where he was proving to be a prodigy. Howard School principal Robert Harris, also the son of free mulattoes who had left the South before the war, was educated in Cleveland and returned to Fayetteville in the late 1860s. He became Chesnutt's mentor and provided a clear view of the middle-class life to which the young man aspired. In 1874, when he was sixteen, the student became an instructor and then served for three years as the assistant of Robert's brother, Cicero Harris, at the Peabody School in Charlotte, teaching in rural schoolhouses during the summer months. At approximately the same time, when seventeen, he began to keep a journal that now provides a remarkably detailed portrait of his personality through 1882—the year before he made his long-planned "escape" from the South and began his new life in the North.

What one finds in the journal is an intellectually, socially, and economically ambitious young man whose dissatisfaction with himself counterpoints with a dynamic self-conception whose limits are defined only by his racial iden-

---

[11] The "aristocrats of color" lifestyle enjoyed by the Chesnutts is fully delineated by daughter Helen Chesnutt in *Charles Waddell Chesnutt: Pioneer of the Color Line* (Chapel Hill: University of North Carolina Press, 1952). For biographical detail and interpretive insights, the editors are also indebted to William L. Andrews, *Literary Career*; Richard Brodhead, *Journals*; and Frances Richardson Keller, *An American Crusade: The Life of Charles Waddell Chesnutt* (Provo: Brigham Young University Press, 1978). The letter to Dr. Park is in the Charles W. Chesnutt Collection, Fisk University Library.

tification and white prejudice against it. With a candor that, in the 16 June 1875 entry, extends to a reflection in German on his intention to cease masturbating, a perfectionist of the Thoreauvian stamp exposes his shortcomings almost as fully as he celebrates his potential for greatness. He is annoyed that his father expects him to share his earnings to help support his family. When associating with rural blacks, he is perturbed that their limited vocabularies, intellectual torpor, and irrational beliefs make it impossible for him to have a substantive conversation with them. A black minister with a taste for alcohol elicits a judgmental response from on high, as does the emotional tenor of the fundamentalist Christianity in the black church. (In Cleveland, the Chesnutts worshiped with white Episcopalians.) Without restraint he characterizes the African-American students he teaches, their parents, and even his fellow townspeople in negative terms that bring to mind the stereotypes employed by nineteenth-century white novelists who are now known principally for their racism. In this vein in his journal, for example, Chesnutt describes his experience during an 1879 train ride when he and another "gentleman," apparently white, are informed that, as the first-class car is full, they must ride in the second-class one since their tickets are for that car:

> It was pleasant enough till we took on about fifty darkies who were going to Norfolk to work on a truck farm. They filled the seats and standing room, and sat in each other's laps for want of seats. As the day was warm and the people rather dirty, the odor may be better imagined than described. Although it was nothing to me, I could empathize with my fellow traveller, who stuck his head out of the window, and swore he would never be caught in such a scrape again.[12]

The qualification, "Although it was nothing to me," is telling not only of the poor rural environments in which he had worked as a teacher but of what he simply takes for granted about "darkies" so different from himself and the white gentleman with whom, it seems, he was "passing."

That he would record this observation is not surprising for another reason. The journal began in 1874 with lengthy entries on the absolute necessity for and particulars of personal hygiene, indicating that by the time he was sixteen or seventeen he had already begun in earnest to develop meticulously the traits that ensured entry into the world of the Harrises and beyond; the toothbrush was as much a passport to the larger world for Chesnutt as it was for the man who later became famous for his references to its power to effect socioeconomic change, Booker T. Washington. That train ride was a memorable and in many ways a defining moment for Chesnutt, in that over twenty years later he would use the scene in *The Marrow of Tradition*, adding a telling detail

---

[12] *Journals*, 112. The lengthy entry (108–19) is undated except for the year, *MDCCCLXXIX*, and it describes the trip that he made to the District of Columbia after his summer vacation from teaching in Fayetteville had begun.

when the mulatto hero of that novel, a physician named Dr. Miller who has elevated himself from the mass in the way Chesnutt had, finds it necessary not to stick his head out of the window but to step outside "upon the platform" for fresh air: "Miller breathed more freely when the lively crowd got off at the next station, after a short ride."[13] Both Dr. Miller and Charles W. Chesnutt were dedicated to helping "their people"; they shared that with the idealized African-American altruists so often featured in the novels by Tourgée that Chesnutt read. But, for Chesnutt, dedication to uplifting the group did not mean seeing himself as standing on the same plane with it.

A recurrent theme in the journal is that the author, who later gave a short story the subtitle "Why the Darkey Loves Chicken" and seriously considered using "De Noo Nigger" as a title, is an African American.[14] He is ineluctably stuck in the same "car" with others to whom he is related by blood, but he never identifies with "them" except when imagining himself as either a spokesperson for the race or as the champion who would "show to the world that a man may spring from a race of slaves, and yet far excel many of the boasted ruling race." Chesnutt continued in this visionary vein on 12 October 1878, "If I can exalt my race, if I can gain the applause of the good, and the approbation of God, the thoughts of the ignorant and prejudiced will not concern me." If he could not be the new messiah, he would at least serve his race and himself as one of the special class of African Americans later described by Du Bois as "the talented tenth." No wonder, in the 1881 journal passage quoted above, Chesnutt concluded that the African Americans he knew viewed him as too "'stuck-up' for colored folks." No wonder that, on 25 June 1880, he should echo Matthew 13:57: "'A prophet is not without honor save in his own country and among his own people,' and I get a great deal more of encouragement from others than from home folks." As in the biblical lands, so in Fayetteville: those uplifted, or to be uplifted by a man assigned that mission, do not always appreciate their deliverer.

Chesnutt did not, of course, develop similar attitudes toward African Americans like himself. About the Harrises, who had returned to the South to educate their people, there were no complaints, and Chesnutt succeeded Cicero Harris as principal in Charlotte in 1877. They appreciated and promoted him; and, the same year, he was called back to Fayetteville for a much better position at the newly established State Colored Normal School. He was moving up the ladder, intellectually, economically, and socially; and in 1878 he could afford to marry the nineteen-year-old Susan Perry, the daughter of a prosperous barber who would later be pictured as the well-heeled, "keen-eyed mulatto" William Nichols in *The Colonel's Dream*.[15] As several literary critics have

---

[13] *The Marrow of Tradition* (Boston: Houghton, Mifflin, 1901), 60–61.

[14] "A Victim of Heredity" was the main title of the former; the latter retained its original title, "Mars Jeems's Nightmare."

[15] New York: Doubleday, Page, 1905, 82.

noted, there are in the Chesnutt canon very few exceptions to the rule: mulattoes like the Harrises, Mr. Perry, and Chesnutt himself comprise the superior caste among African Americans. Talent made the difference, and thus Uncle Julius, the gifted raconteur featured in all of the stories in *The Conjure Woman*, was transformed into a mulatto in 1898 when Chesnutt made his final revisions of his manuscript. The match with the well-educated Susan, who taught at the Howard School, certainly did not hurt Chesnutt's chances for advancement within his circle. At twenty-two, he became one of the preeminent African-American educators in North Carolina, assuming the position of head of the Normal School that Robert Harris had previously held.

Chesnutt had become, in short, one of Fayetteville's most distinguished citizens, which meant, of course, that he had successfully cultivated relationships with the important white residents whose approval was necessary for him to be appointed to that position. George H. Haigh, the white owner of a bookstore frequented by Chesnutt, was a supporter, despite the journal's record of his attitude toward "uppity" domestics who were both reluctant to work as hard as they should and predisposed to stealing from their employers. Dr. T. D. Haigh corresponded with Chesnutt long after he had settled in Cleveland, and was a member of the board that oversaw the Normal School. Also kindly disposed toward Chesnutt was "Professor" Emil Neufeld, who declared that he would not turn away Chesnutt as a student of French and German—even if the association with an African American meant the loss of twenty paying students who were white. According to the journal, Robert Harris told Chesnutt of a conversation with Neufeld in which the teacher had made clear his sympathy: on 25 June 1880, Chesnutt wrote, Neufeld "recognized my ability and accomplishments, and felt that my lot was a hard one, to be cut off from all intercourse with cultivated society, and from almost every source of improvement." As he would in the Cleveland business world and in his cordial relations with the publishers and editors of Boston and New York City, Chesnutt earned the respect and admiration of whites who saw him as one who had, indeed, "exalted" his race. The more liberal-minded found him the embodiment of their fondest hopes for the African American; to George Washington Cable in the late 1880s, Classics scholar Scarborough and Chesnutt were the proof positive of his passionately made claims for the potential equality of all African Americans. The more conservative, too, had nothing to lose by acknowledging this Franklinesque achiever who embodied the virtue of Emersonian self-reliance when displaying his superiority to others of his race. The "Negro Problem" might continue to anger, depress, and— because of its persistent duration—bore the whites with whom Chesnutt came in contact; but gentlemanly Chesnutt himself was an ever-dependable "feel good" stimulus for them.

Privately, however, Chesnutt bristled. The race with which he was linked demeaned him by association. "Passing" as a white man was the means of escape he identified in his journal; therein and in the 1901 article "The White and the Black," he described instances in which he had done so. But the marriage of an honorable man to a woman who was in appearance more obviously African American, the birth in 1879 of Ethel, who took after her mother, and the arrival of the fairer Helen in 1881 closed that avenue. Whites did help him; and he appreciated it. Yet despite his physical appearance, his arduously crafted personality traits, and the polished manners that put him on an equal footing in the most polite society, he would always be an outsider to the "better class of people" to which he obviously belonged but from which he was excluded in Fayetteville. On 7 March 1882, his frustration peaked as T. D. Haigh, Emil Neufeld, and other whites stood revealed for what they actually were:

> I hear colored men speak of their "white friends." I have no white friends. I could not degrade the sacred name of "Friendship" by associating it with any man who feels himself too good to sit at table with me, or sleep in the same hotel. True friendship can only exist between men who have something in common, between equals in something, if not in everything; and where there is respect as well as admiration.

As another self-conscious journalist, Thoreau, did when imagining in *Walden* a world of finer, fairer, and fuller proportions than the too-limiting one before him, Chesnutt then waxed the Platonic idealist by imagining a higher realm of white companionship that he hoped to know someday:

> I hope yet to have a friend. If not in this world, then in some distant future eon, when men are emancipated from the grossness of flesh, and mind can seek out mind; then shall I find some kindred spirit, who will sympathize with all that is purest and best in mine, and will cement a friendship that shall endure throughout the ages.
>
> I get more and more tired of the South. I pine for civilization, and "equality." . . . I think I could serve my race better in some more congenial occupation. And I shudder to think of exposing my children to the social and intellectual proscription to which I have been a victim.

Paradise—civilization, equality, even friendships with whites—was in the North of his imagination. The South, or more precisely Southern whites, had wounded him; and, as both his correspondence and his works written for publication show, he never forgot it nor saw reason to forgive them.

IN 1883, Chesnutt resigned from his position at the Normal School, departing alone for New York City, where he was employed reporting financial news for Dow, Jones, and Company, and where he also wrote a financial-news column for the *New York Mail and Express*. Whether he was "passing" is not known for a certainty, but it is unlikely that the civilization, equality, and friendships with whites of which he had dreamed were immediately made available to a self-proclaimed African American there. Indeed, even though Chesnutt had obtained employment as a writer, he soon found New York incompatible. After six months he left for Cleveland, where cousin John P. Green lived. Green was a state legislator and a friend of John D. Rockefeller, who was sympathetic to African Americans and who wielded influence with the Nickel Plate Railroad, which employed several black stenographers. Such connections undoubtedly had much to do with Chesnutt finding a bookkeeping position there. Chesnutt had made the right move. When transferred to the legal department, he took the opportunity to read law while working as a stenographer for Judge Samuel Williamson, and passed the bar examination in 1887. In the meantime, his son Edwin was born, and the Chesnutt family was reunited in Cleveland in 1884. Further, a part-time writing career had been formally initiated in December 1885 with the publication of a short story into which Chesnutt had poured his Southern frustrations. "Uncle Peter's House" made clear to Cleveland's *News and Herald* readership how the South made it impossible for an African American to do what Chesnutt was gradually accomplishing. In 1887, he began practicing law, in some as yet undetermined way associated with the white law firm, Henderson, Kline and Tolles. At the same time he advertised himself in the city directory as a stenographer, initiating the line of work that would be his principal occupation through the rest of his life. An equally crucial development also occurred that year when he learned that the *Atlantic Monthly* wished to publish a more artful and less lugubrious story than "Uncle Peter's House."

That Chesnutt had mellowed, putting his Southern discontent behind him, is what one might easily infer from a reading of "The Goophered Grapevine." The overwhelmingly white readership of the *Atlantic* was treated to a jolly tale that had to bring Joel Chandler's Harris's delightful Uncle Remus stories to mind, featuring as it did an equally extravagant storyteller, Uncle Julius McAdoo, whose interest was not in anthropomorphized rabbits and foxes but in fabulous effects wrought by African-American conjurers during the old plantation days. It was so congenial and light-hearted a performance that no one could have suspected its author had, only four years earlier, fled the South, following the drinking gourd as resolutely as a runaway slave. None could have imagined the tension that was his as, over several years, he conspired with his journal on an escape plan.

The flight to New York City in 1883 was not a spur-of-the-moment decision, nor even his first attempt at self-liberation. On 31 July 1875, after confiding to his journal that he had "passed" twice that day, he announced pugnaciously, "I believe I'll leave here and pass anyhow, for I am as white as any of them." He declared again on 12 October 1878, "I will go North"; and on 23 April 1879, Chesnutt recorded Dr. Haigh's belief that he could succeed there. On the same day he sketchily described the scenario that he tried in 1883:

> I will go to the Metropolis, or some other large city, and like Franklin, Greely [*sic*] and many others, there I will stick. . . . I can get employment in some literary avocation, or something leading in that direction. I depend principally upon my knowledge of stenography, which I hope will enable me to secure a position on the staff of some good newspaper, and then,—work, work, work! I will trust in God and work. I will test the social problem. I will see if it's possible for talent, wealth, genius to acquire social standing and distinction.

His study of stenography begun in 1875 was, he fully realized well before 1879, the ticket North, though he was wrong in thinking that journalism was the means to all that he wanted. And what he wanted requires comment, in that the multiplicity and grandeur of his expressed desires illuminate the origins of Chesnutt's complex, sometimes conflicted, states of mind seen in his correspondence of 1889–1905. His letters make it clear that he continued to want it all: wealth, social standing, and the recognition of not just his talent but his genius. But there was a fly in the idealist's ointment by 1879. These desires were, on the face of them, selfish. The noble individual Chesnutt aspired to be—and would receive recognition for becoming—could not be so basely motivated by self-interest. The solution to this problem was at hand: as he concludes the above passage, he elevates his self-aggrandizing quest to a higher plane. "This work I shall undertake not for myself alone, but for my children, for the people with whom I am connected—for humanity!" Three steps, that is, will effect his altruistic ascent. First, what he accomplishes will be done for the family. Second, he will serve others of his racial background by achieving success, "exalting" them thus. Third, he will become the benefactor of humanity at large—a wealthy, socially prominent, and universally recognized genius-philanthropist. Although Chesnutt does not refer to Emerson in his journal, his ideal self resembles the independently wealthy, universally admired, and powerfully influential sage of Concord, as much as it differs from that of the socially unambitious and radically anti-materialistic Thoreau.

Immediately after a later journal entry dated "*April 79*," Chesnutt described the unprecedented step he had taken toward these goals. He fashioned an account of "a visit to the City of Washington. . . . By Charles Waddell Chesnutt, Professor of Reading, Writing, Spelling &c in the State Colored Normal School of N.C." After the school term had ended, that is, he went to the District of Columbia, where he contacted acquaintances who might help him find employment.[16] But a government job was not to be had: "The places are all, or nearly all, gifts of political favoritism, and without great influence and some cheek, ability amounts to nothing." Further, his ability was not sufficient: he discovered that he did not have the stenographic expertise necessary for him "to become an official reporter." And so his dream was modified. What he

---

[16] His experience in the second-class car on his way North was described above; see n. 12.

resolved was to return to Fayetteville, develop a greater appreciation of what he already had, and continue his advancement in the field of education. "By industry and economy I shall raise myself still higher in the estimation of my fellow-citizens, and with a permanent situation and an increased salary I hope to be somewhat independent in five or ten years." He foreswore acting as an "aerial architect," determined not to allow his "active imagination" to look into the future any farther than six months. He had learned his lesson.

What he actually did, in fact, was continue to pine for the Canaan north of the Carolinas and to perfect his stenographic skill. He also refined his conception of how it was possible to have it all.

Although stenography remained the obvious means of leaving Fayetteville, and though it served him well when he went to New York and Cleveland, it soon came to pass that the "literary avocation" of the stenographer-journalist figure imagined in 1879 was displaced by the more magnificent one of novelist. The journal preserves three major phases in the development of the self-conception that would be his through 1905. On 26 March 1881 he recorded the greater part of it that had evolved since early 1880. As he finished reading *Vanity Fair* that day, it was clear he was still thinking in terms of fortune and fame. Among all of the things that he could have said about this impressive work by Thackeray, what he noted had more to do with his own need for recognition than anything else. This "first great novel" by Thackeray was important because it was the one with which "he made himself a reputation." The revery that followed reveals Chesnutt once again a thrall to his "active imagination." It also provides an important key to understanding the autobiographical narrative embedded in Chesnutt's correspondence, as he continued after 1889 to look beyond stenography and law to the sublimest of possible gratifications:

> Every time I read a good novel, I want to write one. It is the dream of my life—to be an author! It is not so much the *monstrari digito* [recognition by others], though that has something to do with my aspirations. I want fame; I want money; I want to raise my children in a different rank of life from that which I sprang from. In my present vocation, I would never accumulate a competency, with all the economy and prudence, and parsimony in the world. . . . But literature pays—the successful. There is a fascination about this calling that draws a scribbler irresistibly toward his doom.

It is likely that readers of his letters will at least once wonder why, given the frustrations he faced, Chesnutt did not simply throw in the towel and enjoy the "competency" that his stenography business did provide him. After all, by the mid-1890s, a well-heeled Chesnutt no longer had the welfare of his children as a motivation for literary production; in 1899 he could afford to announce to editor Walter Hines Page that he had retired from business to

devote all of his time to writing. He did so, however, on the assumption articulated here: literature pays the successful, and in October 1899 he was looking
forward to the royalties for not one but three books that appeared before the
end of the year. In his mind, he would soon be richer than the stenographer
who had amassed enough capital to become a full-time author, or he would at
least break even within a few years.

The initiation of this line of thought is, happily, dated in the journal. On 16
March 1880, Chesnutt—whose starting salary as the head of the Normal
School would be the handsome sum of $75 per month—was astonished:
"Judge Tourgée has sold the 'Fool's Errand,' I understand, for $20,000." The
mind-boggling figure, he reflected, did not, of course, include royalties on
sales. In a lengthy rumination on what was involved in Tourgée making "himself rich and famous" by writing in such a charmingly didactic way about the
abuse of African Americans in the South, Chesnutt spells out the logic that
possessed him through 1905:

> why could not a colored man, who has lived among colored people all his
> life; who is familiar with their habits, their ruling passions, their preju-
> dices; their whole moral and social condition; their public and private
> ambitions; their religious tendencies and habits;—why could not such a
> colored man who knew all this, and who, besides, had possessed such
> opportunities for observation and conversation with the better class of
> white men in the south as to understand their modes of thinking; who
> was familiar with the political history of the country, and especially with
> all the phases of the slavery question;—why could not such a man, if he
> possessed the same ability, write a far better book about the South than
> Judge Tourgée or Mrs. Stowe has written? Answer who can!

Here was how he could gain all that he wanted in one fell swoop. Self-interest
would be served: *Uncle Tom's Cabin* and *A Fool's Errand* had made their authors wealthy celebrities. The need for heroically humanitarian behavior
would be met, as well: both works were designed to redeem mankind and had
been acknowledged as having most definitely contributed to the ongoing per-
fection of the human race. Huge earnings and fame had tainted neither the
authors nor their holy purpose. And, in the Gilded Age imagination of a
largely self-educated young man in the hinterlands, who had to know more
about the South than the woman from New England and the Ohioan who
lived for only a short while in North Carolina, it was self-evident that he could
even more dramatically show how the illumination of moral principle and
the taking of hefty profits were compatible motivations. On 29 May 1880,
Chesnutt added a final refinement. The emphasis thus far had been, perhaps,
too worldly; it was time to right the balance between profit and principle. He
assured his journal that any perception of ignobility was unwarranted: "If I do

write, I shall write for a purpose, a high, holy purpose. . . . The object of my writings would be not so much the elevation of the colored people as the elevation of the whites"; he was ready to "head a determined, organized crusade" against racism.

This did not show in 1887 in "The Goophered Grapevine." But that was a part of the 29 May 1880 plan, whereby Chesnutt in his writings would mask his condescension toward unregenerate white readers, affably befriend them and win their confidence, and by insinuation effect a "moral revolution." The "trumpet tones" used by the abolitionists would not work: "the subtle almost indefinable feeling of repulsion toward the negro, which is common to most Americans—and easily enough accounted for—, cannot be stormed and taken by assault; the garrison will not capitulate: so their position must be mined, and we will find ourselves in their midst before they think it." He would win "social recognition and equality" for the African American by accustoming "the public mind to the idea; and while amusing them . . . lead them on imperceptibly, unconsciously step by step to the desired state of feeling."

Those already familiar with "The Goophered Grapevine" and the later stories in which Uncle Julius spins his fantastic yarns will note the affinity between him and his creator. Julius addresses his white auditors, John and Annie, with a similar intent. His storytelling is pragmatic, wholly unaffected by any folderol about art for art's sake. Almost every time Julius holds forth, his purpose is the manipulation of John and Annie to serve his own needs: personal profit, the acquisition of an unfinished ham, the employment of a relative, and so on. Chesnutt's ends were, in part, inarguably more noble: the diminution of dislike for both mulattoes and what he termed the "full-blooded"; and the recognition of the civil rights guaranteed African Americans by the United States Constitution, particularly the fourteenth and fifteenth amendments. This cannot be discounted. Still, he was, in fact, acting as Julius did, using his art for the purpose of seduction; and his method worked marvelously well. His greatest strength as an author is to be seen in his Irvingesque ability to charm the short-story reader; and, like Irving, he took great pride in his skill as a wry humorist. Had he abided by this method throughout his writing career, had he not succumbed to the temptation to take up the trumpet of the abolitionists that he correctly judged anachronistic in 1880, his "tragic mulatto" novel, The House Behind the Cedars, might have fared better in the marketplace in 1900. As it was, the "soft-sell" strategy was wholly cast aside in 1901 as his rage over white chicanery in North Carolina became evident on virtually every page of The Marrow of Tradition. In his first published short story of 1885, "Uncle Peter's House," Chesnutt's anti-Southern animus was expressed with restraint, his tone melancholic rather than choleric. His last published novel, The Colonel's Dream, revealed that his enmity had become so strong that it could not be contained in 1905, when it was essential that he make up for the disappointing sales of *Marrow*. This fictional denunciation of incorrigibly base North Carolina ends with the once-idealistic white hero who tried to improve it returning forever to the North, as did Tourgée's no longer naïve principal almost a quarter century earlier, when he terminated a like "errand" to the same state. That Chesnutt named his *idéaliste manqué* hero Colonel French seems his testimony to the recently deceased Tourgée, whose alter ego in the autobiographical *Errand* was a "fool" with a Gallic surname, Servosse.

Weak sales of all three novels account for the terribly ironic way in which this collection of letters ends. By 1905 Chesnutt had become a name, to be sure. When the literary world then celebrated Mark Twain's seventieth birthday at Delmonico's Restaurant in New York City, a partner in the Doubleday, Page firm that had published *The Colonel's Dream*, Walter Hines Page, integrated the gathering by securing Chesnutt an invitation. In the company of George Washington Cable, William Dean Howells, Richard Watson Gilder, and numerous other luminaries, Chesnutt indeed "exalted" his people. As will be seen in the letter with which this volume concludes, he had arrived in the grand manner; but his career as a professional author had already run its course. After he returned to Cleveland, he began his lapse into obscurity.

As THIS collection begins in 1889 with a long series of letters addressed to George Washington Cable, Chesnutt could not, of course, anticipate the arc of his rise and fall traceable by late 1905, or foresee the crucial role Cable would play in determining the unhappy outcome of his writing career. That he was already an *Atlantic* author was the card Chesnutt had recently played to get the attention of the well-known writer and lecturer when he visited Cleveland to deliver a speech. His trump card, however, was the announcement that belied his appearance: this *Atlantic* author disclosed that he was a "colored man"; and that rivetted Cable's interest on him.[17] He thus became Chesnutt's mentor, counseling him on the revision of his long short story "Rena Walden," which proved the Ur-text of *The House Behind the Cedars* years later, when Walter Hines Page became Chesnutt's advisor.

Chesnutt, it is soon clear in his correspondence with Cable, was very much the naïf in regard to how the publishing world works and what professional authorship entails, despite his previous literary attainments. The provincial author of "The Goophered Grapevine" and "Po' Sandy" had produced publishable work whose quality is manifest; but his link to the literary world in early 1889 was the postal service. Now guided by a seasoned veteran with good connections at another first-rate magazine, *The Century*, Chesnutt's future seemed even brighter, for he had found a means of accelerating his progress toward the realization of his cherished dream: to become the new Tourgée, the

[17] Cable preserved the moment in his diary; see 10 January 1889 to Cable, n. 1.

equal of Harriet Beecher Stowe, or the peer of Cable himself, whose 1879 collection of short stories, *Old Creole Days*, and 1880 novel, *The Grandissimes*, dealt with race and were commercial successes. The belletristic life that he wanted is what Cable had; and Cable appeared eager to expedite his passage to Parnassus.

There is another side to the story as it developed over the next few years, just as there were two sides to Chesnutt's personality as a writer: the congenial and the mordant. In this subplot one finds the ultimate cause of Chesnutt's demise as a literary figure.

Until he began to correspond with Cable, Chesnutt's writings had been literary rather than political, wholly unconcerned with the need for social change when featuring white characters, and gently reformist in character when focused upon blacks. "Uncle Peter's House" was only mildly propagandistic in its sentimental appeal for recognition of the African-American hero's simple humanity; "The Goophered Grapevine" barely suggested criticism of white attitudes toward blacks. Cable, on the other hand, had become a vociferous critic of racism whose *The Silent South* (1885) would soon be followed by another collection of essays entitled *The Negro Question* (1890); and, in 1889, we find Cable more interested in coaxing Chesnutt to become his ideological ally than in nurturing the artist. The opportunities he provides Chesnutt to contribute to the noblest of causes cannot be resisted, and Cable thus effects a complication in the course of seductive writing for whites that Chesnutt had plotted in 1880. In May 1889, Chesnutt's first essay—the indignant exposure of racism and its effects upon those of mixed racial ancestry that is "What Is a White Man?"—was published. Simply stated, the angry polemicist whose voice would eventually displace that of the congenial, witty, and ingratiating storyteller of 1887 was fathered and encouraged by Cable at this time, and given numerous opportunities to debate the issues as a participant in an "Open Letter Club" that Cable had recently formed to facilitate national discussion of race-related topics. "Dave's Neckliss," typical of Chesnutt's seductive fiction, was written by the congenial Chesnutt for the October 1889 issue of *Atlantic Monthly;* the next month, he judgmentally focused upon the sins of the white fathers in "The Sheriff's Children" for the more politically oriented readers of *Independent*.[18]

[18] True, "Dave's Neckliss" pathetically records the unmerited suffering of a slave named Dave who is wrongly convicted of stealing a ham, but the tale ends with a gothic twist so bizarre that it invites a comedic interpretation, thus undercutting its "seriousness." Further, sympathy for blacks is qualified as another slave is depicted as at least as inhumane as the white owner who pushes Dave into insanity by making him wear a ham suspended from his neck. In addition, Uncle Julius, who narrates Dave's tale, does so for the purpose of making his auditor, the white Annie, not want to eat any more of the ham that she has on her dining-room table. When the ploy works and Julius carries it home with him, his cleverness may be acknowledged by the chuckling reader; but Julius' self-serving manipulation of a sensitive white woman, whose sympathy for blacks is exemplary, renders him a less than attractive character. In short, Chesnutt's "messages" regarding both

By the mid-1890s Chesnutt was no longer under Cable's tutelage, and the O.L.C. was a thing of the past. On the literary side, Cable had not proven much of a mentor, and his connections in the publishing world had not benefited the aspiring author at all: Cable placed for publication none of the work Chesnutt had sent him. Their occasional correspondence remained friendly; but a much less deferential Chesnutt had emerged, as did a more argumentative wielder of words who, when his hackles were raised, was as confident as Cable in his ability to pronounce the truth without mincing qualifications.

ONE'S attitude toward the story that unfolds in these letters has to be, it seems, one of ambivalence. That so talented a man should channel his energies into vigorous and sometimes strident pleas for and demonstrations of the rightness of viewing the African American in a new way cannot be seen in a negative light. Booker T. Washington's conciliatory approach to the race problem certainly needed to be complemented by a more insistent African-American voice, and attorney Chesnutt was adept in formal argumentation, not to mention the stinging use of sarcasm when exposing logical fallacies. His use of the flail was masterful.

On the other hand, Chesnutt did display a gift for the "soft sell": he could picture African Americans more attractively, and more pathetically, than Washington, humanizing them more fully than Dunbar in short stories such as "The Wife of His Youth," "A Matter of Principle," "The Passing of Grandison," and the majority of the Uncle Julius tales. The point to be inferred from such pieces was unthreatening to the dominant white readership of the time: these people pictured are different from whites in easily identified aspects but ultimately not different at all in regard to the essentials of what it means to be human. For his middle-class white readers of *The Wife of His Youth and Other Stories of the Color Line* (1899), he not only made the perhaps surprising revelation of the existence of an African-American bourgeoisie but demonstrated that its values and aspirations were identical to theirs. That Chesnutt became more militant as the years passed was not a personal shortcoming, and this development certainly will not be viewed as such by those convinced that confrontation was, and is, the only means of obtaining social justice. Yet, it is unfortunate that he had to pay so high a price—his literary career—for his principle-motivated protests.

Ironically, in 1894 a more market-wise Cable was cannily trimming his sails before the "storm" that Booker T. Washington hoped his people could

---

the plight of blacks and the attitudes of whites are so qualified by conflicting signals that the complex ambiguity of Chesnutt's art is what is noteworthy. Rather than make a polemical point, the story—if read seriously—only raises the question of how members of the two races should interact. At the most, it provides food for thought. "The Sheriff's Children," on the other hand, is straightforwardly didactic and coldly accusatory in its portrayal of a victimized mulatto.

weather, writing increasingly apolitical, popular romances. *John March, Southerner* (1894) was reconceived by Cable when *Century* editor Richard Watson Gilder accused him of having abandoned his art for the sake of writing a tract on the race problem; Cable even developed in that novel a portrait of the mulatto with unattractive personality traits guaranteed to please prejudiced Southern readers. *Strong Hearts* (1899), *The Cavalier* (1901), and *Bylow Hill* (1902) were not written by the fire-eater Chesnutt once knew. As the new century began, Chesnutt, unlike his one-time mentor, did not correctly judge the limitations of sympathy for the African-American predicament, and the need for a would-be popular author to work within those limitations. He chose a way of "exalting" his people that simply failed to effect "the elevation of the whites" who were not interested in paying to be scolded. Chesnutt did achieve in 1901 one of the high ambitions of his North Carolina years: in *The Marrow of Tradition* he had grasped true nobility as he played David to the Southern Goliath. Doing so, however, finally meant falling on his sword before he could behead this bête blanche, for Houghton, Mifflin was thereafter no longer interested in publishing his minimally profitable novels. When he did the same with Doubleday, Page four years later in *The Colonel's Dream*, his sword was taken away from him. One wonders what might have been had Chesnutt heard the clarion call to arms but persisted in his plan for a white readership, to "lead them on imperceptibly, unconsciously step by step to the desired state of feeling." The man who had delighted both black and white readers in 1898 with the widely praised *Atlantic* short story, "The Wife of His Youth," might have had it all if he had continued to write in the same vein.

Letters of
Charles W. Chesnutt

1889–1905

PART I
CABLE'S PROTÉGÉ IN
1889–1891

❧

An "Insider" Views the
Negro Question

❧

*I am under the impression that a
colored writer of literature is something that
editors and the public would be glad to
recognize and encourage.*

George Washington Cable

❧

My Dear Mr. Cable:—

I have written something on the Negro question, which at your kind suggestion, I enclose to you herewith.[1] I do not know that there are any new ideas in it, or that the old ones are expressed with sufficient originality to merit attention.[2] I have tried to write it as well as I could, with the limited time I have been able to devote to it, though I am painfully aware that it could be improved upon. Perhaps there are some things in it which you may not think it wise to publish. I have kept pretty closely to your view of the subject, as I understand it, which seems to me the correct one; and I have doubtless, and unavoidably, trenched upon ground which you have covered.[3] I have indicated by pencil marks on the margin certain passages which it occurs to me you might think better left unsaid; and I am quite willing to accept your advice and suggestions. This is my first attempt at a serious composition of this description, and I would not have ventured to trouble you with it, but for your friendly offer, of which I trust you have not since repented.[4] The difficulty I meet with in writing upon this question is not a dearth of ideas, but rather a superabundance of them, and it is quite possible that I have written too long an article.

If you can place the enclosed (in its present shape, or with such emendations as you may suggest, or choose to make in the way of omissions), where it will be read, I will feel that I have tried to do something in a good cause.

There could hardly be any question that the writer of such an article is a colored man; and it has been suggested to me by a gentleman of some literary standing and authority, that a knowledge of that fact would adversely affect my chances for literary success.[5] I hardly think so, for I am under the impression that a colored writer of *literature* is something that editors and the public would be glad to recognize and encourage. I may be mistaken, but if your opinion agrees with mine, I am not afraid to make a frank avowal of my position, and to give the benefit of any possible success or reputation that I may by hard work win, to those who need it most.

As the reading of my MS will occupy a good deal of your time, I will not trouble you with a longer letter, but remain

Very respectfully yours,
Chas. W. Chesnutt.

TLS: LNHT

[1] George Washington Cable (1844–1925) was born in New Orleans and during the Civil War served in the Fourth Mississippi Cavalry. By 1885, however, this novelist and short-story writer had migrated from Louisiana to Northampton, Mass., in part because of hostility triggered by his unflattering portraits of creoles and championing of African Americans in his works. His essays in *The Silent South* (1885) and *The Negro Question* (1890) focused on the need for reform in the South

and urged an end to racial discrimination; like Chesnutt, he was particularly sympathetic to the idiosyncratic problems of the mulatto, as may be seen is his most memorable novel, *The Grandissimes* (1880). Cable first met Chesnutt on 21 December 1888 in Cleveland, where he was the principal speaker at the Congregational Club's Forefathers' Day celebration. Beginning quirkily with the announcement that he was "a man in haste" with "only a few slender memoranda," Cable delivered a brief after-dinner speech emphasizing the fact that the Pilgrims had fled oppression and that their descendants should not oppress others by limiting suffrage—whereupon he declared that he had to catch a train and departed before the festivities were formally concluded ("Forefathers' Day," *Cleveland Leader and Morning Herald*, 22 December 1888, 3). His diary entry for the 21st (LNHT) reads: "As I turned to go to my room a man said 'Is this' &c. I said it was. He said his name was Chestnut [sic]. Wanted to go to my room to ask me a question. I thought him an unskilful interviewing reporter, and met his proposition coldly. Asked him to state his question. He began that he had contributed some stories to the *Atlantic Monthly*—I said, 'come upstairs.' Up there he began thanking me for my political papers and surprised me with the statement that he was a 'colored man.' We talked an hour. He is very bright. Is a court stenographer here. I think he will be very valuable in our Open Letter Club work." The short-lived Open Letter Club (defunct by late 1890) had recently been conceived by Cable as the means of discussing racial problems through circulating essays and reactions to them among a national membership that would be stimulated into joining the debate. Cable was quick to see that Chesnutt's unique contribution would be the articulation of the African American's own point of view on the race question.

[2] Chesnutt's essay, "An Inside View of the Negro Question," makes six points: the African American "knows what he wants"; "does not ask for social equality with white people"; "knows that his cause is just" and is "recognized before the great tribunal of the world"; "believes that *now* is the time to settle this question"; is convinced that "means of its solution are simple"; and "is confident of the ultimate success of his cause."

[3] Although Chesnutt does not make explicit his familiarity with it, Cable's pamphlet of thirty-two pages, *The Negro Question*, appears to be the expression of Cable's viewpoint referred to here. Published by the American Missionary Association in 1888, and in 1890 lending its title to Cable's book of essays on race problems, this pamphlet was distributed by Cable to potential contributors to the Open Letter Club such as Chesnutt.

[4] Chesnutt's publications, dating from 1885 on, were all short fictions that appeared in the magazines *Tid-Bits*, *Puck*, and *Atlantic Monthly*; others were distributed to newspapers by the S. S. McClure Syndicate.

[5] The "gentleman" appears to have been Albion W. Tourgée, with whom Chesnutt was corresponding by 1888. See the postscript of 26 September 1889 to Tourgée, in which Chesnutt alludes to his point of view on this matter and relates that the editors of two magazines, *Independent* and *Atlantic Monthly*, knew that he was African-American.

George Washington Cable

◦

Feb'y 2, 1889

My Dear Mr. Cable:—

MS. received, with accompanying note. I have adopted your suggestions literally, and have given the paper the title last suggested by you. I have only to look at the re-written MS. to see that your cuts have enhanced the dignity and effectiveness of the paper, and thereby more than compensated for any loss made by the excisions.[1]

I will forward you in a few days several type-written copies of the MSS., of which you are at liberty to make any use you may see fit.[2]

Thanks for the criticisms contained in your marginal notes: they will be of value to me in other ways than in connection with this article. I return the MS. herewith, and hope to be able at some time, to express to you in person my thanks for your favors to me.　　　　　　　　　　Very respectfully yours,

Chas. W. Chesnutt.

ALS: LNHT

[1] Chesnutt's manuscript on "the Negro question," sent on 10 January, was returned by Cable with a cover letter dated 30 January. Cable proclaimed, "You have written a noble essay"; and he asked Chesnutt to approve suggested revisions as well as cuts which brought it "down nearly to 5000 words." Chesnutt was advised not to delay in returning the essay to Cable for placement with a magazine: "There are reasons why the article should find publication as soon as possible." In a postscript, Cable advised Chesnutt to "let the matter of the race of the author rest as you find it now in your M.S. It is very interesting as coming declaredly from a man of color. Why not call it 'The Negro's View of the Negro Question?' 'Inside View' is indeterminate. Or how is, 'The Negro's Answer to the Negro Question?'" Chesnutt adopted the latter as his new title.

[2] Cable requested "two or three (or even more) copies" for distribution through the Open Letter Club.

George Washington Cable

༅·

February 12, 1889

My Dear Mr. Cable:—

I enclose herewith three copies of "The Negro's Answer to the Negro Question" as per your suggestion.

I would have sent them sooner, but have really not had time to write them until now. I shall be very glad to have you place them where they may possibly do some good.

Professor Scarborough,[1] of Wilberforce University (a colored institution of this state), and the author of a series of Greek textbooks published by A. S. Barnes & Co. of New York,[2] if I am not mistaken, has an article in the March *Forum*.[3] I have not read it yet, and do not know what it is about, but I mention the fact because the Professor is a Negro, and a full-blooded one at that;[4] perhaps you know him already—he is a scholar and a gentleman.

The article by Professor Wright of Berea College in the last *Independent* but one, I believe, was a good one;[5] and the Negro question, I am convinced, will become a more and more prominent subject of discussion until there is a radical departure at the South in the right direction.[6]

Very respectfully yours,

Chas. W. Chesnutt

ALS: LNHT

[1] William Sanders Scarborough (1852–1926) was an educator and political activist best known at this time for aiding the passage of 1887 legislation ending segregation in Ohio's public schools. He was graduated from Oberlin College in 1875. He served as head of the Payne Institute at Cokesbury, S.C. He was next appointed a professor of Latin and Greek at Wilberforce University in Ohio; dismissed from that school in 1892 because of an increased emphasis on the teaching of practical rather than "intellectual" subjects; and then reappointed in 1897. He became the president of Wilberforce in 1908. Like Chesnutt, he disagreed with Booker T. Washington in regard to the latter's heavy emphasis on manual-labor training rather than "higher education" for African Americans. See his "Educated Negroes and Menial Pursuits," *Forum* 26 (December 1898), 434–40, where he acknowledges the need for the acquisition of job skills but champions the value of intellectual refinements.

[2] Scarborough had written one textbook, *First Lessons in Greek: Adapted to the Greek Grammar of Goodwin and Hadley* (1881). That he "has nearly completed his second . . . which will be issued next spring" was reported in *Cleveland Gazette,* 2 November 1889, 1.

[3] His article in *Forum* was "The Future of the Negro"; see 1 March 1889 to Cable, n. 1.

[4] A description of Scarborough's genetic inheritance of "unmixed blood" appeared in "Conspicuous Examples," *Cleveland Gazette,* 9 November 1889, 1; but both of Scarborough's parents were multiracial in ancestry, according to the *Dictionary of American Negro Biography,* ed. Rayford W. Logan and Michael R. Winston (New York and London: W. W. Norton, 1982), 546.

[5] W. E. C. Wright, in "Two Roads Before the South," *Independent* 41 (31 January 1889), 4–5, criticized Henry W. Grady for his 1887 speech at the state fair in Dallas, Tex., in which he advocated white supremacy. Citing other expressions of supremacist sentiment in Virginia and North Carolina, Wright observed that the predictable outcome would be perpetual racial strife; and he argued for an alliance in which the needs of both races are met.

[6] Cable forwarded a copy of the essay to Lorettus S. Metcalf, editor of *Forum,* who declined it; see 22 February 1889 to Cable.

George Washington Cable

Feb'y 22/89

My Dear Mr. Cable:—

I return herewith Mr. Metcalf's letter. I appreciate his words of commendation, and am sorry he could not accept the article. I shall read Prof. Scarborough's article with interest, and revise my MSS. in view of it.[1] I was thinking that the title of my article, "The Negro's Answer &c," might sound rather large in view of the fact that Scarborough is, I presume, speaking in the same character: but I can tell better when I have read his paper. If you succeed with the *Century,* I shall regard it as a very good change from the *Forum.* I presume the *Century* is read by ten people to the *Forum's* one.

The "Symposium" in this week's *Independent* is a revelation to me, and confirms me in a theory I have had for some time, i.e., that just about the time that the Negro got ready to assert himself and demand his rights, he would find nothing to do—the white people would have done it all.[2] The most encouraging thing about it all is that these men are the teachers of the white youth of the South. The influence of one Haygood,[3] or Baskervill,[4] extending over a long period of time and acting upon receptive and plastic minds, will more than offset the fervid rhetoric of a score of Gradys[5] and Eustises[6] and Morgans,[7] and I more than suspect that your example and your influence have done more than any other one thing to stimulate the growth of the school of thought represented by the *Independent's* Symposium.

Very truly yours—
Chas. W. Chesnutt.

I am glad that you asked Scarborough to write.[8] I think there is a good deal of latent talent, literary and otherwise, among the colored people of this country, which needs only a decent degree of encouragement and recognition to stimulate it to activity. Yours &c.,

C.W.C.

ALS: LNHT

[1] Cable had sent a copy of "The Negro's Answer" to Lorettus Sutton Metcalf (1837–?), founder and editor of *Forum*. In his 16 February reply (LNHT), immediately forwarded to Chesnutt by Cable, Metcalf declared: Chesnutt's "article is certainly excellent, and if I had not secured a paper from a Negro [Scarborough] I would use it gladly. But not only have I obtained a contribution from a Negro, but my writer covers some of the ground that this one traverses, so that I could not publish this without making my series repeat itself considerably." Cable assured Chesnutt that he was continuing to work in his behalf: "I am now trying the *Century*. It would be well to revise your paper and take out whatever Scarborough had treated identically. . . . Your paper will easily find a publisher." Scarborough's essay is described in 1 March 1889 to Cable, n. 1.

[2] The symposium entitled "Shall the Negro Be Educated or Suppressed?" appeared in *Independent* 41 (21 February 1889), 225–27. The eight participants were responding to Atticus G. Haygood's "Senator Eustis on the Negro Problem," *Independent* 40 (8 November 1888), 11,425–27, which was a rebuttal of Louisiana Senator James B. Eustis's essay, "Race Antagonism in the South," *Forum* 6 (October 1888), 144–54. After observing that the inferiority of the African American was as much a recognized fact in Massachusetts as it was in the South, Eustis had argued that "the Negro problem" in the South was a concern of the Southern states alone. Haygood replied that it was, instead, a matter for national attention, particularly in regard to education. The respondents to Haygood were Professor William M. Baskervill (Vanderbilt University), George W. Cable, Professor Charles Foster Smith (Vanderbilt), Professor Robert T. Hill (University of Texas), Professor F. C. Woodward (University of South Carolina), W. M. Beckner (editor of the *Winchester* [Ky.] *Democrat*), John H. Boyd (Durant, Miss.), and Julius D. Dreher (president of Roanoke College, Salem, Va.). Cable had also rebutted Eustis directly in "A Simpler Southern Question," *Forum* 6 (December 1888), 392–403. Cable saw Eustis' position—that the African American is naturally incapable of achieving equality with whites and that whites must be supreme in a Southern situation in which the only alternatives were white or black dominance—as irrelevant to the main question at hand: whether African Americans are to be guaranteed the equal rights that are already theirs by law. Cable thus articulated what became a constant perspective in Chesnutt's statements about the franchise: such rights do not depend upon personal or racial identity but "one's simple membership in the community."

[3] Atticus G. Haygood (1839–1896) was a graduate of Emory College and a Methodist Episcopal chaplain in the Confederate army. He served as president of his alma mater (1875–1884) and was made a bishop in 1890. Author of *Our Brother in Black* (1881), he became in 1883 an agent of the Slater Fund that supported the education of African Americans, and his speeches in its behalf were collected in *Pleas for Progress* (1889).

[4] William M. Baskervill (1850–1899) was a professor of English at Vanderbilt University and Cable's personal friend. He served as the secretary of the Open Letter Club.

[5]Henry Woodfin Grady (1850–1889) was a journalist who became part-owner of the *Atlanta Constitution* and was distinguished by his zeal for progress in the "New South." He was also well known for his insistence on the necessity of white supremacy. Typical are his comments in "The South and Her Problems," a speech delivered at the Texas State Fair in Dallas on 26 October 1888: "The clear and unmistakable domination of the white race . . .—that is the hope and assurance of the South"; "the white race must dominate forever in the South, because it is the white race, and superior to that race by which its supremacy is threatened" (*Joel Chandler Harris' Life of Henry W. Grady Including His Writings and Speeches* [1890], 99 and 101).

[6] James Biddle Eustis (1834–1899) was a New Orleans attorney who served in the Confederate army and became deeply involved in politics during the Reconstruction period. A state legislator, professor of law at what is now Tulane University, and U.S. senator, he represents to Chesnutt the Southern Democrat opposed to full civil rights for African Americans.

[7] John Tyler Morgan (1824–1907) was a brigadier general in the Confederate army, a U.S. senator from 1876 until his death, and a white supremacist who, from 1886 to 1888, fought against the Blair education bill for eliminating Southern illiteracy. He was the author of "Negro Majorities: Shall They Rule?" *Forum* 6 (February 1889), 586–99. Observing that in thirteen contiguous states "nearly 40 per cent. of the inhabitants are Negro" and that in three "the Negroes outnumber the whites," Morgan reflected on how repugnant was the possibility of future "Negro supremacy" and how rash was the experiment of granting suffrage to African Americans. A champion of states' rights, he saw the solution of the problem in the hands of "the people of the States," who "under the Constitution," determine who is qualified to vote. Particularly galling to Chesnutt must have been Morgan's evaluation of mulattoes. After expressing his opinion about the lower "intellectual, moral, and social condition of the Negroes," Morgan described "Negroes of mixed blood" as "inferior among the race to which they belong."

[8] Cable appears to have encouraged Scarborough in the same way he did Chesnutt, in order to have both provide the tangible proof of the intellectual capabilities of African Americans.

George Washington Cable

March 1, 1889

My dear Mr. Cable:—

I have read Prof. Scarborough's article in the March *Forum*.[1] He has a clear grasp of the situation; his article is well written, though it might have had a little more fervor. I don't believe that emigration to the West will do the Negroes in the South a great deal of good, for the reason that those who go will probably be the most advanced of them instead of the lowest, and it is not difficult to foresee the effect upon a people of a steady drain of its best blood.[2] While Scarborough and I have written on the same subject, and our views upon it are substantially the same, I am not able to see, at first glance at least, that we have treated any special topic identically. I will go over it more carefully, however; and if, as sponsor to my essay, you have time or inclination to make any further suggestions in regard to it, they will be gratefully received and respectfully considered.[3]

Thanks for the Open Letter pamphlet containing Dr. Haygood's Reply to Eustis; I shall endeavor to send Mr. Baskervill a number of such names as are desired.[4]

Very truly yours,

Chas. W. Chesnutt

ALS: LNHT

[1] "The Future of the Negro," *Forum* 7 (March 1889), 80–89, answers James B. Eustis, who saw African Americans as having made very little progress since the Civil War despite the extraordinary amount of support given them (see 22 February 1889 to Cable, n. 2). Scarborough begins by restating Cable's more sanguine view expressed in "What Shall the Negro Do?" *Forum* 5 (August 1888), 627–39—addressed to African-American readers of that journal who are the proof of the progress that has been made by the race. Scarborough then turns to the situation in the South, where the African American is terrorized because the whites are fearful of "Negro domination." He laments the fact that immigrants, "the largest part ignorant and degraded," are given full freedom while African Americans are not. The first step toward improvement of the conditions in the South, he argues, is the extension of full civil rights to all, effected by federal intervention if necessary. Further, if conditions in the South fail to improve, African Americans should consider the possibility of migrating to the West, where one may be "a man among men and not simply a Negro." As Chesnutt did in his own essay, "The Negro's Answer," Scarborough makes it clear that he is an African-American author; and he again exploited the "insider's" point of view in "The Negro Question from the Negro's Point of View," *Arena* 4 (July 1891), 219–22, where he dismisses the idea that African Americans desire "Negro supremacy."

[2] This is an ironically self-referential statement, given Chesnutt's own flight from the South to New York City and then Cleveland in 1883.

[3] Cable next sent "The Negro's Answer" to *Century*; see 10 April 1889 to Cable, n. 1.

[4] Cable printed three thousand copies of Haygood's essay (see 22 February 1889 to Cable, n. 2) and sent them to the Club members, soliciting reactions and mailing the symposium consequently assembled to those who had requested the pamphlet from William M. Baskervill (see 10 April 1889 to Cable, n. 2). Chesnutt is here responding to an undated request from Cable that he help distribute the pamphlet and send Baskervill a list of potential Club members. He did so. On 9 March 1889, turpentine merchant A. H. Slocomb of Fayetteville, N.C., acknowledged receipt of the pamphlet that Chesnutt sent him and provided the names of ten men who might be put on Cable's mailing list (see 3 May 1889 to Cable, n. 3.)

George Washington Cable

⟨∾⟩

March 4th, 1889.

My dear Mr. Cable:—

Permit me to trouble you long enough to read this letter, in regard to a personal matter.

I have been chiefly employed, during the past two years, as a stenographic reporter in the courts of this county, intending to use this business as a means of support while awaiting the growth of a law practice, there being reasons why this process might be a little slower in my case than in some others. But by a very natural process, the thing I have given most time to has hindered instead of helping that which it was intended to assist. As a consequence I have built up a business, almost entirely as a stenographer, which brought me in last year an income of two thousand dollars.[1]

But there is a bill pending in the legislature of this State (it has already passed one house) for the appointment of two official stenographers for this county. There are five or six men now engaged in doing this court work, and probably all of these will be applicants for these positions. I have perhaps more than a fighting chance—certainly that—for one of them. If I should secure it, it would pay a salary of $1500 a year, with fees to the probable amount of $1000 or $1500 more; and it would in all probability occupy fully all my time.

In the event of a failure on my part to apply for or to secure one of these appointments, I shall be compelled to turn my attention to other fields of labor. And my object in writing to you is to inquire your opinion as to the wisdom or rashness of my adopting literature as a means of support.

I am aware that I am perhaps asking you a question, an answer to which you have very meager data to base upon; and I realize that I am perhaps presuming on a very slight acquaintance with a busy man. But I will risk the latter, and say as to the former, that I can turn my hand to several kinds of literary work—can write a story, a funny skit, can turn a verse, or write a serious essay, and I have heretofore been able to dispose of most that I have written, at prices which fairly compensated me for the time spent in writing them, as compared with what I could have earned in the same time at something else. I have even written a novel, though I have never had time to revise it for publication, nor temerity enough to submit it to a publisher.[2] I have a student's knowledge of German and French, can speak the former, and could translate either into grammatical English, and I trust into better English than many of the translations which are dumped upon the market.[3]

I am also impelled to this step by a deep and growing interest in the discussion and settlement of the Southern question, and all other questions which affect the happiness of the millions of colored people in this country. But life is short, and any active part that one would take in this matter ought to be begun, it seems to me, while something of the vigor and hopefulness of youth remains. I am only 31, but time flies rapidly. It seems to me that there is a growing demand for literature dealing with the Negro, and for information concerning subjects with which he is in any manner connected; his progress in the United States, in Brazil, in the West Indies, in South America, and in other lands, the opening up of Africa—it seems to me that in these subjects there is a vast field for literary work, and that the time is propitious for it; and it seems to me a field in which a writer who was connected with these people by ties of blood and still stronger ties of sympathy, could be *facile princeps*, other things being equal; or in which such a writer of very ordinary powers could at least earn a livelihood.

If I could earn twelve or fifteen hundred dollars a year at literature, or in some collateral pursuit which would allow me some time to devote to letters, I think I should be willing to undertake it in any event, and certainly in the event of my failure to apply for or to secure one of the appointments above referred to. If from your own experience and knowledge of the literary life you think it likely that I could make a success in it, or if you know or hear of any such employment as I have suggested, and will take the trouble to write to me upon the subject, I will be under greater obligations to you than I am already.

Yours very truly,
Chas. W. Chesnutt.

TLS: LNHT

[1] As Chesnutt indicates, admission to the Ohio Bar Association in 1887 did not offer so much pecuniary promise for an African American as did stenography. He later described in "Uncle Wellington's Wives" (1899) a Mr. Wright, who was "for a long time the only colored lawyer in North Carolina": "His services were frequently called into requisition by impecunious people of his own race; when they had money they went to white lawyers, who, they shrewdly conjectured, would have more influence with judge or jury than a colored lawyer, however able."

[2] On 5 July 1880, Chesnutt entered a "plan for a novel" in his journal: an octoroon is studying for the ministry at a college in the South; the daughter of the college president and he fall in love but they cannot marry; years later, she nurses him back to health in Africa; they wed and "live happily, etc. etc. ad infinitum" in "a clime free from prejudice." There is no evidence, however, of his having executed this plan. Thus, Chesnutt is very likely referring to his "Rena Walden" manuscript, actually a "tragic mulatto" short story that would be revised several times and finally published in expanded form in 1900 as *The House Behind the Cedars*. See 26 September 1889 to Tourgée where Chesnutt relates that he is writing a novel.

[3] Since the 1870s Chesnutt had been pursuing a course of self-education, including not only German and French but Latin and Greek. He eventually became most proficient in French, and his 1880s journal entries witness his trials in writing German.

George Washington Cable

ᐧᐁᐧ

April 10, 1889.

My dear Mr. Cable:—

Your two letters were duly received,[1] also Symposium pamphlet.[2] I have been very busy since my return to Cleveland,[3] which must be my excuse for not having written to you sooner.

I enclose several type-writer copies of excerpts from pamphlet.[4] There are not many short sentences in the symposium. I suspect I have written too much, but that is a defect easily remedied. There are other good things, which could not be used, at least some of them, without garbling them. I have written in one copy the name of the author of each group of sentiments; if you do not desire to quote names, of course they can be rubbed out and the copy used. If I had not already delayed this so long I would try to write a suitable introductory paragraph, but I think perhaps you would prefer to do that, as you said nothing about it in your letter.

I have not yet succeeded in procuring you any engagements in this part of the country. I am writing to several parties to-day, and shall ask them for immediate replies.[5]

I have not yet decided upon my plans for the Summer; in any event, it will be impossible for me to come to Northampton before the Summer. As to whether I can come then, or move to Northampton permanently, I must have some further time to consider.[6] I fully realize the importance of the work, and would like nothing better, personally, than to be in it. In any event, I shall devote more or less time to it. In the meantime, do not let yourself be embarrassed for want of proper assistance on my account. Whatever you can send me here to do, I will gladly give precedence, wherever possible, over my other work.

I will send you later in the day, or to-morrow, a list of names for the O.L.C. pamphlets. Shall I see your "Haunted House in Royal Street" in the *Century* soon?[7]

Very truly yours,

Chas. W. Chesnutt.

TLS: LNHT

[1] Chesnutt refers to 1 and 5 April letters from Cable. Cable reported in the former that "*Century* can't use the Open Letter on the color line. *North American* not heard from—shall write them today." "The Negro's Answer to the Negro Question" was rejected by *Century* editor Richard Watson Gilder (1844–1909), who wrote to Cable on 13 March 1889 (LNHT) that "Mr. Chesnutt's . . . is a timely political paper—so timely & so political—in fact so partisan—that we cannot handle it. It should appear at once somewhere." The essay was then sent to *North American Review*.

[2] The "Symposium pamphlet" sent to Chesnutt on 5 April was a publication of the Open Letter Club entitled *Shall the Negro be Educated or Suppressed?* It contained the eight responses to Atticus G. Haygood's "Senator Eustis on the Negro Problem" originally published in the *Independent* (see 22 February 1889 to Cable, n. 2), to which were added three new essays by Seth Low (Brooklyn, N.Y.), P. D. Sims, M.D. (Chattanooga, Tenn.), and Joseph Holt, M.D. (Portland, Ore.).

[3] Chesnutt visited Cable in Northampton, Mass., in mid-March, and on 17 March he demonstrated his stenography skills by producing a transcription of the City Hall Bible Class conducted by Cable. It was published as "Blind Bartimeus," *Northampton Daily Herald*, 18 March 1889, 2. Chesnutt may have also transcribed the next Sunday's presentation for that newspaper: "In Review: Mr. Cable's Sunday School Talk," 25 March 1889, 2.

[4] On 5 April, Cable asked Chesnutt to "make a selection of good, trenchant sentences" from the pamphlet "to be given to newspapers as extracts," and he requested six typewritten copies. Chesnutt, that is, was performing the same kind of Open Letter Club work as William M. Baskervill in Nashville and Cable's east-coast protégée, Adelene Moffat (see 2 September 1889 to Moffat, n. 1).

[5] On 1 April, Cable announced that he was thinking of beginning a lecture tour in late April, inquiring if Chesnutt might secure engagements for him between Oneida, N.Y., and Chicago from 24 April to 3 May. He offered him a commission for each $100 lecture secured.

[6] On 5 April, Cable alluded to the possibility of Chesnutt working with him that summer: "I shall be glad to hear what your summer plans are. . . . You ought to be in this noble work." Chesnutt's reply makes it clear that Cable offered him a full-time position.

[7] This was one of Cable's nonfiction tales based upon past instances of anti-African-American racism in New Orleans (see 2 September 1889 to Moffat, n. 4). In "Personal," *Northampton Daily Herald*, 1 March 1889, 4, it was reported that "Mr. Cable is now at work on a story entitled 'The Haunted House of Royal Street'"; Chesnutt very likely read the piece in manuscript when visiting Cable in March. The O.L.C. is Cable's Open Letter Club.

George Washington Cable

ᧁ

May 3, 1889.

My dear Mr. Cable:—

I regret to say that, after mature deliberation, I have reached the conclusion that I could not afford to come to Northampton for any sum which, judging from the figures you have already mentioned, you would probably feel justified in offering me.[1] The contingency which immediately inspired my first letter to you did not happen—that is, the appointment of official stenographers—so that my business is not affected in that direction. My earnings, for the month just ended, as per memorandum lying before me, are just $250.65. I have just made a change in my business which will, I hope, enable me to increase the income from it with less work on my part individually. So you will see that even $1200.00 or $1500.00 a year would, in comparison, be a sacrifice of half my income—a sacrifice which I, personally, would not hesitate to make, in view of the compensating advantages, but which my duty to my family, and other considerations which would perhaps not interest you, constrain me not to make.

I hope, however, to still do what I can in the good cause of human rights, and am not likely to grow lukewarm in it, for if no nobler motive inspired me, my own interests and those of many who are dear to me are largely at stake. But I hope still to find opportunities, and I shall write and speak and act as occasion may require.

I have written to the *North American Review* asking for something definite in regard to the acceptance of my article, but have as yet received no answer.[2]

I enclose you a list of names of gentlemen who will be valuable additions to the list of those to whom Open Letter Club pamphlets are sent.[3]

My office arrangements are now such that I can give prompt attention to copying other work, and as I have already said, you can command me for assistance in anything where distance will not be too great an obstacle. Reiterating my regret at feeling forced to the conclusion I have reached, I remain

Very respectfully yours,

Chas. W. Chesnutt

P.S. Please note the change of address.[4]

C.W.C.

TLS: LNHT

[1] On 13 April 1889, Cable asked Chesnutt to make his decision about a position at Northampton: "I do not know that we can meet each other on the pecuniary basis, but I will try, if you will." On 22 April, from Utica, N.Y., he again queried Chesnutt with some urgency, explaining that he would not return to Northampton until 6 or 7 May but that a response should not be delayed since it would be forwarded to him from his home.

[2] "The Negro's Answer to the Negro Question," previously rejected by *Forum* and *Century*.

[3] On a separate sheet, Chesnutt provided these "Names for Open Letter Club Pamphlets": Rev. Joseph Clapp, Newton, Catawba Co., N.C.; Prof. Geo. W. Williams, State Normal School, Fayetteville, N.C.; and Prof. J. S. Leary, Shaw University, Raleigh, N.C. He also listed eight others whose address was Fayetteville: Dr. S. J. Hinsdale, Dr. H. P. Hodges, Dr. W. C. McDuffie, H. R. Horne, R. W. Hardie, W. S. Kingsbury, S. C. Rankin, and A. H. Slocomb. Chesnutt noted that the "above are all prominent men, and all but two of them are white."

[4] Chesnutt had moved his office from Room 8, 219 Superior Street, where he appears to have been associated with the Henderson, Kline and Tolles law firm, to 30 Blackstone Building.

George Washington Cable

May 24, 1889

My dear Mr. Cable:—

The *North American Review*, after keeping my essay on the Negro Question an unconscionably long time under the circumstances, has returned it with the usual polite regrets.[1] I fear the public, as represented by the editors of the leading magazines, is not absolutely yearning for an opportunity to read the utterances of obscure colored writers upon the subject of the Negro's rights; a little of it I suspect goes a long way.

I see from the papers that the chapter of Southern outrages is not yet complete, but the work of intimidating voters and killing prominent negroes on trumped-up charges (the true character of which is not discovered until after the killing) still goes merrily on.[2]

Your story of Salome Miller was very interesting, and yet one could not help thinking, while reading it, what a still more interesting work of fiction might have been made of it. I suppose the story of "The Haunted House in Royal Street" will soon appear. I hope you have secured a good secretary, and still regret that circumstances would not permit me to serve you in that capacity.[3]

Very truly yours,
Chas. W. Chesnutt.

ALS: LNHT

[1] On 22 April 1889, Cable urged Chesnutt to write the editor of *North American Review* about the status of "The Negro's Answer."

[2] Chesnutt is referring to the killing of a prominent African-American Republican in Forest City, Ark., on 19 May. An altercation developed on 18 May when A. M. Neely and another speaker, G. W. Angram, made what were viewed by white Democrats as incendiary, pro-black

domination speeches in behalf of two African-American candidates in a school board election. The death of three Caucasians was the result. Neely, his brother, and father took refuge in a building; when the latter two were allowed by a mob to leave, Neely was rushed and shot to death ("The Forest City Riot," *New York Times*, 20 May 1889, 1).

[3] On 30 May, Cable attempted to console Chesnutt for the *North American Review* rejection of "The Negro's Answer." Assuming that Chesnutt saw their cause—rather than personal success—as most important, he pointed out that the "Southern question" was receiving a good deal of attention in the press. He then reflected that Chesnutt's essay would have been accepted by *Forum* had not Scarborough's been taken first, and assured him that he had yet another plan for its publication. He went on to avail himself of Chesnutt's willingness to participate in the Open Letter Club, asking him to write a summary of a letter received from a Mr. Bidwell of Weatherford, Tex., and then refute Bidwell point by point. To Chesnutt's reaction to "Salome Müller,"—which appeared in *Century* 38 (May 1889), 59–69—Cable responded on 30 May: "don't found fiction on fact. . . . Found your fictions on truth, but stay away from actual occurrences of historical value."

Mary Adelene Moffat

∾

September 2, 1889.

Miss Moffat:—

Your favor of August 28th received.[1] Please say to Mr. Cable that I will endeavor to send him during the present week the information he wants in regard to North Carolina laws.[2] I think I shall be able to get it all from our Law Library here; if not, I shall have to write to a friend in North Carolina, which may require a few days longer.[3]

Please say to Mr. Cable that I read his "Haunted House," "Attalie Brouillard"—if that is correct—and the *Independent* paper with the pleasure I always derive from his writings;[4] also that the *Independent* accepted a story of mine last week, and that another will appear in the October *Atlantic*.[5] I shall be very glad to hear from Mr. Cable when he has leisure to write.

Very respectfully yours,
Chas. W. Chesnutt.

TLS: LNHT

[1] Mary Adelene Moffat (1862–1956), Cable's personal secretary and then co-worker in his Home Culture Club headquartered at Northampton, first heard Cable lecture in 1887 during the fifth session of the Monteagle Sunday School Assembly, a Tennessee version of the Chautauqua founded by her father. The following year she abandoned her plans for a career in teaching; an idealist devoted to the values articulated by Cable, she worked with him until 1907. Like Baskervill in Nashville, Moffat facilitated correspondence among members of the Open Letter Club until its demise in 1890.

[2] In a 28 August letter, Moffat communicated Cable's request that Chesnutt write a paper on a subject they most likely discussed during his March 1889 visit to Northampton: "the origin, wording and effects of those laws in North Carolina that take county and town governments out of local hands." Chesnutt's compliance ultimately led to a confrontation with Alfred M. Waddell and Baskervill (see 14 November 1889 to Moffat), and it may have been one of the primary causes of

the disbanding of the Open Letter Club, since it made it clear to Baskervill that he was out of harmony with Cable on the subject of social equality for African Americans (see 17 October 1889 to Cable, n. 2).

[3] See 9 September 1889 to Cable, n. 6.

[4] "The Haunted House in Royal Street," *Century* 38 (August 1889), 590–601; "Attalie Brouillard," *Century* 38 (September 1889), 749–57; "The Nation and the Illiteracy of the South," *Independent* 41 (29 August 1889), 1106–7.

[5] "The Sheriff's Children," *Independent* 41 (7 November 1889), 30–32; "Dave's Neckliss," *Atlantic Monthly* 64 (October 1889), 500–8.

George Washington Cable

Sept. 9, 1889.

My dear Mr. Cable:—

I enclose you herewith a paper on County Government in North Carolina. I could not gather, from Miss Moffat's note, whether you simply wanted me to collate material for use in connection with something you are writing on southern political methods, or whether you wanted something complete in itself. I thought most likely it was for the former purpose, and have therefore thrown it together rather crudely, after spending half a day in the law library looking up the law. If you should wish to use it as coming from me, and there is time, I would like to have it back again, unless you think it good enough in its present shape. You are entirely welcome, however, to make whatever use of it may be best for the "cause," which from present indications,—the shootings in Mississippi and Louisiana, the whippings in Georgia, and the burning at the stake in Kentucky, not to mention such trifles as burning postmasters in effigy—, would seem to be in rather a bad way.[1] If things keep on at this rate much longer, I shall be compelled to believe, with Judge Tourgée, that serious and widespread race troubles in the South are not improbable in the near future.[2] Such conflicts would probably result to the injury of the negroes, but as sure as there is a heaven and an earth the white people of the South are sowing a crop from which they will reap an abundant harvest of hatred; the plant has already attained a vigorous growth, and what its fruit will be none can tell.

I take the liberty of enclosing you the Ms. of a story, entitled "Rena Walden." If it is not asking too much of you, will you kindly read it, and tell me what you think the chance would be of its acceptance by the *Century*?[3] Its local color is certainly new; it deals with a class similar to your Louisiana quadroons, but of course not so romantic.[4] The hardest point I had to decide in connection with the story was what to call my heroine's mother. I couldn't call her "Mrs. Molly" and be consistent, because she was really called "Miss," by those people who gave her any title at all—and "Mrs." was an unknown term to all but people of the highest culture. And yet "Miss" as the title of an unmarried woman, looks a little out of place.[5] I did not have your practically noncommittal French "*Madame*" to fall back upon. While I have n't the "nerve" to ask for suggestions from you, yet any that you might have time to make on that or any other point would be gratefully appreciated, and you need not fear you would be establishing a dangerous precedent, for I am quite aware of the value of your time and the manner in which it is taken up.

I have written to-day to North Carolina for a copy of the new election law referred to in the enclosed article, and will send it to you when I receive it.[6]

Hoping to hear from you at your convenience,[7] I remain

Very respectfully yours,
Chas. W. Chesnutt.

TLS: LNHT

[1] See 2 September 1889 to Moffat, where Chesnutt acknowledges Cable's request for information on county government in North Carolina. The specific dimension of the "cause" to which Chesnutt refers is the need to insure equitable application of the law and the protection of African Americans' rights that it offers. The essay Chesnutt sent Cable has not been located, but the concern of both men was that, in North Carolina in 1889, county commissioners were not directly elected by their constituents. Rather, justices of the peace were put into office by white state legislators, and these justices determined who would serve as commissioners. An explanation of the situation, together with Chesnutt's expression of concern that these commissioners would not extend equal protection of the law to African Americans, very likely comprised the substance of the paper sent to Cable. (See the description of county governance provided by Alfred M. Waddell, 14 November 1889 to Moffat, n. 2.)

[2] In *An Appeal to Caesar* (1884), Tourgée argued for an end to racial discrimination, repeatedly raising the specter of violent rebellion on the part of African Americans if reforms were not made. This remained a distinctive theme of his writings on the race question.

[3] "Rena Walden" is possibly the "novel" that Chesnutt first mentioned to Cable in his 4 March 1889 letter.

[4] Influenced by transatlantic "local color" writers such as Sir Walter Scott and Robert Burns, and by Americans such as Tourgée and Cable, Chesnutt here identifies "Rena" as an indication of his relationship with the popular "Regional" school of American literature.

[5] Molly is the unwed mother of the heroine, and thus the question at hand.

[6] In an unlocated letter, Chesnutt wrote to North Carolinian Charles N. Hunter, editor of *Progressive Educator*, who promised to forward a copy on 13 September 1889. Hunter described it as a modified version of the election law in South Carolina: one applying to become a registered voter is required to state the date and place of his birth, the last precinct in which he voted, and present residence. Hunter viewed this as a de facto proscription of voting rights for many African Americans since they would not be able to provide this information. "How many Negroes in N.C. can give *date* and *place* of birth?" The inevitably white registrars would be the sole judges of eligibility; worse, they would be able to "go behind the returns" by rejecting "the whole or any part of the vote returned as they see fit."

[7] See 14 November 1889 to Moffat, where Open Letter Club discussion of North Carolina county government begins in earnest.

Albion W. Tourgée

✧

Sept. 26, 1889.

My dear Sir:—

I do not know that I ever acknowledged receipt of your kindly letter in answer to the one in which I thanked you for a compliment paid.[1] I found in your letter not only great pleasure but much encouragement.[2] I think with you that the colored people ought to erect a monument to John Brown, and I hope to see it done, though hardly for some years. Recent developments seem to indicate that they are learning to act unitedly; in a few more years, say a decade, they may have attained, as a class, that pitch of enlightenment, that degree of confidence in themselves, which will make it possible to carry out successfully such an enterprise; the example set by their white fellow-citizens in the matter of the Washington and Grant monuments is not exactly an inspiring one.[3]

I take the liberty of sending you a copy of the October *Atlantic*, which contains one of my stories, which if you read it, I hope you may think the best of the series. I think I have about used up the old Negro who serves as mouthpiece, and I shall drop him in future stories, as well as much of the dialect.[4] The punishment of tying the stolen meat around the thief's neck was a real incident of slavery—in fact I think it hardly possible to imagine anything cruel or detestable that did not have its counterpart in that institution.[5] The setting of that incident is of course pure fiction. I tried in this story to get out of the realm of superstition into the region of feeling and passion—with what degree of success the story itself can testify.[6]

I presume you saw an article of mine in the *Independent* in June; that paper has accepted from me a Southern Story, dealing with a tragic incident, not of slavery exactly, but showing the fruits of slavery.[7] It is not in dialect, and while it has a moral, I tried to write as an artist and not as a preacher. I had a humorous dialect story in the June *Overland*, a rather out-of-the-way publication which it hardly pays to write for.[8]

I read with much interest your stirring weekly letters in the *Inter Ocean*.[9] I sincerely hope some of the Southern fire-eaters read them and profit by them. Recent events do not show, however, that the Southern whites have learned much; they certainly have not forgotten how to insult and oppress the Negro, and they still possess their old-time facility with the shot-gun and the cowhide. I see no remedy for the disease but for the colored people to learn to defend themselves.[10]

I have had some thoughts of collecting in book form the stories I have published in the *Atlantic*, with some others I think as good, which have seen daylight elsewhere. If you have time to answer this letter, perhaps you would be kind enough to advise me from your own experience, whether such a book would be likely to pay for itself, or whether it would be of sufficient value as an advertisement to justify me in paying for it? I have been writing a good deal this Summer, among other things a novel which I shall try to inflict on the public sooner or later. With kindest regards, I am

Yours very respectfully,
Chas. W. Chesnutt.

P.S.—

You said to me that you thought the fact of color would hurt me in literature—the knowledge of the fact rather. Perhaps it might with the public. It has not with the *Independent*—on the contrary I think it has helped me with that journal. I do not think it has hurt me with the *Atlantic*. The editors of both journals are aware of my connection with the colored race. The road to success in literature is not, I imagine, an easy one, and perhaps, if I have the patience and the industry to pursue it, the fact of color may in the course of time prove to be a distinction instead of a disadvantage.

Yours, etc.
C. W. Chesnutt.

ALS: NWefHi

[1] Born in Ohio, Albion W. Tourgée (1838–1905) ended in 1861 a brief stint as a teacher in New York State to become a Union soldier, and he participated in several major battles. Like Chesnutt two decades later, he was admitted to the Ohio bar. In 1865 he began a practice in Greensboro, N.C. He became a judge in 1868, and he was an energetic participant in the Reconstruction; like Chesnutt, he saw an essential role for the federal government to play in the establishment of equal rights for African Americans. He was an important Republican figure during the 1868 North Carolina Constitutional Convention, where he had much to do with the institution of a greater degree of local government and a diminution of the power of the white state legislature. In part because Tourgée was very visibly associated with the "Carpet-bag" régime and thus earned the enmity of Southern whites, he decided in 1879 to return to the North. He lived in Mayville, N.Y., until 1897 when he became the United States Consul in Bordeaux, France. A polemical journalist and the editor of two unsuccessful journals (*Our Continent*, 1882–1884, and *The Basis*, 1895–1896), Tourgée wrote six novels dealing directly or indirectly with the Reconstruction. His present reputation rests largely on *A Fool's Errand* (1879)—one of the novels that inspired Chesnutt to pursue a literary career (see his journal entry for 16 March 1880).

[2] While this is the earliest known letter to Tourgée, Chesnutt's correspondence with him was well advanced: on 8 December 1888, Tourgée wrote to him, "Few things have given me greater pleasure than your letters." The more recent compliment paid, to which Chesnutt refers here, was a reference to "Chestnut's [*sic*] curious realism" in "The South as a Field for Fiction," *Forum* 6 (December 1888), 404–13; and in an 8 December letter Tourgée apologized for its brevity: "I did not dare make the reference more explicit lest it should do you an injury. The fact of color is yet a curse the intensity of which few realize." Alluding to what he viewed as the distasteful kind of literary realism then advocated by the influential novelist and critic William Dean Howells, Tourgée went on to praise Chesnutt's highly imaginative variety of "realism" as more "true to nature" because free from "the fettering ideas" and "narrow rules" which result in the "falsest and sorriest" literature. He encouraged Chesnutt to persist in the belief that, through his art, he "will do much to solve the great question of the hour—the greatest question of the world's history—the future of the negro."

[3] In his 8 December letter, Tourgée expressed his hope that the "colored race" would build a

monument to Brown by 1900, funding it by a contribution of one penny per person per year, with the rest of the cost made up by whites.

[4] The "mouthpiece" character in "Dave's Neckliss" is Uncle Julius McAdoo, who had spun his fanciful yarns in "The Goophered Grapevine," *Atlantic Monthly* 60 (August 1887), 254–60; "Po' Sandy," *Atlantic Monthly* 61 (May 1888), 605–11; and "The Conjurer's Revenge," *Overland Monthly* 13 (June 1889), 623–29. It was almost ten years before Chesnutt again published a story with Julius in it, "Hot-Foot Hannibal," *Atlantic Monthly* 83 (January 1899), 49–56.

[5] In "Dave's Neckliss," the principal character is a slave falsely accused of stealing a ham. His punishment is the shackling of a ham to his neck, and he eventually goes mad, seeing himself as a ham that should be hung in the smokehouse. That is, he hangs himself.

[6] Chesnutt is here self-consciously describing himself as an African-American artist in the terms employed by Tourgée in his 8 December letter: "I incline to think that the climacteric of American literature will be negroloid in character,—I do not mean in form—the dialect is a mere fleeting incident, but in style of thought, intensity of color, fervency of passion and grandeur of aspiration. Literature rather than politics, science or government, is the [medium] in which the American negro—not the African for there is really but little of the African left—will win his earliest perhaps his brightest laurels." See n. 2, where it is clear that Tourgée saw Chesnutt and himself as practitioners of realism in literature; it is as clear here, however, that his aesthetic values were as romantic as they were didactic.

[7] The article was "What Is a White Man?" *Independent*, 30 May 1889, 5–6; the short story to be published was "The Sheriff's Children."

[8] "The Conjurer's Revenge."

[9] From 21 April 1888 through 5 January 1895 Tourgée wrote a weekly column, "A Bystander's Notes," for the Chicago *Inter Ocean*.

[10] Chesnutt expresses Tourgée's point of view here; see 9 September 1889 to Cable, n. 2.

George Washington Cable

·∾·

Oct. 4, 1889.

Dear Mr. Cable:—

Your letter returning the MS. of "Rena Walden" and enclosing statement of Gov. Chamberlain's views on the Negro Question was duly received.[1] I have tried to answer Gov. Chamberlain's argument on the line you suggested, with what success you can determine from the enclosed type-writer copy, which I made in duplicate, as it was about as easy. It's funny about Chamberlain: he himself led the black vote of S.C. tolerably well, and had hopes, as the recent history of his administration states, of bringing to a successful issue the experiment of providing good government even out of unpromising materials, until his attempt was nipped in the bud by the very methods which he now approves and justifies.[2]

I cannot properly express my thanks to you for your wise and kindly criticism of "Rena Walden." Every suggestion is to the point, and I had purposely dodged some of the additional work necessary—because it was hard, and because I wanted to keep the story within a certain length. I suppose, however, it is a species of willful murder to kill a story for lack of words. I have doubts about my ability to make of the story all that you suggest, but I shall do my best, and then let you see the result. I am glad you think the story a good one in outline; I was afraid it would suffer from the lack of white characters in it. The elaborations you suggest will increase its length several thousand words; indeed, I think it could be rounded out into a "novelette" if not a novel.[3]

I have read of your article in the *Congregationalist*, though I have not had an opportunity to read it.[4] The Christian Church now has a fine opportunity to demonstrate whether it will be really the Church of Christ, and teach what He taught, or whether it shall be merely a weak reflection of society. A good many people are watching with deep interest the course of the Congregational and Episcopal churches in this matter.

Very truly yours,
Chas. W. Chesnutt

TLS: LNHT

[1] Daniel Henry Chamberlain (1835–1907) was born and educated in Massachusetts. During the Civil War he was a lieutenant in the Fifth Massachusetts, an African-American regiment. Afterwards, he settled in South Carolina where he practiced law and became active in Republican politics. Elected governor in 1874, he was known by his admirers as a foe to corruption and proponent of good government. Democrats, however, charged him with malfeasance in office, and his narrow reelection in 1876 was a cause for civil disorder. He abdicated on 10 April 1877, and South Carolina was returned to Democrat rule. Cable had solicited from Chamberlain an essay on "the Negro Question" for the Open Letter Club. He sent it to Chesnutt on 26 September 1889 with a request that makes clear his partisan purpose for founding the Open Letter Club: he asked Chesnutt to write a response pointing out Chamberlain's "sophistries," enclosing the text of his own criticism of Chamberlain's piece as "a kind of hint and stimulation" for Chesnutt. (Cable would treat Alfred M. Waddell in the same manner, again giving an adversary the false impression he was merely the coordinator of debate; see 14 November 1889 to Moffat, n. 2.) Chesnutt's critique, acknowledged as received in an undated letter sent from Nashville, has not been located. For later expressions of Chamberlain's views, see "The Race Problem at the South," *New Englander* 52 (June 1890), 507–27, and "Reconstruction in South Carolina," *Atlantic Monthly* 87 (April 1901), 473.

[2] Chesnutt is referring to Walter Allen's laudatory history, *Governor Chamberlain's Administration in South Carolina: A Chapter of Reconstruction in the Southern States* (1888). Chamberlain "led the black vote" in that he was a Republican for whom African Americans voted in two gubernatorial elections, in opposition to the white supremacist Democrat party whose Wade Hampton (1818–1902) replaced Chamberlain as governor in 1877. The comparatively more benign Reconstruction era situation of African Americans in South Carolina ended with the abdication of Chamberlain. The new trend set in motion was toward the limitation of their political power and civil rights. Two points made in Chamberlain's unlocated essay for the Open Letter Club can be inferred from Cable's criticism of Chamberlain's reasoning, which he sent Chesnutt along with the essay (see n. 1). Chamberlain had argued that suppression will continue until the African American is educated, and that "an inferior race cannot maintain an ascendancy." Cable's retort was that "the Negro can never be educated until we stop suppressing him," and that the goal of educating African Americans is not to put the race "in the ascendancy" over whites.

[3] Since, in his 4 March 1889 letter to Cable, Chesnutt claimed to have already written a novel, his speculation that "Rena" might be made into a novella or novel reflects either his having forgotten the earlier and too-grand claim for the size of it or the existence of another, unidentified manuscript that Chesnutt considered a novel. What is clear is that Chesnutt is here reconceiving "Rena" in light of Cable's suggestions. Cable's 25 September 1889 letter was a thoroughgoing

criticism, indicating that he viewed the story as far from finished. Cable found that it began well, but the "weakness of insufficient labor" manifested itself soon after page 8. He encouraged Chesnutt to do more with regard to depicting "the grotesque, ludicrous, pathetic and barren conditions of colored society." Chesnutt should present such actualities truthfully to cultivated white readers, treating these elements "with proper tenderness and fraternal charity" but being careful not to "assert and ask too much of these qualities" since the prejudices of his readers must be taken into account. The character Frank's attendance at a party Cable judges "badly slighted," a "good opportunity overlooked"; the contrast between Rena's dreams and the actualities of her situation should be artfully emphasized more; and the "white lady's visit" can be managed "with much better effect." Lastly, the melodrama of the grand finale should be made more powerful: "Page 30 ought to be simply tremendous."

⁴ Cable lamented the failure of "the two State bodies of Congregational churches in Georgia, white and colored" to form a union in "Congregational Unity in Georgia," *Congregationalist* (Boston) 74 (26 September 1889), 317. Noting that the African-American group rejected a plan that did not eliminate racial caste distinctions but provided for "separate local bodies," Cable opined that the proposal was "really a plan for putting forth a maximum of profession with a minimum of performance." He hoped that the matter would be eventually resolved by adherence to "the Divine Master's teachings."

George Washington Cable

ᴥ

Oct. 17, 1889.

Dear Mr. Cable:—

I return the MS.¹ It contains my ideas, and I am quite willing to let it go in its present shape. If it would not interfere with your plan, however, I would suggest one or two changes:—

The repetition of the word "because" might be avoided by putting it at the end of the main proposition, followed by a dash, instead of at the beginning of each argument.

Is not the second argument a little obscure? I thought of this: "This suppression, as practiced, is not confined to the Negroes who are not educated, but bears down with equal weight upon the educated Negro."

It seems to me that the eighth and ninth propositions are rather minor propositions to support the seventh, than directly in support of the main proposition, and might be marked (a) and (b), leaving the tenth and 11th to be called the 8th and 9th.

I do not insist upon these changes, as perhaps your arrangement may be imperative in connection with the other papers.² It has occurred to me that the word "suppress" might be replaced with something else in one or two places with a gain in strength and no loss in clearness, though that, with the rest, I leave to you.

                                                        Yours very truly,
                                                        Chas. W. Chesnutt.

TLS: LNHT

[1] Chesnutt is referring to his Open Letter Club reply to Governor Chamberlain's essay on the "Negro Question." See 4 October 1889 to Cable, n. 2, where it is clear that the key concept referred to here, "suppression," was also of cardinal importance in Chamberlain's essay.

[2] As indicated on a postcard to Cable sent by Baskervill on 15 March 1890, Chamberlain's essay, Chesnutt's response (unlocated), and Baskervill's own were distributed from Nashville to the Open Letter Club members in early March 1890. Baskervill explained at length in a 24 February letter to Cable (LNHT) that he sided with Chamberlain against Chesnutt, knowing that he was opposing Cable as well. Baskervill's letter to Cable and an undated draft of his "open letter" (LNHT) invite additional inferences about Chamberlain's position (see 4 October 1889 to Cable, n. 2) as well as Chesnutt's: that Chamberlain and Baskervill favored a solution of the "Negro problem" by the individual states, while Chesnutt proposed federal intervention; that they saw better conditions for African Americans being contingent upon them becoming "better Negroes" in "work, in industry, in economy, in thrift, in honesty, in chastity," while Chesnutt argued the unqualified right to enjoy better conditions immediately; that they felt African Americans would fare better politically if they did not vote en bloc as Republicans since both parties would then solicit their support, while Chesnutt may have argued that Democrats were the African American's enemies; and that they favored an educational qualification for voting, while Chesnutt insisted upon the franchise as an absolute right for all males.

Albion W. Tourgée

࠵

Oct. 18, 1889.

My Dear Sir:—

Yours of Oct. 12th received, and I thank you cordially for your offer to write me a preface. I am more than likely to recall it to you as soon as I have time to look after the matter of getting out a book.[1]

Thanks also for the copy of *Frank Leslie's*. I saw it copied just now, with proper credit, in a newspaper published by a colored man for circulation among colored people,—a roundabout way of saying a "colored" newspaper.[2] Your labors are appreciated by those you seek to benefit.

Yours very truly,
Chas. W. Chesnutt.

TLS: NWefHi

[1] In 26 September 1889 to Tourgée, Chesnutt announced his plan to collect his short stories as a book.

[2] The reference is to "Our Semi-citizens," *Frank Leslie's Illustrated Newspaper* 69 (28 September 1889), 122–23. Tourgée's writings were frequently reprinted in the *Cleveland Gazette*, though not in this case. The African-American newspaper to which Chesnutt refers has not been identified.

Mary Adelene Moffat

་ར་

November 14, 1889.

I thank you for the opportunity of reading Hon. A. M. Waddell's letter.[1] His statement of the County Government system, though brief, is correct; and from it may be readily gathered what Mr. Waddell does not directly say—that it centralizes the government of the State in the hands of the legislative majority, and entirely takes away the power of any local majority of the opposite political party.[2]

I cannot quite agree with Mr. Waddell in regard to the degree of corruption which characterized the Carpet-bag County governments. They were not all corrupt, nor were the corrupt all equally corrupt, nor was the financial condition so bad as he puts it. In fact, Mr. Waddell's own letter bears me out in this statement. On the second page of his letter he says: "The result (of carpet-bag government) was that in a very short time they (the Eastern counties) were overwhelmed with debt and ruined financially." On the same page, in the following paragraph, he says that the result of the return to the old or centralized system, "was wonderful, for those which had been bankrupted were in a very few years out of debt, paying dollar for dollar, and their securities at par." I submit that the two statements do not harmonize perfectly: the ruin which could be so easily repaired could not have been so deep-seated or complete, especially when the fact is taken into consideration that the recuperative power of the South was very small for many years after the war. It must also be borne in mind that the carpet-bag governments found the South bankrupt—the country was impoverished, the local treasuries empty, the industries paralyzed. The reorganization of the State and County governments, the establishment of a common-school system for the whole people, (a fact for which the carpet-bag governments must be given credit), were necessarily expensive; and a public debt was not a new thing in history.

To say that the misgovernment and corruption of the carpet-bag governments was unparalleled in history is a strong statement. The government of New York City under the Tweed *regime*,[3] the financial methods, or lack of method, of many of the Central and South American governments, the notorious corruption of Russian local administration, are instances which invite comparison. And the recent defalcations of the State Treasurer's of Kentucky and Louisiana suggest that even if the white people of the South have a monopoly of personal honesty and political integrity, the supply is unfortunately not large enough to go around.

But the greatest mistake which Mr. Waddell, and indeed most Southern writers on this subject make, is in ascribing the mistakes and the corruption of carpet-bag rule to the Negroes. That these things were mostly due to the rapacity of corrupt and unscrupulous white men seems to be overlooked.

Mr. Waddell himself would be the last to say that the Negroes either engineered or profited to any great extent by the several considerable jobs which disgraced carpet-bag rule in North Carolina. The Negroes had no competent leaders among themselves; they received neither advice nor assistance from the Southern white people, who were indeed rather gratified at seeing them sink deeper and deeper into the slough of incompetency, for successful government by the Negro would have been a shock to their preconceived notions, and harder to bear than even the worst misgovernment.

And that is the root of the whole trouble in the South. The white people not only do not wish to be governed by Negroes, whether well or ill; (and it is very natural and proper that they should not wish to be governed entirely by Negroes, who as a class are undoubtedly inferior in ability to govern); but they do not want the Negroes to share with them the power which their numbers and their citizenship justly entitle them to. The white people are willing to curtail their own liberties very materially, as they do by the North Carolina system of County government, in order that they may entirely eliminate the Negro as a political factor.

I do not believe this is necessary to good government in the South, and especially in North Carolina even under present party divisions; for in that State there is a higher average of intelligence among the colored people and a larger number of whites throughout the State who are in political sympathy with the Negroes, than perhaps in any other Southern State except Virginia. But laying partisan considerations aside, one half of the time and ingenuity spent in conciliating the Negroes, in winning their friendship and confidence, that is now employed in subverting their rights under cover of law, would enable the white people of North Carolina and of the whole South to govern by the supremacy which superior wealth, station, education and experience in public affairs would naturally give them. This method of controlling the Negroes has never been tried. It would require some concessions on the part of the whites. It would require a change of attitude toward the colored people; it would require such a recognition of their political and public rights as would disarm their distrust of the whites. It would require, too, a cessation of such utterances as the following from the New Orleans *Times-Democrat* of November 5, 1889:—

> When Gov. Hill, upon his recent visit to Atlanta and Chattanooga, told the people in his public addresses that the settlement of the race issue is a mere matter of money, that astute politician did not know what he was talking about. . . . The race issue is a natural antagonism; it springs from innate differences between the Negro and the Caucasian, and has nothing whatever to do with education or the lack of education. To the Negro varnished with such learning as he is capable of acquiring, there is even a more pronounced antipathy than to the Negro of the cotton-field and the kitchen.[4]

No one would deny that a state of things such as I have spoken of, if it could be brought about, would be better for both races than the present system of suppressing the Negro by hook or crook, to which system, by the way, the recently enacted election law of North Carolina is a subtle but effective "clincher."[5] Until the policy of conciliation has been tried and has failed, there will not be in the minds of fair-minded people any sufficient excuse for a system which is avowedly based on a denial of the principles of "pure democracy"—a doctrine so highly lauded by the Southern whites in the abstract, and when it enlarges their own powers or privileges, and so completely ignored by them when it conflicts with their notions of so-called Anglo-Saxon superiority.[6]

But pardon the length of my letter. Your correspondent, as I happen to know, is an able attorney as well as a veteran politician, and has presented his side of the case to you in its strongest light. But in the saving clause of his letter, where he foresees a possible future when the Negroes will not (to paraphrase his language by the slang of the day) regard "public office as a private snap," there seems to speak the fair-minded man rising above the advocate, and looking forward to a time when the laws will be employed to extend rather than to restrict the liberty of the citizen.[7]

Very respectfully yours,
Chas. W. Chesnutt.

TLS: LNHT

[1] Neither the 13 November autograph draft nor the typed version of this letter sent to Moffat includes a salutation. Alfred Moore Waddell (1834–1912) was a North Carolina attorney and active Democrat who began his tenure of eight years as a member of the U.S. House of Representatives in early 1871. During the 1898 state election, he would prove one of the principal white supremacists using "Negro dominance" as the theme precipitating the defeat of the state's "fusion" government of Republicans and Populists, which had since 1894 effected a greater degree of African-American participation in politics. He is still seen as one of the main figures who caused the Wilmington, N.C., race riot of 10 November 1898 (see 11 November 1898 to Page, n. 2.) After the riot, he and his followers violated democratic processes with a coup d'état: they proclaimed Waddell the new mayor, and the other offices were filled in the same manner. It should be noted that Waddell's *Some Memories of My Life: 1907* (1908) discloses the personality of a sophisticated native son whose racism does not stand in high relief.

[2] With 9 September 1889 to Cable, Chesnutt enclosed a rough draft providing information on the North Carolina county government system requested by Cable. At that time, Cable appears to have solicited an "open letter" on the subject from Waddell. On 7 November 1889, Cable asked Chesnutt to respond to Waddell's comments and send his Open Letter Club contribution to Moffat in New York City. Cable, that is, wished to appear to Waddell as though he was not directly involved in the debate that he was, in fact, initiating. Hardly the objective intermediary, Cable gave clear signals to Chesnutt regarding how a rebuttal should be designed: "The new phase of this North Carolina problem seems to require something to show, first, that the corruption and bankruptcy of the eastern counties was exaggerated—due to the determination of the [Democrats] to bankrupt their opponents—or that at any rate, the change of county governmental form was not necessary to an extrication from corruption and bankruptcy was not really resorted to for that purpose mainly." Waddell's 31 October 1889 letter to Cable (LNHT) read thus:

I received this morning your favor of the 28th inquiring about "County Government" in North Carolina and will give you in brief its history.

From 1776 to 1868 the local government of Counties was in the hands of the Justices of the Peace who met in the County Court and transacted the County business. These Justices were elected by the Legislature, and all the public business was done by them in the open Court where any citizen had a right to be heard.

When "Carpet Bag" government was instituted in the State the system was changed to a government by County Commissioners, elected by the people, (as all Justices and other officers were under that government), and thereupon that shameless corruption, which is unparalleled in history, began. The 27 Eastern Counties contained an overwhelming negro vote—a large majority in most of them—and these were completely controlled by the corrupt leaders, who thereby got possession of those Counties and others. The result was that in a very short time they were overwhelmed with debt and ruined financially—County "script" was reduced to from 15 to 25 cts on the dollar in the hands of anybody but "the ring," who bought at those rates and redeemed at par. Offices were multiplied, and filled with the most ignorant and purchasable of the population. —Well, it is a long and humiliating story.

In 1875 a Constitutional Convention was called, when a return to the old system was adopted, except that the Justices elected by the Legislature instead of governing in a body now elect the County Commissioners. The result of the change on the finances of the Counties was wonderful, for those which had been bankrupted were in a very few years out of debt, paying dollar for dollar, and their securities at par, and have remained so ever since. It was simply the uniform experience of every State or municipality where the two kinds of government—negro and Anglo-Saxon—have been tried.

Of course there has always been complaint of a want of "liberty" by the advocates of the Carpet Bag system in the Eastern part of the State.

In the Western part of the State, where there are very few negroes, there is, of course, some reason (for those who believe in pure Democracy—that every office, of every kind, everywhere, ought to be filled by election under a system of universal free suffrage) to complain of the present system as one which deprives the white people of local self-government; but, so far as I know, there has not been a single instance of any complaint that there was *corrupt* government. It has been purely a matter of party ascendancy with them.

And, really, there would be no objection to electing the County Commissioners by the people in the West, but, of course, the system must be uniform in every part of the State, and it would be madness to re-establish the Carpet Bag system in the Eastern Counties, *now* at least, or until the negroes learn that the power to elect public officers does not embrace the right to use the public funds at will.

I do not believe there would have been any especial objection to the new system, if it had not, from the start, been the source of such infamous mis-government and corruption; but the experience of it for a few years renders a return to it impossible, unless an unexpected political revolution occurs.

[3] William M. "Boss" Tweed (1823–1878) was a Democrat New York politician best known for his corrupt Tammany Hall "ring" in New York City.

[4] Chesnutt here extracts the gist of "Gov. Hill and the Negro," New Orleans *Times-Democrat*, 5 November 1889, 4. David Bennett Hill (1843–1910) was active in Democrat politics in the state of New York and was elected to several local and state offices. At this time he was serving as governor (1885–1891).

[5] In January 1889 an election law reform bill modeled upon one passed in South Carolina the previous month was introduced in the North Carolina legislature ("North Carolina Legislature," *New York Times*, 18 January 1889, 1). Because it imposed an educational requirement for voting, its passage into law on 7 March effected the disfranchisement of many African Americans ("Ballot Reform in the South," *New York Times*, 8 March 1889, 1).

⁶ What Chesnutt hoped for began to become a reality in North Carolina in 1894, when a "Fusion" of Republicans and Populists began the process of restoring county government to local control, passing legislation in 1895 and 1897 which thwarted Democrat intentions to continue minimizing both the degree to which African Americans were a significant factor in elections and the number of political and judicial positions occupied by them. In 1898, however, the Democrats regained office, recentralized control of county government by returning appointment power to the white legislature, and commenced to impose restrictions on voting that effectively disfranchised African Americans.

⁷ What Chesnutt does not mention in his discussion of the previous system of county governance established by Tourgée and others at the state's 1867–1868 constitutional convention is that his family was a direct beneficiary: his father, Andrew Chesnutt, served as a justice of the peace and county commissioner in 1868–1870.

George Washington Cable

◦◦

December 30, 1889.

Dear Mr. Cable:—

Your letter received. I am glad to learn that you are back at your desk, for one can confidently expect that under such circumstances something valuable will be added to literature, and to Open Letter Club work.[1] I have noticed the handsome volume in which your "Strange True Stories" have been issued.[2]

My business has been so absorbing for the last two months that I haven't been able to touch either the story or the article on Southern school matters since I saw you;[3] the leading man in the business I devote most of my time to, court reporting, has quit the business, and I have had a large part of his work, which with my own has given me all I have been able to do, even with the assistance of my sister. I mention this merely as an excuse for neglecting what I realize is higher work, and work which I would prefer to do.[4] But I hope to get at both very soon, perhaps this week, and try to finish them up. I will make use of the clipping sent me, and return it to you in a few days; many thanks for it.[5]

I see our Southern friends are very much worked up over the fact that you stopped with Mr. Napier at Nashville, and the *Memphis Appeal* solemnly declares that you are the most thoroughly despised man, among Southern people, in the United States;[6] I presume you can stand it if they can. The horrible affair at Barnwell, S.C.,[7] almost offsets the refusal of the legislature to repeal the civil rights bill and to pass the law requiring railroads to furnish separate accommodation for colored passengers. It is supposed that the railroad companies worked against the measures proposed by the Governor in his message, and defeated them. It is indeed a hopeful sign that the people of the South are beginning to consider their pockets before their prejudices.[8]

I hope you had a successful tour in the West. Mr. Kennan lectures here Thursday night, and I hope to hear him.[9]

Very truly yours,
Chas. W. Chesnutt.

TLS: LNHT

[1] Cable wrote Chesnutt on 27 December, indicating that he was back at his desk in Northampton doing Open Letter Club work and anxious to see Chesnutt's revision of "Rena Walden" and a "paper" on Southern school funding. Cable had just completed what is referred to by Chesnutt below as his Western lecture tour.

[2] Cable's *Strange True Stories of Louisiana* included three race-focused stories previously read by Chesnutt: "Salome Müller, the White Slave" (24 May 1889 to Cable), "The 'Haunted House' in Royal Street" and "Attalie Brouillard" (2 September 1889 to Moffat).

[3] The story is "Rena Walden," which Cable read in manuscript and which Chesnutt, on 4 October 1889, indicated he planned to expand in light of the criticism and suggestions Cable had sent him. Cable is not known to have given a lecture in Cleveland in November; but he then visited there long enough for the two to discuss "Rena" and the article on Southern schools. The latter essay does not appear to have seen print, and the manuscript has not been located.

[4]Chesnutt's sister Lillian (1871–?) came to Cleveland from Fayetteville, N.C., in 1888. She was employed by him, first as a typist and then as a stenographer, until 1892 or 1893.

[5] Cable's 27 December letter indicates that the unlocated clipping relates to the distribution of public education funds. At TNF is a three-page typed transcription of a Fort Worth *Gazette* article on funding in Texas, complete with a county-by-county account of how much was spent on whites and blacks (the November 1889 issue of the *Gazette* in which the article appeared is not extant). The point made by the article was that large amounts of public money have been spent, or squandered, on the education of the state's African Americans.

[6] James Carroll Napier (1845–1940) was a Nashville attorney and a prominent Republican politician. Cable's dining with this African American proved a sensation in Nashville, and he was attacked by white journalists as a renegade and traitor ("The Gossiper," Nashville *American*, 10 December 1889, 4). The *American* continued to criticize Cable, "who has lived in the South long enough to know the folly and wickedness of inspiring ignorant negroes with vain dreams of social equality" ("Cable and Negro Equality," 15 December 1889, 4), triggering additional attacks and defenses in not only Southern newspapers but in those published outside the region. The Nashville representative of the Open Letter Club, William M. Baskervill, was mortified because of his widely known connection with Cable; indeed, Cable was his house guest when the visit to Napier's home occurred. Baskervill scolded him for his inflammatory behavior in an 8 January 1890 letter (LNHT). The solution of the "Negro problem," Baskervill explained, is retarded whenever the impression is given that social equality is the reformer's goal. Baskervill himself did not favor social equality in that it might lead to intermarriage between the races: "I abhor miscegenation, for it would be a degradation of our race without any great resultant good to the other race." (Chesnutt, of course, came to see interracial marriage as the ultimate means of solving "the race problem": see "The Future American," *Boston Evening Transcript*, 1 September 1900, 24.)

[7] Eight African-American men were taken from the jail of Barnwell County, S.C., and shot to death on 28 December 1889. Six were suspected of murdering the son of the owner of the plantation on which they lived; the other two were suspects in a separate case concerning the death of another Caucasian male. In "Prominent Citizens Tell the Story" (Columbia, S.C., *Daily Register*, 29 December 1889, 1), an explanation was offered: "These several brutal murders of prominent white

men by negroes caused a state of indignation and resentment among our people that can be better imagined than described, but cannot be imagined by any one not present in our midst."

[8] In his 1889 address to the South Carolina state legislature, Governor John P. Richardson proposed that "the General Statutes be carefully amended" to allow "separate but equal accommodations for passengers of the two races" on railroad cars ("South Carolina's Debt," *New York Times*, 28 November 1889, 5). Chesnutt here expresses his pleasure over the fact that, on 20 December, the House of Representatives rejected the railway car segregation bill offered by the governor, in part because of the financial reason that Chesnutt cites: "that to carry out its provisions would subject the railroads to great hardships and expense, and, on the other hand, there was no necessity for it, as the colored people, with few exceptions, travel in second-class cars, and, as a rule, are well behaved" ("Race Prejudice Allayed," *New York Times*, 21 December 1889, 5). Chesnutt, however, was too optimistic about the South Carolina legislature refusing to repeal the "civil rights bill," that is, the Civil Rights Act passed by Republican lawmakers in 1869. This act was an application at the state level of the Fourteenth Amendment of the U.S. Constitution, prohibiting discrimination on public conveyances and in the matters of accommodations and entertainments. Chesnutt appears not to have been aware that on 21 December the South Carolina Senate reconsidered the repeal of the act and ordered a third reading of the measure ("General Assembly," Columbia, S.C., *Daily Register*, 22 December 1889, 1). When the legislative session ended on 24 December, the railroad companies were not required to provide separate cars for African Americans but the law requiring Fourteenth Amendment protections for that group had been expunged. Further, as an editorial writer put it, the people of South Carolina did, regardless of statutes, expect the railroads to separate black and white passengers in individual cars and, when cars were crowded, to employ separate ones for African Americans ("The Civil Rights Act," Columbia, S.C., *Daily Register*, 24 December 1889, 2).

[9] George Kennan (1845–1924) was an explorer and author who became an expert on Russia and the cruelties of the Romanoff Government. His exposé, *Siberia and the Exile System* (1891), described the excesses of the imperial autocracy and contributed to the overthrow of that regime.

George Washington Cable

⌒

February 3, 1890.

My dear Mr. Cable:—

I have been able to devote a few days almost entirely to literary work, and I took up my unfinished story first, although I suspect you regard the article on Southern schools as of more importance. I have cut the story down from about 20,000 words to 14,000, without eliminating a single incident that I can at present think of, but simply by following the line of condensation suggested by you when you were at my house.[1] I have adopted your suggestions with regard to Rena's speech and appearance, and I think I have made a compact story of what was before a rather rambling collection of thoughts. I have studied to reduce the number of words, but I do not see where I could do so further except in the preliminary descriptions, and then not without loss to the story.

If you can get the *Century* people to read the manuscript, and if otherwise available to make a concession in regard to the length, it will be a favor which I can appreciate if not return. The story has been read in its crude form to several people of taste and culture, as well as to some plainer people, and it seems to strike a chord of sympathy. I hope it will be as successful with the editor you send it to. If by reason of its length or any other cause you think it or find it unsalable, I will try my hand at it again, and will thank you for any further suggestions.

I am now going to work at the article on Southern schools. I have just received a copy of the Report of the Com'r of Education for 1887–'88, the latest of the series, just recently issued; and with the data I already have on hand I think I can write a readable and reliable article; at least I shall try. I shall send it to you when completed, which I think will be very soon.

Very respectfully yours,
Chas. W. Chesnutt.

TLS: LNHT

[1] On 4 October 1889 Chesnutt indicated to Cable that he was planning to expand "Rena." But it appears that, during Cable's visit to Cleveland in November, they agreed on the desirability of an abridgment.

George Washington Cable

Feb'y 4th, 1890.

My dear Mr. Cable:—

In my letter to you of yesterday I forgot to mention something that strikes me as either a remarkable coincidence or a rather bold plagiarism. The February number of the *Century* contains a contribution by H. S. Edwards, entitled "How Sal Came Through." About three years ago I published in a Washington paper, called *Family Fiction*, a story entitled "How Dasdy Came Through."[1] It was about a colored girl who had a sweetheart. Another girl with a new dress and hat cut her out and caught the fickle swain, to Dasdy's great chagrin. There was a revival in progress at the colored church, and her mother advised her to seek the consolations of religion. Dasdy went to the mourners' bench for several evenings, and managed to "come through" one night just at a time when her successful rival, clad in the new dress and hat, was standing near her. In the irresponsible frenzy of her "coming through," Dasdy tore the new dress to shreds and made a wreck of the new hat. The remedy was efficacious, and when Dasdy came out next Sunday in a new dress and all the odor of a freshly-acquired sanctity, the fickle 'Dolphus returned to his first love. If that isn't the story in the *Century*, then I haven't read it correctly. It is padded more than mine, told in a different style, and illustrated—some of the cuts are caricatures—but the substance is the same, even the name. Of course it may be only a coincidence, but it is certainly a curious one. I have a printed copy of my story, which is signed with my own name.

I don't know just how editors look upon such an adaptation, but I mention this to you as a matter of curiosity. Perhaps it might be doing the author a service for somebody to drop him a hint to quit writing when he has used up his own stock of ideas.

Yours very truly,
Chas. W. Chesnutt.

TLS: LNHT

[1] Harry Stillwell Edwards (1855–1938) was a Southern novelist and poet who, like Chesnutt, made broad comical use of African-American stereotypes. Edwards' "How Sal Came Through" was published in *Century* 39 (February 1890), 578–85; Chesnutt's "How Dasdy Came Through" appeared in *Family Fiction* on 21 February 1887. *Family Fiction* has not been located, and thus the pagination is not known. On 6 February, Cable replied: "Plagiarism is such a futile vice and so dangerous, that it is little short of insanity to attempt it. Before imputing it one must have overwhelming proof that it is not a coincidence, but the deliberate intention to deceive."

George Washington Cable

‹◇›

Feb'y 18, 1890

Dear Mr. Cable:

I send you by this mail copy of a paper entitled *Family Fiction*, containing story "How Dasdy Came Through." It is a poor sketchy sort of affair, and it is quite possible that the writer of "How Sal Came Through" never saw it, or having seen it forgot that he had seen it, and reproduced the plot unconsciously. However, if you will read my sketch first, you will perceive the correspondence. The *Century* story is dramatic, and evidently carefully studied—(mine is neither)—so carefully studied in fact that it almost suggests an effort to make it as unlike mine as possible, assuming of course that the writer had read mine. The events of my story are laid since the war, in town, among yellow people, so to speak; the other seems to be laid before the war, in the country, among black people. In my sketch, the mother suggests religion as a solace for disappointed love; in the other the suggestion comes from the young mistress. The climax is varied a little. In my opinion, the latter story is as skilfully and effectually changed as it would be possible to vary a story without telling another. Or perhaps, less invidiously speaking, if I were going to adapt somebody else's story, I would vary it in just that way. I don't wish to charge the writer of "How Sal Came Through" with plagiarism; and yet I have enough of the literary instinct to resent plagiarism in the abstract, and still more when it is from a contemporary writer, and that writer myself.[1]

Kindly pursue the course you suggested, and tell me what you think. If you conclude it is a plagiarism, consider it your own discovery and do as you like about it.[2] If you think it merely a coincidence, and perhaps hardly that, my lips are sealed on the subject. To say anything would be much ado about nothing, perhaps, in any event, for I don't think much of the story in either form.

Has the Open Letter Club published another pamphlet? I must ask a little longer indulgence for my article on Southern schools; the subject is not likely to become untimely for some years to come.[3]

Yours very respectfully,
Chas. W. Chesnutt.

P.S. Absence from the city has prevented my sending you this paper sooner.

ALS: LNHT

[1] That is, Chesnutt does not wish to charge Edwards with the act of plagiarizing; but he resents plagiarism, especially when he is the contemporary writer who originated the work that was plagiarized.

[2] Cable accommodated Chesnutt by acting as intermediary with Richard Watson Gilder, editor of *Century*. See 15 April 1890 to Cable, n. 1, for Gilder's response.

[3] Chesnutt indicated to Cable on 3 February 1890 that he was turning to this article, apparently intended for Open Letter Club distribution; but he worked on "Rena Walden" instead. He finally enclosed a draft of the piece with 29 March 1890 to Cable.

George Washington Cable

❧

March 29, 1890.

My Dear Mr. Cable:—

Yours of the 21st received. I have not yet been able to elaborate as careful a paper as I would wish, but I send you herewith the result of my labors.[1] It takes time and deliberation to do statistical work, and I have not been in a position to give this paper the necessary attention without neglecting something else. My paper is brief and by no means exhaustive. You can make use of it in its present shape under my name, if you think it worthy, or you can use it in any way you see fit. I also send you by express to-day the rather meager memoranda from which I have prepared it, including the latest report of the Com'r of Education;[2] if you can use them in adding to what I have written, I shall be glad to have you do so. In any event, kindly return me all except the Commissioner's Report, which please keep, as by some chance my congressman has sent me two of them.

I received a copy of your address to the Massachusetts Club.[3] It is a clear and able presentation of the Southern question in a new light—the hopeless struggle for pure government without free government.

I do not comprehend how a fair-minded opponent, however radically he might differ from you, could find anything harsh to say in reply to so fair and courteous an argument; if any one can lift the race question out of the mire of prejudice and partisanship into the clear light of reason and patriotism, I think you are the man. I don't agree with you, however, in the plea for one more chance for the Southern Democrats to deal fairly with their political opponents; it is true that something would be gained by a delay of Federal interference, and if the delay were long enough continued no Federal interference would be necessary to protect the Negroes in their rights. It is easy enough to temporize with the bull when you are on the other side of the fence, but when you are in the pasture with him, as the colored people of the South are, the case is different. I take it that every citizen is entitled to such protection as the government can extend to him in the enjoyment of his rights, and that he is entitled to that protection *now*, and whenever his rights are invaded.[4] I sincerely hope the present Congress will pass a wise and practicable federal election law, and that the President will have brain enough and backbone enough to enforce it.[5] The ever lengthening record of Southern wrongs and insults, both lawless and under the form of law, calls for whatever there is of patriotism, of justice, of fair play in the American people, to cry hands off and give the Negro a show, not five years hence or ten years hence, or a generation hence, but *now*, while he is alive, and can appreciate it; posthumous fame is a glorious thing, even if it is only posthumous; posthumous liberty is not, in the homely language of the rural Southerner, "w'u'th shucks."

I was wondering what had become of "Rena Walden"; I hope the *Century* people will look with favor upon it. I should experience much satisfaction in seeing it in print. I presume from what you say about the Edwards matter that the *Century* story was open at least to suspicion of plagiarism; I only wish that my story had been told as well as Mr. Edwards told it; I am afraid that a comparison of the two will give the *Century* people such a poor opinion of my literary skill that they will consider it too great a loss of time to read "Rena."

Yours very truly,
Chas. W. Chesnutt.

P.S. Will you kindly send me another copy of your speech to the Reform Club? I want it for a gentleman of character and influence who is very much interested in the Race question.
Yours &c.,
C.W.C.

P.S. I have written a title in pencil; perhaps you can think of a better.[6]
C.W.C.

TLS: LNHT

[1] Chesnutt refers to the article on Southern schools requested by Cable (unlocated).

[2] The report for 1887–1888, referred to in 3 February 1890 to Cable.

[3] Cable spoke before the Massachusetts Club in Boston on 22 February 1890. The text of his speech appeared in the *Boston Journal*, 24 February 1890, 1, as well as in pamphlet form, *The Southern Struggle for Pure Government. An Address . . . Delivered Before the Massachusetts Club, Boston, on Washington's Birthday, 1890* (1890).

[4] In his speech, Cable enumerated the restrictions imposed upon African Americans by South-

ern Democrats, but he avoided incendiary language and employed an optimistic, conciliatory tone. He emphasized the need for all to stop blaming one another and make a fresh start. He saw no immediate need for federal intervention in the Southern states, suggesting that they be given two years to begin eliminating Jim Crow laws. Should there not be significant progress by that presidential election year, however, the new president should be called upon to take effective action. Chesnutt, in responding to Cable with a more radical demand for immediate implementation of full civil rights for African Americans, articulates a theme running through his later correspondence with Booker T. Washington, and his tone with Washington is anticipated here.

[5] As in the Open Letter Club situation involving Chamberlain and Baskervill (see 17 October 1889 to Cable, n. 2), Chesnutt again espouses a federal-intervention solution to problems in the South.

[6] The title of the article on Southern schools is not known.

George Washington Cable

◦◦◦

April 15, 1890.

My dear Mr. Cable:—

I return you Mr. Gilder's letter.[1] I would, merely from curiosity, (and I think pardonable curiosity in this instance), like to hear what Mr. Edwards says about that story. I don't press the charge of plagiarism, for it may have happened just as I have said, and as Mr. Gilder, quoting me, repeats. Mr. Edwards is justly entitled to the benefit of the doubt.

I hope Mr. Gilder will ask for my story, and that he may find it available.[2] This Edwards matter might very naturally predispose him a little in my favor, and added to your favorable suggestions may float the story into the desired haven.

I hope you were not very badly disappointed in the paper on Southern schools, and that you may at least find in it and the accompanying documents something useful in the discussion of *the* problem.[3]

I have heard something about Mr. Smiley's proposed "Negro" conference at Lake Mohonk.[4] Whenever you get time to write me a line or two, I would be glad to know whether the conference will materialize or not, and whether or not Mr. Smiley has accepted the suggestion you made to him, or what he has to say about it.[5]

Very truly yours,
Chas. W. Chesnutt.

TLS: LNHT

[1] Concerning the relationship between Chesnutt's "How Dasdy Came Through" and Edwards' "How Sal Came Through" (see 4 February 1890 to Cable), Gilder wrote Cable on 9 April 1890 (LNHT):

Taking the story and the title together, I think it would be no more than just to ask an explanation from Mr. Edwards; but I should not be at all surprised if he had never seen Mr. Chesnutt's story; they are so very different, after all. In style they have not the slightest resemblance; and it would be quite likely that the same subject, which is a typical one, should be hit upon by the two writers separately. The fact that the titles are so much alike would be a positive proof to me that Mr. Edwards had not, *knowingly*, plagiarized. Whether he had seen the story somewhere and had forgotten that he had read it is another question.

May I ask him whether he had seen it when he wrote his?

I also send back Mr. Chesnutt's letter to you dated February 18th. You will notice that Mr. Chesnutt in this letter says of his own story: "It is a poor sketchy sort of affair, and it is quite possible that the writer of 'How Sal Came Through' never saw it, or having seen it forgot that he had seen it, and reproduced the plot unconsciously."

[2] "Rena Walden."

[3] Chesnutt's enclosures have not been located. But, given his close attendance to the *Cleveland Gazette*, a militant African-American weekly edited by Harry C. Smith (see 25 April 1896 to Tourgée, n. 1), it is possible that he forwarded clippings of an untitled editorial regarding the Blair Bill for federal aid to education and an article dealing with a school segregation bill submitted to the Ohio legislature. The editorial, "The 'Separate School' Bill," and the article "Misrepresentation" appeared on p. 2 of the 29 March 1890 issue. The Blair Bill, defeated on 20 March 1890, was also the focus in "The Defeat of the Blair Bill," *Cleveland Leader*, 21 March 1890, 4. Chesnutt's familiarity with the *Gazette* was made clear at a local organizational meeting of an "Afro-American League" on 12 November 1889 (Chesnutt was a member of the "permanent organization committee"): "The most noteworthy remarks of the evening were those of Mr. Chas. Chestnut [*sic*], whose treatment of race troubles and remedies therefor were referred to by several speakers who followed. Mr. Chestnut laid due stress upon the importance of the race journals in this work and of their decision and fearlessness. The *Gazette* he thought second to no Afro-American organ" ("John Pea Green's Mouth," *Cleveland Gazette*, 16 November 1889, 3). On 26 November the organization was formed with the title of the Citizens' Equal Rights League; Chesnutt's friend, William T. Boyd (see 3 September 1895 to Tourgée and 26 October 1901 to Ethel Chesnutt), was elected a member of the Executive Committee, but Chesnutt himself did not become an officer ([Untitled paragraphs], *Cleveland Gazette*, 30 November 1889, 3).

[4] Albert Keith Smiley (1828–1912) was an educator who, in 1879, decided to devote all of his time to managing an inn on Lake Mohonk in Ulster County, N.Y. The same year he was appointed by President Rutherford B. Hayes to the Board of Indian Commissioners; in 1883 he arranged his first annual Lake Mohonk Conference of the Friends of the Indian. African Americans and the denizens of American dependencies eventually came within the scope of the conferences. Cable was invited but did not attend. "The Negro's View of the Race Problem" was the address given by Albion W. Tourgée. John C. Colvert, editor of the *Cleveland Leader*, also delivered a paper on "The Race Problem."

[5] The LNHT Cable collection includes a clipping noting the planned conference, "The Mohawk 'Negro Conference,'" *Cleveland Gazette*, 5 April 1890, 2. Chesnutt appears to have read the same article, for it focuses on the suggestion that Cable made to Smiley: that African Americans be invited to participate despite the problems that accommodations for them might entail.

George Washington Cable

⋘·

May 6, 1890.

My Dear Mr. Cable:—

I enclose you a copy of a communication from the editor of *Family Fiction*, with a newspaper clipping attached, from which you will see that I am not the only person to whom the idea of plagiarism has occurred in connection with Mr. Edwards's story in the *Century*.[1] This editor asks me for my opinion in regard to it. My opinion is that it was a deliberate plagiarism. You did not tell me in your letter what you thought about it, but I gathered from reading between the lines that your opinion does not differ very much from mine; correct me if I am wrong. At the same time, for obvious reasons, I would not wish to write anything to this editor which would lead him to make any editorial utterance reflecting on the character of a *Century* contributor, if thereby I would run the remotest risk of offending or antagonizing the editor of the *Century*. Taking the worst view of this case, there is an implied compliment to me involved in the fact that my plot was considered worth plagiarizing.

If it is not trespassing too much upon your time and good nature, may I ask your advice as to whether I had better discourage this editor from any further action in this matter, or tell him my opinion of it and let him take what course he likes?[2] His paper has a wide circulation, and while comparatively obscure, the story of the mouse and the elephant might not be without application.

Please let me know whether you have sent "Rena Walden" to the *Century*; also whether you received the paper, etc., with regard to Southern schools. The enclosed clipping from the *Cleveland Leader*,—I presume it is an Ass. Press despatch—has some bearing on the subject; and you have probably read of the action taken by the Virginia legislature affecting injuriously the Virginia Collegiate and Normal Institute.[3]   Very respectfully yours,

Chas. W. Chesnutt.

P.S. Please return enclosure.

TLS: LNHT

[1] The editor of *Family Fiction* wrote Chesnutt on 28 April 1890, noting the "close resemblance" of Edwards' story to Chesnutt's "How Dasdy Came Through."

[2] Cable sent to Chesnutt on 9 May a copy of Edwards' 5 May letter to Gilder. Edwards admitted, there "is certainly a remarkable resemblance between the stories, not alone in name, but in incidents. Where Mr. Chesnutt got his facts from I do not know. Mine were obtained from my wife. 'Sal' was a girl who grew up with her, and the scene of the comedy is a plantation belonging to the family. Since receiving your letter, I have questioned my wife, her mother, and her sister, the latter in Sparta, and each separately recalled the facts in the 'Coming Through of Sal.' These constitute the foundation of my story." He continued, "So far as the name or title is concerned, it is known that the history of every old time negro's conversion is called 'his' or 'her coming through.' It is first related in meeting by the convert and then retailed by the congregation—'Did you hear 'bout Tom's Comin' through?'—or 'you ought to hear'd how Sal Came through,' etc., etc. Mr. Chesnutt heard of 'Dasdy's' and I of Sal's, and naturally used the titles as published. To this I may add that I have never before seen Mr. Chesnutt's story, nor do I recollect ever seeing *Family Fiction* or hearing of it, though this need not argue the Magazine unknown, since I am too busy to read much. Of all the stories that I have written this is the only one that resembles any other, and the author of 'How Dasdy Came Through' may be sure that if his work was being used, a title would not have been selected to challenge attention." Cable advised Chesnutt that "all you really need to have established is the fact that your story appeared before Edwards' and that therefore if there was either plagiarisms [*sic*] or unconscious reminiscence it was his and not yours. You can afford to let the public settle the rest. A great many more things look like plagiarisms than really are such. I would discourage the editor [of *Family Fiction*] from further action in the matter. Write him a few very clear line [*sic*] and leave Mr. Edwards under no implication whatever."

[3] On 9 May 1890 (LNHT) Cable replied: "Mr. Gilder has 'Rena Walden' and holds it under consideration. I have the paper on Southern schools and cannot do anything with it for awhile. If

you should want it back let me know. I have not heard of the action of the Virginia legislature. If you have it in print, I would like to file it with your paper on schools." The Virginia Normal and Collegiate Institute had been negatively affected by two recent developments: not only was an all-white Board of Directors appointed by the governor, but the "college," or "higher learning," part of it was eliminated by the Virginia Assembly ("Some Race Doings," *Cleveland Gazette*, 5 April 1890, 1.) The *Cleveland Leader* clipping has not been located.

George Washington Cable

∾

May 23rd, 1890.

My dear Mr. Cable:—

Thanks for your kind letter of May 9th. I enclose you a copy of the letter which I have written to the editor of *Family Fiction*.[1]

Thanks for your good wishes. My business has been very prosperous for the past eight or nine months, and if it continues in anything like its present condition, I shall be able in a very few years to take the chances of devoting myself entirely to literary work, which I earnestly hope to do; meanwhile I look forward to a little leisure for writing during the Summer.

I trust that your kind word in its favor, coupled with such merits as the story itself may possess, will help "Rena Walden" to run the gauntlet of editorial criticism and break into the charmed pages of the *Century*.

May I retain the copy of Mr. Edwards' letter and Mr. Gilder's note? If you wish to have them returned, may I take copies of them?

I have just received a circular, directed in a familiar handwriting, with the Northampton postmark, in reference *Justice and Jurisprudence*.[2] I have ordered the book, which I did not find at our leading bookstore, and look forward with some curiosity to reading it. I think I can guess who inspired it. Is one permitted to know anything further about the "Brotherhood of Liberty"?[3] It is plain that in some form or other, under one name or another, the good work which has as its fountainhead a certain Northampton study goes bravely on. In the meantime some of your admirers are waiting patiently for your next novel, which from what you said to me when in Cleveland, we expect to find not without some bearing upon the question that *Justice and Jurisprudence* deals with.[4]

Sincerely yours,
Chas. W. Chesnutt.

TLS: LNHT

[1] Chesnutt wrote the editor of *Family Fiction* on 15 May 1890 (LNHT): "Your note with enclosed clipping, calling my attention to the story of Mr. Edwards in the *Century*, 'How Sal Came Through,' was duly received. I had noticed the resemblance of Mr. Edwards' story to my story, 'How Dasdy Came Through,' published in *Family Fiction*, February 12, 1887. I have since investigated the matter and do not wish to make the charge of plagiarism against Mr. Edwards, who has accounted for his story in a manner which I must accept as satisfactory."

[2] Brotherhood of Liberty, *Justice and Jurisprudence: An Inquiry Concerning the Constitutional Limitations of the Thirteenth, Fourteenth, and Fifteenth Amendments* (1889). According to its dedicatory address (21), this book "is intended to be a defence of the civil liberty of the whole American people. It presents the claim of the African race with no fairer gloss than naked truth affords. It is especially designed to be a treatise on the true exposition of the noble principle of *equality of rights by due process of law*, which these addressers insist is the great seminal doctrine of the Fourteenth Amendment; and constitutes an impregnable foundation for the civil tranquility, present and future, of a strong, proud, loving, and united people."

[3] Cable is not known to have responded to this query.

[4] Chesnutt is referring to Cable's visit to his home in November 1889. The novel Cable was then writing was *John March, Southerner*, published in 1894.

George Washington Cable

◦⌒◦

June 13, 1890.

Dear Mr. Cable:—

An absence of several days from the city has interfered with my answering your letter returning the MS. of "Rena Walden," which came duly to hand.[1] I thank you very much for sending me Mr. Gilder's letter which I do accept as a "faithful, wise word of friendly counsel."[2] Its faithfulness is obvious, its wisdom I cannot question, though I shall have to study both the letter and the story to avail myself of it, for while there is something lacking, Mr. Gilder only very vaguely intimates what it may be.[3] I do not think I am deficient in humor, though I dare say the sentiment of the story is a little bit "amorphous." It was written under the ever-present consciousness, so hard for me to get rid of, that a very large class of people consider the class the story treats of as "amorphous." I fear there is too much of this sentiment to make mulattoes good magazine characters,[4] and I notice that all of the good negroes (excepting your own creations) whose virtues have been given to the world through the columns of the *Century*, have been blacks, full-blooded, and their chief virtues have been their dog-like fidelity and devotion to their old masters. Such characters exist; not six months ago a negro in Raleigh, N.C., wrote to the Governor of the State offering to serve out the sentence in the penitentiary of seven years just imposed upon his old master for some crime. But I don't care to write about these people;[5] I do not think these virtues by any means the crown of manhood. I have read a number of English and French novels during the past few months dealing largely with colored characters, either in principal or subordinate parts. They figure as lawyers, as judges, as doctors, botanists, musicians, as people of wealth and station. They love and they marry without reference to their race, or with only such reference to it as to other personal disabilities, like poverty or ugliness for instance. These writers seem to find nothing extraordinary in a talented, well-bred colored man, nothing amorphous in a pretty, gentle-spirited colored girl.

But our American writers are different. Maurice Thompson's characters are generally an old, vulgar master, who, when not drunk or asleep, is amusing himself by beating an old negro. Thos. N. Page and H. S. Edwards and Joel C. Harris give us the sentimental and devoted negro who prefers kicks to half-pence.[6] Judge Tourgée's cultivated white negroes are always bewailing their fate, and cursing the drop of black blood that "taints"—I hate the word, it implies corruption—their otherwise pure blood.[7] An English writer would not hesitate to say that race prejudice was mean and narrow and provincial and unchristian—something to which a free-born Briton was entirely supe-rior; he would make his colored characters think no less of themselves because of their color but infinitely less of those who despise them on account of it.

But I am wandering. Mr. Gilder finds that I either lack humor, or that my characters have "a brutality, a lack of mellowness, a lack of spontaneous imag-inative life, lack of outlook." I fear, alas! that those are exactly the things that do characterize them, and just about the things that might be expected in them—the very qualities which government and society had for 300 years or so labored faithfully, zealously, and successfully to produce, the only qualities which would have rendered life at all endurable to them in the 19th century. But I suppose I shall have to drop the attempt at realism,[8] and try to make my characters like other folks, for uninteresting people are not good subjects for fiction.[9]

I cannot find words to thank you for your expressions of kindness and con-fidence in my as yet almost untried powers. I have felt the same thing ob-scurely. Self-confidence is a good thing, but recognition is a better; and next to an accepted MS. there is nothing so encouraging as the recognition of those who have proved their right to criticise. I will endeavor to show that your judgment is not at fault and that it is based on something more than a senti-mental sympathy with a would-be writer circumscribed in a manner so pecu-liar. Mr. Gilder shall see more of my work, and better. I shall write to please the editors, and the public, and who knows but that perhaps at some future day I may be best able to please others by pleasing myself?[10]

I will go right to work on "Rena Walden," and send you a draft when com-pleted. I would not personally send the same story twice to an editor, unless so requested by him; but I will follow your advice in regard to the disposition of this one.[11] I am grateful to Mr. Gilder for his interest in me, which the letter sufficiently attests. I fear I cannot acquire his fine discernment of all ungenu-ineness; that is perhaps the quality which gives his genius its individuality; but I will do my best.

Is the authorship of *Justice & Jurisprudence* a secret? I have read the book, and infer that it is written by a colored man, as it really purports to be. It shows a great deal of research and industry; I have not yet had time to read it so thoroughly as to criticise it justly, but it strikes me as rather wordy and long drawn out. But there is much valuable information in it, which is worth to me a great deal more than the price of the book, which by the way is rather high for a book designed for popular reading.[12]

Yours very truly,
Chas. W. Chesnutt.

P.S. I enclose Mr. Gilder's letter, of which I have taken a copy.

C.W.C.

ALS: LNHT

[1] When Chesnutt expresses strong emotion in his letters, it is typically provoked by outrages perpetrated against the African-American community. His feelings concerning his own situation are normally restrained. The cri de coeur in the present letter is unique, even though Chesnutt toned down several passages in the original draft dated 5 June, as will be seen in the notes below focusing on his revisions. The tonality of both versions, however, is effectively glossed by the original opening of the third paragraph: Chesnutt began it with: "Pardon my earnestness. I write *de plein coeur*—as I feel."

[2] *Century* editor Gilder wrote Cable on 28 May 1890 (LNHT), explaining his rejection of "Rena Walden": "This story of Chesnutts [*sic*] 'Rena Walden' I have read with great care. I'm extremely sorry not to find it feasible. Its subject is new, & the point of view. But somehow it seems to me amorphous—not so much in construction as in *Sentiment*. I could talk to you about it more clearly than I can write. There is either a lack of humor in the author or a brutality in the characters, & lack of mellowness, lack of spontaneous, imaginative life in the people, lack of outlook—I don't know what—that makes them—as here depicted—*uninteresting*. I think it is the writers [*sic*] fault, rather than the people's. The result seems to me a crude study; not a thoroughly human one. I wish I could see more of the author's work—some briefer study. The writing in the opening pages is excellent." In the left margin Gilder added: "The hero & heroine are such frauds both of them that they have no interest—*as here described*. The black boy is better, from a literary point of view & his father."

[3] In the draft of this letter, Chesnutt eliminated a request he apparently considered an imposition on Cable, or a possible sign of both his anxiety and inexperience in the ways of author-publisher relationships: Gilder "says that he can talk about it more clearly than he can write. When you meet him again, will you, if you have time, mention the matter and give me the benefit of what he says?"

[4] In his draft Chesnutt here expatiated on the unlikelihood of any mulatto characters being attractive to American magazine editors and readers: "I suspect that my way of looking at these things is 'amorphous' not in the sense of being unnatural but unusual. There are a great many intelligent people who consider the [mulatto] class to which Rena and Wain belong as unnatural. I had a gentleman with whom I had just dined for whom I had been doing some difficult work, a man of high standing in his profession, of wide reading and as I had thought of great liberality, whom I had heard declare enthusiastically about the doctrine of human equality—which characterizes our institutions, I say this gentleman remarked to me in substance that he considered a mulatto an insult to nature, a kind of monster that he looked upon with infinite distaste, not to say disgust; that a black negro he looked upon with some respect, but any laws which permitted the intermarriage of the two races, or tended in any way to bring the two races nearer together, were pernicious and in the highest degree reprehensible."

[5] In the draft, Chesnutt wrote more passionately, "But I can't write about those people, or rather I won't write about them." He went on to make a self-disclosure appearing nowhere else in his correspondence: "I am a little surprised of Mr. Gilder's suggestion of a want of humor in the writer. Almost everything I have written has been humorous and I had thought that I had a rather keen

sense of humor. But my position, my surroundings, are not such as to make me take a humourous view of life. They rather tend the other way. It has been remarked, and my observation justifies the remark, that a humorous Jew is a rarity. I know a number; they seldom smile, and a real, healthy wholesome spontaneous laugh is something I hardly ever heard from a Jew; the reason is to be sought in their past history. Pardon my references to myself—they are not meant to be egotistical; but, when I first began to think, circumstances tended make [sic] me introspective, self-conscious; latterly I fear they have tended to make me morbid. It may be weakness but my mental health and equipoise require constant employment, either in working or in writing. If I should remain idle for two weeks, at the end of that time I should be ready to close out my affairs and move my family to Europe. The kind of stuff I could write, if I were not all the time oppressed by the fear that this line or this sentiment would offend somebody's prejudices, jar on somebody's American-trained sense of propriety, would I believe find a ready sale in England."

[6] James Maurice Thompson (1844–1901) served in the Confederate army and became a romancer famous for his fierce opposition to literary realism; his *A Tallahassee Girl* (1882), *His Second Campaign* (1883), and *At Love's Extremes* (1885) are sentimental works set in the South. Thomas Nelson Page (1853–1922) was a Virginia attorney whose "Marse Chan," published in *Century* in 1884, established his literary reputation as a writer adept at fictionalizing what he saw as the attractive life of the antebellum plantations. Joel Chandler Harris (1848–1908) was best known for his dialect stories narrated by his Uncle Remus in works such as *Uncle Remus: His Songs and His Sayings* (1881).

[7] The pathos of the mulatto's situation receives heavy emphasis in Tourgée's *Toinette: A Tale of the South* (1874; published as *A Royal Gentleman* in 1881), in which a Caucasian hero cannot acknowledge his love for the fair heroine who is passing as white. Chesnutt, however, appears to be referring specifically to *Hot Plowshares* (1883). Its heroine, attending a school for girls in New England, is astounded to learn that she is not purely Caucasian, and her teachers and fellow students react in various ways to the appalling news that she is tainted by Negro blood—as Tourgée measures the ways in which racist attitudes thus manifest themselves in the North. After the initial response of horror, she resolves to bear the heavy burden of her mixed racial ancestry and to continue her studies—whereupon Tourgée eliminates her problem with the discovery that she is, in fact, wholly Caucasian after all.

[8] Contrary to what Chesnutt infers below from Gilder's letter, Gilder was not a foe to realism any more than the equally genteel and idealistic Chesnutt was; further, both were latter-day Victorians with a taste for sentiment, truthfulness, and high moral purpose in art.

[9] Cable offered encouragement to Chesnutt on 31 May: "I feel you and this story stand in a very important relation to the interests of a whole great nation. If you will be patient and persevering, you can make of yourself a fictionist of a very high order. Your turning point is right before you. If you—with your vantage ground of a point of view new to the world and impossible to any other known writer—can acquire Gilder's clear discernment of all ungenuineness, you will become an apostle of a new emancipation to millions."

[10] In his 17 June 1890 reply to Chesnutt, Cable advised him to be true to his own vision rather than resort to pandering to popular taste.

[11] On 31 May, Cable asked Chesnutt to send him a "new draught as early as possible." In a postscript he wrote: "The things that Gilder objects to are the *last* obstacles between a writer and his success, and almost everyone has to encounter and conquer these adversaries." He explained that many of Gilder's pencil checks simply indicated "phrases that are weak and wordy" and that a more serious matter was the need "to make Rena and her mother grow into the knowledge of their own terrible speciousness."

[12] The volume was priced at $3.00. The racial and personal identity of its author remains undetermined.

George Washington Cable

ᴖ

July 25th, 1890.

Dear Mr. Cable:—

I send you herewith new draft of "Rena Walden." I have endeavored to obviate, so far as I could see them, the things objected to by Mr. Gilder. In the first place I have given the mother more heart, I think to the improvement of the character. A few passages intended to have that effect may be found at the bottom of page 6 and on page 7. On pp. 19 and 20 the dialogue is rewritten with this intention. At the bottom of page 35 and on pp. 36 and 37, the night interview; also the interview at parting, p. 37, are similar passages.

I have also shaded Wain down so that he is not quite so melodramatic a villain, and modified Rena's speech and bearing so that she is not quite so superior a being, leaving her to depend for her interest more on the element of common human feeling. The hint at a rather cold-blooded attempt on the part of the old woman, Wain's mother, to poison Rena, is ascribed to senile idiocy, so to speak.

I have tried to word the dialogue so as to give the people a little more imagination, a little broader outlook. For instance, in one place Mis' Molly says she "would n' lose her daughter for all de riches er Solomon"; and Wain observes that "a ride behin' dat mare would wake de dead," etc. And I have also taken pains to refer in terms to the narrowness of their lives and to trace it to the influence of their surroundings. I have endeavored to have the mother realize, fitfully and vaguely, her own "terrible speciousness"—I think I have used that expression, which is yours, on page 5.

There is a preaching passage on page 10, beginning: "If with the fine analytic mind," and ending with "handiwork," which can be left out if an editor should think best, without disturbing the story. The little apostrophe to dreamland on page 30 I think rather pretty and not strained, though rigid pruning might perhaps require it to be eliminated.

In short, I have re-written the story so that scarcely five pages of the last draught remain unchanged.[1] I am afraid the length is awkward for a magazine, though the story "Little Venice" in the last *Century* was I think longer than this.[2]

I have put so much of my time and my heart in this story, and it has been so well spoken of by the few who have read it (the last was a cultivated gentleman who is very familiar with the best English and French literature, with whom I went on a journey a few weeks ago), that I mean to have it published. I send it to you with *carte blanche*, with only the request that you kindly give it as early attention as your own business will permit. I imagine you mean, if you think it sufficiently improved, to offer it again to the *Century*, although, as I said before, I personally would not have the temerity to do so. If it is not accepted by the people to whom you send it, I shall offer it to the *Atlantic* and if rejected there shall either publish it in book form with some other stories, or re-write it into a longer work.

With renewed thanks for your kindness and appreciation, I remain as ever,

Yours sincerely,
Chas. W. Chesnutt.

TLS: LNHT

[1] Chesnutt appears to have responded to all of the criticisms made by Gilder (see 13 June 1890 to Cable, n. 2). On 17 June, Cable had offered his advice, echoing Gilder: "You will make an enormous improvement in Rena Walden if you will keep clearly in the reader's sight your own fully implied (rather than asserted) recognition of the 'brutality, lack of mellowness, lack of spontaneous imaginative life, lack of outlook,' of the people of the story, with the things you have named as having caused them." He concluded, "In other words you must make the story of Rena Walden very much more what it is already rather than less. You must charge through the smoke and slaughter, not retreat."

[2] Grace Denio Litchfield, "Little Venice: A Story of the St. Clair Flats," *Century* 40 (July 1890), 367–84.

George Washington Cable

September 12, 1890.

My dear Mr. Cable:—

Your favor enclosing MS. of "Rena Walden" was duly received. I have forwarded it to the *Atlantic*, but have not yet learned its fate. I thank you very much for your kindly criticism and encouragement, and realize that it is a much better story from having passed through your hands. And while there is still doubtless room for improvement, the final draft, after your and Mr. Gilder's criticisms, can hardly be compared with the crude sketch first shown you.[1] I thank you for your faith in the story and in me, and hope that time will justify it.

I am looking forward to the time when your own long literary silence will be broken, which I presume will be by your new novel.[2]

Sincerely yours,
Chas. W. Chesnutt.

TLS: LNHT

[1] Cable returned the manuscript of "Rena Walden" with his letter of 18 August. He concluded: "It is improved; but it is not so radically improved that I think it would be other than bad policy to ask Gilder to look at it again."

Nor do I advise taking the risk of a refusal from *Harper's* or *Scribner's*. I would offer it to the *Atlantic*. Your chances of acceptance are best there, and you don't want to diminish them by getting it refused in several other directions. The *Atlantic's* acceptance of it sets it higher in literary standing than *Scribner's* or even *Harper's*.

I return it for you to offer to Aldrich yourself, as I doubt not you will consider it the wiser plan rather than for me to intervene. . . . Don't give it to any second rate concern either for magazine or book publication.

If no first-rate concern will arrange with you, lay it by; it will keep and its day will come; but you can't force it by unworthy publication.

Thomas Bailey Aldrich (1836–1907) was the editor of *Atlantic Monthly*.

[2] Cable was composing *John March, Southerner*.

George Washington Cable

꙳

Sept. 22, 1890.

Dear Mr. Cable:—

"Rena Walden" came back from the *Atlantic* with the following:

"Dear Sir: We are sorry that we cannot find a place for this story—much as we like it in some respects—, and so return it, with thanks for your kindness."[1]

Sincerely yours,
Chas. W. Chesnutt.

TLS: LNHT

[1] Cable responded on 2 October 1890: "I am sorry about 'Rena Walden,' but I hope you will not push into print anything that is unworthy of your pen. We mustn't let any temptation lower our standards. Let us determine to please the best critical judgments we can find and not print till we do. I hope you will lay 'Rena Walden' carefully aside for the present and start anew. By and by you may discover what is the matter with Rena, and will have retained the opportunity to remove the fault."

George Washington Cable

꙳

January 13, 1891.

My dear Mr. Cable:—

Yours of the 29th inst. received.[1] The study of the Southern question is fruitful of surprises, and a great many people who have much to say about it, know really very little about it. I fear that future political action, of which the Mississippi Constitutional Convention will serve as a prototype, will still further curtail the opportunities for education of the colored people in the South.[2]

It seems to me I sent you with my MS. that you refer to, the various pamphlets from which I got my information; I suspect you will find them about your study somewhere, though I will look for them here.[3] There is a later report of the Commissioner of Education, which may slightly alter the figures for 1887-'8—whether for better or worse I do not now call to mind.

My wife and sister join me in regards to you. We remember with much pride and pleasure your brief visit to our home, and would be glad of some future opportunity to offer you better entertainment.[4] My wife has recently presented me with another little Chesnutt, a girl, which makes ours a respectably numerous family.[5]

I will look up any further data I have on the subject of Southern schools, and forward any papers or information I may get upon the matter. I haven't written anything, or rather I haven't offered anything for publication since "Rena" came back to me.[6] My business for the past year has been very absorbing, and has netted me a handsome income. I stand at the parting of two ways: by strict attention to business, and its natural development, I see a speedy competence and possible wealth before me. On the other hand, I see probably a comfortable living and such compensations as the literary life has to offer. I think I have made my choice of the latter, though it will be a year yet before I can safely adopt it. I remain, as ever,   Sincerely yours,

Chas. W. Chesnutt.

TLS: LNHT

[1] Cable wrote Chesnutt on 29 December 1890: "I have at last got around to the subject of school funds in the South and am amazed at the disclosures of the Bureau of Education's statistics, 1887–8. Your N.Y. article, which is before me, is a mere hint of what it points to. Can you tell me how you got the figures of such towns as Birmingham and Montgomery on the matter of colored teachers' pay as compared with amounts paid white teachers? And if so, can I see them?"

[2] The 1890 Mississippi Constitutional Convention disfranchised many African Americans by establishing literacy and property ownership qualifications for voting.

[3] Chesnutt enclosed his article on Southern schools and these pamphlets with 29 March 1890 to Cable.

[4] While Cable may have more recently visited Chesnutt, he was a guest at the Chesnutt home in November 1889.

[5] Dorothy Chesnutt.

[6] Chesnutt informed Cable of the second rejection of "Rena," by *Atlantic Monthly*, in 22 September 1890 to Cable.

PART II

A DREAM DEFERRED,

1891–1896

❧

The Businessman Prevails

❧

I am simply biding my time, and hope in the near future to devote the greater part of my time to literary production.

Houghton, Mifflin & Co.

᰷

September 8, 1891

Dear Sirs:

I desire to be informed on what terms, if at all, you will publish the enclosed MS. volume of stories, containing in all something over 60,000 words. There are eight stories, three of which have been published in the *Atlantic Monthly*, at the dates noted on the first page of each respectively. (These stories I hereby ask your permission to reproduce.) Of the remainder, one was published in the *Overland Monthly*, and one in the *Independent*.[1] The others are new stories.

I would call the volume "Rena Walden and Other Stories," or simply "Rena Walden," that being the story for the sake of which I wish to publish the volume.

The published stories have been favorably noticed, and the story "Rena Walden" has received favorable criticism in high literary quarters.[2] I can send letters and notices if desired.

There is one fact which would give this volume distinction—though I must confess that I do not know whether it would help or hurt its reception by critics or the public. It is the first contribution by an American with acknowledged African descent to purely imaginative literature. In this case, the infusion of African blood is very small—is not in fact a visible admixture—but it is enough, combined with the fact that the writer was practically brought up in the South, to give him a knowledge of the people whose description is attempted. These people have never been treated from a closely sympathetic standpoint, they have not had their day in court. Their friends have written of them, and their enemies; but this is, so far as I know, the first instance where a writer with any of their own blood has attempted a literary portrayal of them. If these stories have any merit, I think it is more owing to this new point of view than to any other thing.

I should not want this fact to be stated in the book, nor advertised, unless the publisher advised it; first, because I do not know whether it would affect its reception favorably or unfavorably, or at all; second, because I would not have the book judged by any standard lower than that set for other writers. If some of these stories have stood the test of admission into the *Atlantic* and other publications where they have appeared, I am willing to submit them all to the public on their merits.

I want, of course, the best terms you can offer, and unless I can better them elsewhere I would prefer that your house bring out the book; the author having been first recognized by you (so far as any high class publication is concerned), and the imprint of your house having the value that it has. The question of terms is an important one to me. I offer this for publication because I understand that the volume of short stories is more favorably received by the public now than ever before.[3] The copyright I would procure and retain for myself.

I would be quite willing to reduce the number of the stories and leave out any that might be suggested, always excepting the longer one, "Rena Walden," and some further slight revision will be needed. I would want the volume bound in cloth. The order of the stories of course will be for future consideration. Please advise me as early as convenient on what terms, if any, you will undertake the publication, and oblige,   Yours very truly,

TDU: TNF

[1] "The Goophered Grapevine," "Po' Sandy," "Dave's Neckliss," "The Conjurer's Revenge," and "The Sheriff's Children" were previously published. The first three appeared in *Atlantic Monthly.* 18 November 1891 to Houghton, Mifflin indicates that one of the new stories was "A Victim of Circumstances." "Rena Walden" is the seventh, and the title of the eighth is unknown.

[2] Although Chesnutt indicates clearly his awareness that *Atlantic Monthly* was published by Houghton, Mifflin, he does not appear to know that those who would read his book manuscript were very likely the same individuals who had already rejected "Rena Walden" for the magazine.

[3] Although Houghton, Mifflin did publish collections of short stories, the refrain one finds in the firm's letterbooks (MH:P) is that such collections were especially risky ventures rather than promising investments.

Houghton, Mifflin & Co.

⌒

Nov. 18, 1891.

Dear Sirs:—

I am in receipt of your favor in which you so gracefully decline to undertake at this time the volume of stories which I offered for publication. But the letter is so nicely worded that I was almost—not quite—as well pleased as if you had accepted it.[1]

You say you doubt if my own interests would be best regarded by a publication at this time. If you meant merely my pecuniary interests, that was a secondary consideration with me, as I could perhaps afford to assume all the expense of its publication if necessary. But if you meant that unsuccess, which the conditions you mention would seem to point to at this time would do me harm, and injure my chances for future success, I of course recognize that your experience and standing as publishers give your opinion unquestionable authority. If it is not asking too much, would you be kind enough to tell me on which of those two grounds your advice to me was based? And also, for my own information, what the expense of getting out such a book would have been, in case you had accepted it on the terms least favorable to me?[2]

As I feel at present I shall probably accept your suggestion to publish more stories before putting forth a book. The only question with me is that the money returns from literature are so small and so uncertain, that I have not had the time to spare from an absorbing and profitable business to devote to it, and therefore my stories are so far between that the reading public has forgotten my name before they see it again. I thank you for your words of commendation. I think most of the stories in the MS. sent you have either been published by you or offered to you for publication. There is one, however, "A Victim of Circumstances" which has not been offered anywhere; it is not a particularly cheerful story, but I would be glad to have you accept it for the *Atlantic* if you think it suitable; if not please return it with the rest of the MS. to me.[3] I enclose 50¢ for postage which I presume will about cover the amount required. If it is not enough, please send the package by express.

Again thanking you for your advice, which I feel disposed to follow, I remain

Very truly yours,

TCU: TNF

[1] On 27 October, Houghton, Mifflin declined the collection of short stories: "an examination both of your book and of our accounts with the several collections of stories . . . issued the past year leads us to question the wisdom of our undertaking the book" and "we doubt if your own interests will best be regarded by a publication at this time." While the firm expressed its liking for some of Chesnutt's stories, it encouraged him to build a larger following of readers "for a year or two more." It would be glad to consider publishing a volume when Chesnutt had a greater number of attractive stories from which the editors might choose.

[2] Francis J. Garrison replied on 21 November to the first question by assuring Chesnutt that the advice to refrain from publishing a book of stories at present was not based upon pecuniary considerations but concern that Chesnutt should receive proper "recognition as an author." He then responded to the request for an estimation of cost: 1,000 bound copies would cost $600.00, plus $150.00 or $200.00 for advertising. Chesnutt would make 62½¢ per copy sold.

[3] On 21 November Garrison reported that "A Victim" was not accepted.

Albion W. Tourgée

·◦·

April 18, 1893

My dear Judge Tourgée:—

Permit me to thank you for the compliment in the *Inter Ocean* of April 8th. Such a statement from such a source is enough to make one determine that he will not permit such a gift to be entirely smothered, even by success in other lines.[1] That I have not ceased altogether to write you may see from reading the story I send you by this mail.[2] It is not as good as some other things I have written, and the publication in which it appeared, *Two Tales*, has suspended since the story appeared; I hope there was no relation of cause and effect between the two events.

The desire and intention on my part to write is, if anything, stronger even than when I was writing most. I am simply biding my time, and hope in the near future to devote the greater part of my time to literary production. But as I have large and pressing family obligations, I have felt it best to do first the duty nearest to me, and to provide for any peradventure of failure or tardy success in the literary life before I undertook it. I have written much that has never seen the light of day, and that has not even been offered for publication. The kindly appreciation of yourself and other gentlemen who have read such things as I have written, and the fact that many people who could not command the same recognition, are making a living in literature—these two things put together certainly have no tendency to discourage me. The only question now, is whether or not I could command a better market, for the kind of matter I could produce most readily and willingly, in this country or in England; and whether or not, in either case, it would not be better for me to live near my best market.[3] For when I do go into literature, I propose to apply to the financial side of it the same business principles I have applied to my other affairs, and to seek the best and most profitable market, knowing that a hearing once secured anywhere will be a hearing secured everywhere.

May I trouble you to drop me a line with the names of the publishers of the two books reviewed by you in the *Inter Ocean*—*Dessalines* and the other.[4] I should be glad to buy them and read them and write a word of appreciation to the authors.

I am glad that Southern editors note with interest and evidently read with care your articles on Southern affairs, as is clearly indicated by their notices of the Birthday edition of the *Inter Ocean*.[5] You do not need my assurance that your efforts in behalf of the colored race are more and more appreciated by them as they advance in education and self-respect.

Thanking you again for your kind words, and hoping you may be amused by my story, I remain,

Very truly yours,

Chas. W. Chesnutt.

TLS: NWefHi

[1] Chesnutt is referring to Tourgée's comment in "A Bystander's Notes," Chicago *Inter Ocean*, 8 April 1893, 4. As he praised two books by African-American authors (see n. 4), Tourgée complimented Chesnutt thus: "Aside from newspaper articles, some controversial pamphlets, volumes of sermons and speeches, the colored people of the United States can scarcely be said to have produced any literature. This is not surprising nor at all discreditable to them. . . . [A] race by law barred from the fields of literature for two centuries, needs at least the lifetime of a generation in which to produce good literary work. The wonder is not that it came so late but that it came so soon, and is of such simple, genuine quality. Except Mr. Chesnutt, who [sic] brief novels [sic] were something marvelous in their unpretentious realism, of which there are no more because prosperity in other fields has smothered his rare gift, hardly any colored writer has made a serious attempt in the realm of fiction, and not one has ventured upon good-tempered, keen, yet kindly, discussion of present conditions with any specific attempt at literary excellence."

[2] "A Deep Sleeper," *Two Tales*, 11 March 1893, 1–8.

[3] See 13 June 1890 to Cable, where Chesnutt describes English and French novelists as able to treat characters of African ancestry with less self-conscious regard for their race than American writers can.

[4] The two volumes positively reviewed by Tourgée were: William E. Easton's *Dessalines, A Dramatic Tale: A Single Character from Haiti's History* (1893); and Anna J. Cooper's *A Voice from the South: By a Black Woman of the South* (1892).

[5] On 25 March 1893 the *Inter Ocean* celebrated its twenty-first year of publication with a mammoth "Birthday" issue; and Tourgée, in his two hundred fifty-second installment of "A Bystander's Notes" (6), celebrated both the newspaper and his long-standing relationship with it. Laudatory statements about the *Inter Ocean*, originally appearing in mainly Northern newspapers, were quoted in subsequent issues; Chesnutt is referring to other comments he had seen in Southern newspapers.

Albion W. Tourgée

⌒

November 21, 1893

My dear Judge Tourgée:—

I received your letter of several days ago, and it has been the subject uppermost in my mind ever since.[1] I am also in receipt of your note this morning requesting an immediate answer.[2]

It is needless for me to say that I recognize the need of such a journal. The demand for it, however, is a different matter, and were it not for the large roll of the Citizens' Rights Association,[3] I would doubt the existence of such a demand, so far as white people are concerned; although I am well aware that colored people who think at all, are interested in whatever favors them. The only question for me, therefore, is whether I shall take a certain amount of the stock, with the prospect or the certainty, as the case may be, of becoming associate editor of the *National Citizen*.

As to the editorship, I am free to say that I should like it, and should manage to find a certain amount of time to devote to it. My business, on the scale on which I conduct it, is very absorbing, and will be especially so for the next eight months, unless all signs fail; yet in this cause I would be willing to sacrifice somewhat of comfort and leisure. I have always looked forward to the literary life, although not specially in the direction of journalism.

This leaves only the financial part of your proposition for consideration. As to my investing $2,500.00, that is out of the question. I have been earning money in excess of my expenditures for only the past five years. With my savings I have purchased a comfortable home, which is worth some four or five thousand dollars. And my surplus since paying for that, I have invested in other ways—in land and in securities of other kinds, never keeping more than a few hundred dollars in the bank to meet current expenses. My investments, while conservative, are nevertheless to some extent of a speculative character, and while I expect them to be very profitable in a comparatively short time, yet I am sure I could not close them out at present without loss rather than profit; and I am only just now started in on what I hope to be a profitable season's business, after my regular dull season during the Summer time, which always depletes to a large extent my current expense fund.

With regard to the least sum which you mention, $500, I should feel somewhat differently. If you had written to me without reference to the position of associate editor, I should have subscribed for one or two hundred dollars worth of stock and sent in a subscription for some five or ten copies of the paper. I do not suppose you want an associate editor merely for ornament. I certainly would not care to be a mere figurehead in such an enterprise, even for the honor of having my name coupled with such a distinguished one as your own. I am willing to put in my work and take my chances in that regard, and to contribute to the capital to the extent of the $500.00, provided the same can be paid in several instalments, in the manner in which stock subscriptions to new enterprises are generally paid; provided I am named as associate editor, and that in reply to this you tell me you have received such responses to your circular as would justify me in taking that course. In saying this I have in mind the sentence in the printed circular in which you state that "you are not putting in any money and cannot advise others to do so without positive assurance" etc.[4] Five hundred dollars is not a large sum in the abstract, but it represents a good deal of hard work in my case, and the magnitude of my family makes me perhaps unduly cautious in disposing of it.

I shall await a reply, and give you a definite answer immediately upon hearing from you. If I had known of this matter several months ago, I would have had more available cash, and would have had time to see you and talk with you. I might have come up to Mayville last Saturday, when I could have discussed the matter more fully; and I should like to come toward the end of this week, say Saturday, if the matter is not too pressing, and if you are inclined to consider my proposition at all favorably.[5] In any event, I will take $100.00 worth of stock, and guarantee at least ten subscriptions. I have not had time, since receipt of your letter, to work up the matter among my friends, as your letter caught me at a very busy time.

Very respectfully yours,

Chas. W. Chesnutt.

TLS: NWefHi

[1] In an unlocated letter, Tourgée offered Chesnutt an editorial position with and opportunity to invest in the periodical he was attempting to found, *The National Citizen.* Tourgée did not succeed in this endeavor, abandoning it in 1894.

[2] On 20 November 1893, Tourgée indicated that he had not received a reply to his "letter of some days ago." He urged Chesnutt to respond: "You are my first choice as associate editor on account of your literary ability."

[3] In late 1891, Tourgée founded the National Citizens' Rights Association which quickly developed a membership in the thousands. By 1893, however, the "large roll" to which Chesnutt refers had dwindled; by 1894 the N.C.R.A. was no longer so significant an organization except insofar as it provided Tourgée the means of claiming widespread support for his political activism.

[4] That is, positive assurance of a sufficient number of investors.

[5] In light of the succeeding letters to Tourgée, it appears that Chesnutt did not visit Mayville in November, despite Tourgée's 23 November invitation to do so (NWefHi).

Albion W. Tourgée

↶

November 27, 1893.

My dear Sir:—

I am in receipt of your last letter, to which I did not respond by telegraph, as I could not assume the responsibility of raising the sum you mentioned.[1] As I said in my former letter, I cannot see my way to furnish it myself, and it would take some time to communicate with others in reference to the matter. A newspaper venture, even under the most favorable auspices, is always a speculation, and if this one should not succeed, there would be nothing whatever to show for the money, except the memory of an effort in a good cause. Nevertheless, I am willing to risk something, and I presume there are others who will do the same. But I would regard it as a risk and would prefer to confine my investment to what I could afford to lose. While you have infinitely better opportunities for feeling the public pulse than I have, yet in my intercourse with the best white people of one of the most advanced communities of the United States, with whom my business brings me in daily contact, I do not remember but once of hearing the subject of the wrongs of the Negro brought up, except by myself; and when brought up by me, as it has often been, I have observed that it is dismissed as quickly as politeness will permit. They admit that the present situation is all wrong, but they do not regard it as their personal concern, and do not see how they can remedy it. They might subscribe to such a journal, if personally solicited, a number of them, but I fear that a publication devoted entirely to a discussion of one topic, so to speak, even so important a one as citizenship, would have a tendency to repel the average white man rather than attract him.[2]

I quite believe that you could make such a venture successful, if any one could; but I am free to admit that I have been somewhat discouraged at the outlook in the Southern States. As to the Northern States, it seems to me that the people have about made up their minds to give the Negro equal rights so far as the laws can effect it, and then to let him paddle his own canoe.

I can quite appreciate your reluctance to go into such an enterprise without ample capital. As I have said, I am willing to do something and to urge others to co-operate. But I am very busy at present; in fact, this is my busy season and I am just now busier than usual; and to assume the responsibility of saying I will raise the sum of $2,500.00, especially in view of the present "hard times," would be undertaking more than I can see my way clear to doing.

There are several colored men of my acquaintance who have more means than I, and who are just as deeply interested in this matter. I think it will be easy to secure their co-operation. One of these is Mr. S. R. Scottron, 598 Monroe Street, Brooklyn, N.Y. Mr. S. is a man of some means, has a proprietary interest in some patents for inventions of his own, and travels for a brass fixture manufactory in New York. He is a man of intelligence, of ideas and of considerable culture. He has always read your letters in the *Inter Ocean* with eager interest.

Mr. F. J. Loudin, Ravenna, Ohio, is a man of comparatively large means. He is the principal stockholder in a shoe manufactory at Ravenna, and has for many years managed a troop of jubilee singers, having spent a number of years in Europe and Australia in that business.[3] I know that he is very much interested in the welfare of his race and liberal of his means in promoting it; and I am informed by his most intimate friend that he is a constant reader and admirer of all you write on the question of citizens' rights.

I will write to these gentlemen, and think that if you will do the same, they can be induced to subscribe for stock.

Regretting, dear sir, that I cannot immediately and fully accept the very flattering offer you make me,—for I consider it a great honor to be asked to co-operate with you so closely,—and assuring you that I will do all I can without assuming any burdensome responsibility, to forward your plan, I remain,

Very sincerely yours,

Chas. W. Chesnutt.

TLS: NWefHi

[1] On 23 November (NWefHi), Tourgée laid out his argument for the likely success of *The National Citizen* and the necessity of investment in it by individuals like Chesnutt. He wanted to be able to approach Caucasian investors with the guarantee that African Americans were involved in the enterprise—further pursuing the policy of encouraging the development of African-American activism that he established when forming the National Citizens' Rights Association.

[2] Chesnutt is not willing to gamble that members of the N.C.R.A. care enough about the "Negro problem" to invest, as Tourgée on 23 November declared they would, three dollars for every one given by African Americans. It is probable as well that Chesnutt was skeptical of Tourgée's expectation that "the colored people can and will take $25,000, in stock and give us 10,000 subscribers."

[3] Frederick J. Loudin (1842/3?–1904) was an Ohioan who moved to Tennessee after the Civil War and became a member of the Fisk University Jubilee Singers prior to their 1875 tour of Great Britain. He assumed the responsibilities of manager and director of the company in 1882. His profits from a six-year world tour enabled him to become the largest stockholder in a shoe manufactory in Ravenna, which was renamed the F. J. Loudin Shoe Manufacturing Company (see "A Great Career," *Cleveland Gazette*, 12 November 1904, 1). Scottron—who later wrote to Chesnutt on the stationery of the Brooklyn School Board—is not so visible a figure, but Chesnutt's characterization of him squares with his letter to the editor, "The Treatment of the Negro," *New York Times*, 30 June 1901, 6. Scottron commended the *Times* for its editorial, "White and Negro in the South," 25 June 1901, 6, which criticized Southern hypersensitivity to outside interference in its management of the race problem and ridiculed the notion that only Southerners can understand the African Americans in their region. Scottron agreed that those of his race cannot be abandoned to "the tender mercies of the South." When Chesnutt and he began their correspondence is unknown: in two letters, Scottron praised *The Wife of His Youth and Other Stories of the Color Line* (19 December 1899) and *The Marrow of Tradition* (21 January 1902).

George Washington Cable

∾

April 11, 1895

My dear Mr. Cable:—

I received your letter in reply to mine soliciting a contribution for the *Lakeside Magazine*,[1] and am sorry you were not able to write for it, though I hardly expected you would be.

I thank you for the kind suggestion that I again enter the literary field. I have never abandoned it in fact, though I have not published anything since a story that appeared a couple of years ago in *Two Tales*, a defunct Boston venture.[2] But I wrote last year a novel of about 60,000 to 70,000 words.[3] I had not completed my revision of it when the Fall business came on with a rush, and diverted me from it. I expect ere the Summer is over to finish it.

Several days before I received your letter I had taken up the MS. of "Rena Walden" with a view to re-writing it. I found myself much better able to realize the force of some criticisms of it that were made four or five years ago, when you were good enough to interest yourself in it. I have recast the story, and in its present form it is a compact, well-balanced novelette of 25,000 to 28,000 words. With four or five years of added study of life and literature I was able to see, I think, the defects that existed in it, and I venture now to regard it not only as an interesting story, but as a work of literary art. I shall offer it for publication in a magazine, and whether successful in that or not, shall publish it in book form. I hope to write many stories, and would like to make a worthy *début* with this one.

My years of silence have not been unfruitful. I believe I am much better qualified to write now than I was five years since; and I have not used up a fund of interesting material which I might have expended on 'prentice work. Furthermore, I have saved from ten to fifteen thousand dollars since I was with you at Northampton, and have the feeling of security which even a little of this world's goods gives, so that I can now devote more time and, if necessary, some money to securing a place in literature.[4]

Thanking you again for your kindly and inspiring wish, I remain, as ever,

Yours very truly,

Chas. W. Chesnutt.

P.S. I have read your *John March, Southerner*. It is a great book, but does not appeal to me, for obvious reasons, quite as much as *The Grandissimes* or *Old Creole Days*. But I realize that the truthful historian must portray all phases of life, if he would be true to his art.[5]

C.W.C.

TLS: LNHT

[1] On 4 March 1895, Cable declined to write for *Lakeside Magazine*, the publication of Lakeside Hospital in Cleveland: "my literary engagements, positive and urgent, are crowding me so that I am now and shall be for months using hours for labor which my physician urges me to give to rest

and recuperation." He then exclaimed, "I long to see you again in the literary field. It would mean so much!"

² "A Deep Sleeper."

³ Chesnutt most likely refers to "Mandy Oxendine," later submitted unsuccessfully to *Atlantic Monthly* as a "long story" of 50,000 words (see 13 February 1897 to Page).

⁴ Chesnutt visited Cable in Northampton in 1889, when his business prospects seemed dim and he was considering taking a position as Cable's secretary. See 3 May 1889 to Cable.

⁵ *John March, Southerner*, a novel published in late 1894, focused on life in post–Civil War South but did not deal with the condition of those with mixed racial backgrounds in the markedly sympathetic way that was typical of Cable's earlier writings. Indeed, it offered a mulatto character whose lack of scruples may be interpreted as Cable's concession to Southern arguments regarding the corruption of which African-American political figures were capable during the Reconstruction.

Richard W. Gilder

᠅

April 11, 1895

Dear Sir:—

Several years ago I sent you, through Mr. G. W. Cable, a story entitled "Rena Walden". You were kind enough to read it, and expressed a willingness to see more of the author's work. You also suggested that the story be re-written along certain lines indicated by you. The attempt was made, but was not successful; in fact the story was not sensibly altered.

After five years' study of life and literature, I have recast the story of "Rena Walden," having always in mind your criticism and suggestions. It is now a novelette of about 25,000 words. I would not venture to send it to you again without asking in advance whether you would be willing to reconsider it.

I have written considerably more since this story was written, but with one exception have offered nothing for publication, having been mainly absorbed in other pursuits. I always believed in this story *as a story*, and hope that it may now find favor in some one's eyes as a work of art as well.

If you would be willing to read this story again with a view to its publication in the *Century*, if found available, I shall be glad to forward it when I hear from you to that effect. It seemed to interest you before,¹ and I am sure it is in every way an improvement on the former version.²

Very respectfully yours,
Chas. W. Chesnutt

TLS: NN-B

¹ See 13 June 1890 to Cable, n. 2.

² On 17 April, Gilder agreed to reconsider "Rena" but advised Chesnutt that there would not be "room for a story of that length for several years, and we fear that it would be lost time." Whether Chesnutt sent him the manuscript is not known.

Albion W. Tourgée

ᖾ

April 27th, 1895

My dear Judge Tourgée:—

A friend of mine handed me a copy of *The Basis*, your new journal, the other day, and I have hastened to place myself in the list of subscribers. The form in which the *Basis* appears is neat and convenient, and the principles and policy of the new journal are just what would be expected with you at its head. You are the one writer in the United States who ought to have an organ of his own, in which to express his views fully and freely; and I venture to hope that your present arrangement will give full scope to your editorial powers, with greater profit and less risk than your plan as at first proposed.[1]

I see that you make most liberal offers of prizes for literary efforts. I trust they will be productive of the best results, both in quality of the work drawn out and in the increase of the circulation of the *Basis*. If I can find time between now and the limit fixed for the close of the competitions, I may take a "sky" at one of the prizes.[2] In the meantime I will do all I can to promote the circulation of the *Basis*; I already have the promise of several subscriptions.

Very truly yours,
Chas. W. Chesnutt.

TLS: NWefHi

[1] Tourgée had previously failed to found *The National Citizen*, after inviting Chesnutt to serve as associate editor and soliciting his personal investment (see 21 and 27 November 1893 to Tourgée). His new venture, *The Basis*, was short-lived: it appeared from March 1895 to April 1896.

[2] Chesnutt's work never appeared in *The Basis*.

Albion W. Tourgée

ᖾ

June 25, 1895

My dear Judge:—

I am in receipt of yours of June 14th enclosing three (3) certificates of stock in the *Basis*.[1] Before making any effort to dispose of them, I should like to know what has become of the *Basis*? Has it suspended, or been changed to a monthly, or what? I ask because I have not received a number for several weeks.

I was sorry I did not see you while you were in Cleveland. I did not learn for a day or two after you had gone, that you had been here, although I had supposed I read the papers every day. I did not have time to attend the sessions of the convention you attended.[2] I shall not let such another opportunity pass, however.

Yours very truly,
Chas. W. Chesnutt.

ALS: NWefHi

[1] When he responded on 8 May 1895 (NWefHi) to Chesnutt's congratulations for the appearance of *The Basis*, Tourgée took the opportunity to celebrate his own "faith, courage, and ability to command support." He also enclosed "one certificate of our convertible stock-options." Unlocated are a subsequent letter to Tourgée, the 14 June reply from Tourgée accompanied by three certificates of stock, and another letter to Chesnutt written on or after 21 June to which Chesnutt is responding below in his second paragraph.

[2] Tourgée was in Cleveland to attend the annual convention of the National League of Republican Clubs, 19–21 June 1895.

Albion W. Tourgée

September 3rd, 1895

My dear Judge:—

A little business and a good many Summer distractions of one sort or another have prevented my answering sooner your letter of some weeks since enclosing three additional certificates of stock in the *Basis*. I have not sold the stock, but I enclose herewith a check for the $15.00 necessary to pay for same. I also enclose five of the coupons, for which please send the *Basis* for one year each to the following addresses:

A. J. Chesnutt, Fayetteville, N.C.
T. J. Shauter, 615 Society for Savings Building, Cleveland, O.
Mr. J. E. Benson, 45 Henry Street, Cleveland, O.
Mr. W. T. Boyd, 33 Maple Street, Cleveland, O.[1]
Hon. John P. Green, 121 Quincy Street, Cleveland, O.[2]

I shall probably be able to add to this list in the course of time. I am not surprised that you should have felt a little disappointment at the apparent lack of zeal for the *Basis* among colored people.[3] I think it is accounted for not by indifference to their own fate or a lack of appreciation for those who are trying to serve their best interests but by the fact that their own efforts in behalf of their race are distributed over so wide an area. Every step they win is by hard work, and there are many ways and places where they can inch their way along on a much lower plane than the high moral level on which the *Basis* finds its field. Quite a number of them, realizing the fact that they are poor and that poverty is almost a crime in the United States, are doing their best to rise above that reproach. They are working along the line of their schools and churches and their own newspapers—which, though they do not begin to compare with the *Basis* in literary quality, are already in the field. I see they have just secured the indictment of the proprietors of a place of amusement in Pittsburgh where discrimination was practiced against them.[4] In politics they are kept on the alert to secure the few offices and appointments they are able to get. They are traveling and lecturing at home and abroad, and are securing a respectful hearing in many quarters.

I think that as the *Basis* becomes more widely known, it cannot fail to take rank as an authority—as *the* authority—on all matters pertaining to the rights of the citizen. The colored people know quite well what their wrongs are, and can imagine in a crude way, the remedy for them. But if the *Basis* can in any degree move the white people of this country from their open hostility or shameless indifference to the rights of the colored people, it will have justified its existence and won the lasting gratitude of all who are connected with or interested in this class of our citizens. If they will not listen to the burning words of the *Basis*, it is simply because they do not wish to hear.

Since I last wrote you the *Basis* has appeared regularly every Saturday and has been my most welcome visitor.[5]

Cordially yours,

Chas. W. Chesnutt.

TLS: NWefHi

[1] Andrew Jackson Chesnutt was Charles' father. Thomas J. Shauter was a stenographer with an office in the Society for Savings Building, where Chesnutt's was also located. James E. Benson was the proprietor of a barber shop and was involved in Cleveland real estate ventures as well. William T. Boyd was the owner of a very successful delivery service; he was a "blue vein" mulatto and a prominent figure in the Social Circle group of Cleveland, whose condescending attitudes toward dark-skinned African Americans Chesnutt would satirize in "The Wife of His Youth" (1898) and "A Matter of Principle" (1899).

[2] See 7 December 1897 to Green, n. 1.

[3] The letter in which Tourgée expressed his disappointment over a dearth of African-American subscribers and investors has not been located.

[4] At the entrance to Schenley Park, opposite the Carnegie Library, was the Pittsburgh Casino at which police "turned all colored people away." On 2 September a grand jury returned a "true bill" against the owners, and they were charged for a misdemeanor ("Negroes' Rights Upheld," *Cleveland Leader*, 3 September 1895, 1).

[5] In an undated draft (NWefHi), Tourgée acknowledged receipt of $15, accepted Chesnutt's explanation for minimal attention being given by African Americans to his weekly, and argued that they should use all such opportunities to form associations with Caucasians. That he thought it would be "worth almost everything to have had a colored associate Editor" for *The Basis* implies that he had again offered Chesnutt a position.

S. Alice Haldeman

∽

February 1st, 1896.

Dear Madam:—

I am in receipt of your favor of January 24th, and take pleasure in answering it.[1]

I fear I cannot assist you to make much of a showing with regard to American colored writers. Literature is largely the fruit of culture, and culture is the flower of wealth and leisure—not in the individual necessarily, but in the race. I do not need to say to one who takes sufficient interest in the colored people to write about them, that wealth and leisure are to them yet in the future.

There are very few American colored men who have written anything which could really be dignified by the name of literature; there have been commendable efforts however in that direction. You are doubtless familiar with the name of Phyllis Wheatley,[2] the poetess of colonial and revolutionary times, who won much recognition, and who was not only a negro of full blood but was brought from Africa when a child; and you have no doubt read of Benjamin Banneker,[3] the negro astronomer and almanac maker, of Maryland, I believe, who flourished about the same epoch or perhaps a little later. You can find a sketch of the life of either in any good library or encyclopedia.

Since the war there have been other efforts. Mr. James M. Trotter, who was recorder of deeds during President Cleveland's first term, some years ago wrote a book on *Music and Some Musical People*;[4] Rev. Alexander Crummell of the Protestant Episcopal Church, Washington, D.C., a man of much learning and power, has published one or two volumes of sermons;[5] a couple of young men in Detroit one of whom is named Anderson, have recently published a novel; and a Texan has written an epic poem of more or less merit.[6] Various ministers and bishops of the different colored churches have issued compendiums of information, chiefly biographical, which are of interest to colored people almost exclusively.

In journalism colored people in this country have made considerable progress. There are very many newspapers among them, of which perhaps the most prominent is the *New York Age*, edited by T. Thomas Fortune, who writes for other New York papers besides, and has published a book entitled *Black and White*, a discussion of the race problem.[7] *The Cleveland Gazette* of this city has also lived for a long time and has considerable influence among the people for whom it is chiefly intended.[8]

None of these productions however can be classed as literature in the higher and finer sense of the term. They are efforts in the right direction and constitute the promise I hope of better things to come in a brighter future. There have been some efforts in the line of pure literature, however, which, while they have not attracted much attention have yet been of the right stamp.

There is a young colored man formerly of Dayton, Ohio, by the name of Paul Dunbar, who has written poems in the James Whitcomb Riley style, which have been widely copied in the newspapers and have brought him into considerable notice. I think he is at present employed on a Chicago daily.[9] I read in the newspaper the other day that "James Edwin Campbell, the colored dialect poet and story writer, died in Pomeroy, Ohio. He was employed on a Chicago daily and was visiting his parents at the Ohio town."[10] As I had not heard of Mr. Campbell before, I might say right here that I do not speak as an oracle, but only from such information as I have, and there may be other colored writers of merit of whom I have not heard. Colored people are somewhat sensitive about advertising the fact of their color, and also labor under the impression that it would interfere with their literary success, and may not therefore make the fact known in every instance, even to their publishers.[11]

As to myself, I doubt whether I could call myself much of a negro, although I have always been more or less identified with the colored people. I am really seven-eighths white, but I have never denied the other, and would be quite willing for the colored people to have any credit they could derive from anything I might accomplish. My works however are principally yet unwritten, or at least unpublished. Such fugitive pieces as I have given to the world however, have perhaps gained recognition in higher authors' quarters than the productions of any other acknowledged colored writer in the United States, and have won for me the personal acquaintance and friendship of some of the most widely known literary men of the country, among whom I may instance Mr. George W. Cable and Hon. A. W. Tourgée. I ought perhaps to write more and mean to do so, although of recent years my professional occupations have absorbed the greater part of my time; I am an attorney by profession and it is difficult for a man to serve two masters.[12] If you care to look them up you will find stories of mine in the *Atlantic Monthly* for the following dates: August, 1887, May, 1888, and October, 1889. If you will look through the bound volumes, or the indexes of the New York *Independent* along about the same period from 1887 to 1892 or 1893, you will find several stories and essays contributed by me to that publication.[13] I also contributed just previous to that quite freely to the columns of *Puck*,[14] the newspapers in the S. S. McClure Syndicate,[15] the *Overland Monthly*,[16] and other publications of lesser note. My later works, except a story published in a Boston magazine about two years ago,[17] have not yet been sprung upon the world; some of them are written however and the world will have a chance to determine their fate in the not distant future.

So much for America. But in other lands and under more favorable circumstances the fact has been demonstrated that people of more or less negro blood are capable of great things in literature. The two most conspicuous instances and quite enough to establish the principle, are the Dumas family in France and Alexander Pushkin (Poushkin) in Russia. Alexander Dumas *père* the most popular writer of the romantic school in France, the author of *Monte Cristo* and *The Three Guardsmen*, left nearly 1,000 volumes bearing his name, and it may be safely said that he was the most conspicuous literary figure during his lifetime in the most conspicuously literary nation of the world. He was a quadroon, his father Gen. Dumas, a mulatto, being himself a person of distinction. The son of Alexander Dumas, of the same name, recently deceased, has been recognized as the leading French dramatist, and he has been conspicuous in the literary life of France since he published his first novel at the age of 18, and especially since he won fame in the early 20's as the author of *La Dame aux Camelias*. The pedigree in the history of these people, and one or two others of the same family and blood but of lesser note, can be found in the biographical dictionaries and encyclopedias in any good library.[18]

Alexander Pushkin, who died while yet a young man some time between 1860 and 1870, was the greatest of Russian poets.[19] His grandfather was a full-blooded negro, attached to the court of one of the Russian emperors. I ran across a beautiful translation of some of his shorter stories the other day. You will find his biography in any biographical dictionary, and if you don't find his pedigree or his African descent referred to in the first one you look at, you will probably find it in the next. People of the stamp of the Dumas and Pushkin rank so high that people lose sight of their origin, except as a mere matter of information and interest. The United States is perhaps the only country in the world where man's color is the paramount consideration in fixing his social and civil status and determining what opportunities he shall have in life.

Several colored men have distinguished themselves as actors, the most conspicuous being Ira Aldridge, and any biographical dictionary will tell you more about him.[20]

I trust what I have written may be of some assistance to you, and so far as I am personally concerned I trust that at some time in the future you may have the opportunity to buy some of my writings at the book stores. I do not think at this moment of any colored scientist of note in the United States; the gifts of the colored people seem to run rather toward *belles lettres* than toward science and mathematics. Whether this is merely the result of circumstances or the indication of a tendency I do not know.

Yours respectfully,

TCU: TNF

[1] Mrs. S. Alice Haldeman of Girard, Kan., was very likely related to and possibly the mother of Anna Marcet Haldeman (1888–1941). The latter married Emanuel Julius in 1916, sharing his leftist political beliefs and using her wealth in 1919 to make possible his becoming the copublisher of the Socialist newspaper *Appeal to Reason*. In 1922 he founded the cheap, mass-production paperback reprint company, Haldeman-Julius, whose "Little Blue Books" were widely distributed from Girard. In her letter to Chesnutt, Haldeman identified herself as President of the Girard Board of Education and a member of the Reading Club before which she was to present a paper, "What Has the Negro Done in Science and Literature?"

[2] Phillis Wheatley (1753?–1784) was the slave of Boston merchant John Wheatley and author of *Poems on Various Subjects*, published in London shortly after she was manumitted (1773).

³ Benjamin Banneker (1731–1806) was a self-taught mathematician, astronomer, and scientific assistant to the survey of what became the District of Columbia. His astronomical calculations were published in a popular series of almanacs, and, like Wheatley, Banneker was focused upon by abolitionists as a case in point regarding the intellectual potential of slaves.

⁴ James Monroe Trotter (1842–1892), the son of a freed slave, taught in Ohio and served in the Fifty-fifth Massachusetts Regiment during the Civil War. His service secured him an appointment in the Boston post office; he was made Recorder of Deeds by President Grover Cleveland in 1887. *Music and Some Highly Musical People* (1878) is a largely nonracial study revealing Trotter's essentially Victorian appreciation of musical compositions in the western cultural mainstream. His praise of African-American musical accomplishments was energetic, though: he emphasized the idea that spirituals of the kind performed by Fisk University's Jubilee Singers represented the only distinctively American music thus far produced.

⁵ Alexander Crummell (1819–1898) was an Episcopal minister and one of the most scholarly African Americans of his generation. He lived in England from 1848 to 1853; studied at Queen's College, Cambridge; and did not return to the United States until after years of service as a minister and teacher in Liberia. In 1873 he founded St. Luke's Church in Washington, D.C., and was a frequent lecturer before African-American audiences, speaking against segregation and disfranchisement. His collections of sermons and speeches include: *The Relations and Duties of Freed Colored Men in America to Africa* (1861), *The Greatness of Christ* (1862), and *Africa and America* (1891). Chesnutt dramatically underestimates the number of publications by Crummell.

⁶ Using the pseudonym "Sanda," William H. Anderson (1857–?) and Walter H. Stowers (1859–?) coauthored *Appointed: An American Novel* (1894). Anderson wrote for the Detroit *Free Press* and the New York *Globe* prior to 1883, when he became one of the founders of the Detroit *Plaindealer*. Stowers, a stenographer, was also one of its founders. The Texan poet is unidentified.

⁷ Timothy Thomas Fortune (1856–1928) was born to slave parents in Marianna, Fla. In 1868, threats by the Ku Klux Klan necessitated the family's move to Jacksonville, Fla. Largely self-educated, he worked for the *People's Advocate* newspaper in Washington, D.C., set type in New York City, and became a New York *Globe* editor. In 1884 he began publication of the *New York Freeman*, which became in 1887 the *New York Age*, of which he was a coowner until 1907. Militant in his demands for equality, Fortune's controversial editorials had much to do with the success of this leading African-American newspaper. His *Black and White: Land and Politics in the South* (1884) was a radical critique of Southern society and its economic system.

⁸ See 25 April 1896 to Tourgée, n. 1.

⁹ Paul Laurence Dunbar (1872–1906) edited the black weekly newspaper Indianapolis *World* from late May until early August 1895. To become a professional artist, he was willing to pay for the publication of his first book, *Oak and Ivy* (1893)—as was Chesnutt (see 8 September 1891 to Houghton, Mifflin). The cost of his next collection of poems, *Majors and Minors* (1895), was also underwritten—by Dr. H. A. Tobey and other Toledo Caucasians. This second book, after attention was drawn to it by William Dean Howells in *Harper's Weekly*, ensured his widespread popularity. Like James Whitcomb Riley (1849–1916), Dunbar employed dialectal language and traditional poetic forms immediately accessible to the popular readership; he focused mainly upon the subject matter of commonplace African-American experience and themes of universal import to which white readers could easily relate; and his tone was often sentimental.

¹⁰ James Edwin Campbell (1867–1896) was an Ohio teacher and an active Republican politician; in 1887 he became the editor of the *West Virginia Enterprise*. That year he published his first book of poems, *Driftings and Gleanings*. In 1893 he was named the first principal of the West Virginia Collegiate Institute. His major poetical work, *Echoes from the Cabin and Elsewhere*, was published in 1895.

¹¹ See Chesnutt's expressions of concern about the advisability of making his racial background public: 10 January 1889 to Cable and 8 September 1891 to Houghton, Mifflin.

¹² The greater part of Chesnutt's business had been stenographic, rather than legal, since 1889.

¹³ For these *Atlantic Monthly* short stories, see 8 September 1891 to Houghton, Mifflin, n. 1.

Independent published "What Is a White Man?" and "The Sheriff's Children," as well as "A Multitude of Counsellors," 43 (2 April 1891), 4–5.

[14] Chesnutt's contributions to *Puck* between 1887 and 1891 have been collected by Sylvia Lyons Render in *The Short Fiction of Charles W. Chesnutt* (Washington, D.C.: Howard University Press, 1981).

[15] Chesnutt's short stories distributed by the S. S. McClure newspaper syndicate in the mid-1880s are also collected in Render.

[16] "The Conjurer's Revenge."

[17] "A Deep Sleeper."

[18] Alexandre Dumas *père* (1802–1870) was the son of General T. Alexandre Dumas (1762–1806) and the author of the two works noted by Chesnutt, whose full titles are *Le Comte de Monte Cristo* and *Les Trois Mousquetaires* (both 1844). The son of Dumas *père* and grandson of the general was Alexandre Dumas *fils* (1823–1895). His *La Dame aux Camelias* was published as a novel in 1848 and transformed into a play in 1852.

[19] Pushkin was born in 1799 and died in 1837.

[20] Ira Frederick Aldridge (1807?–1867) obtained acting experience with New York City's African Theater and went on to earn acclaim in Great Britain and the European continent as one of his era's greatest actors. He became an English citizen in 1863.

Albion W. Tourgée

⌒

April 25, 1896

Dear Sir:—

Will you kindly look at the subscription list of the *Basis* or have some one do so, and see if I have given correctly the address of MR. JAMES A. JOYCE, of this city, as a subscriber to the *Basis*? It should be NO. 20 VAN NESS ST., Cleveland, O. If it is otherwise shown in your list, the mistake was doubtless mine in sending on the name. I hope the *Basis* is doing well.

Permit me as a citizen of this State, desirous of social order and good government, and also as one of those for whose benefit the work was in part at least undertaken, to thank you for your kind collaboration with our Mr. H. C. Smith in securing the passage through the State legislature of the anti-lynching bill.[1] It can do no harm, and if it did no more than simply to express by the mouth of its legislature the condemnation by the State of the abominable practice which has done so much to disgrace the country, it would be worth all the labor that has been spent in promoting its passage. You will never get an adequate reward in this world for your efforts in behalf of the oppressed and the humble, but you believe in a hereafter, and I hope there is one, if for no other reason than that you and those like you may receive their reward.

Sincerely yours,
Chas. W. Chesnutt.

TLS: NWefHi

[1] Harry C. Smith (1863–1941) was for twenty-seven years the editor of a weekly newspaper, the *Cleveland Gazette*, which focused exclusively on the concerns of African Americans—from the frequently outraged point of view of Smith himself. A political activist as well as writer, he served three terms in the Ohio state legislature at the turn of the century and was for four years the state's oil inspector. His political savvy was especially evident when, during the 1896 presidential election, he led five hundred African Americans in a demonstration of support for Governor William McKinley; on the other hand, his lack of self-restraint resulted in his alienation from powerful Republicans in Ohio in 1897, and he did not enjoy presidential patronage. Smith regularly reprinted and commented enthusiastically on Tourgée's writings in the *Cleveland Gazette*; he was a major supporter of Tourgée in his opposition to Jim Crow legislation, one of the fruits of which was the recently passed state law against lynching.

PART III
PAGE'S PROTÉGÉ IN
1897–1899

·❧·

The Reëmergence of the
Artist and Prophet

·❧·

*I am not easily discouraged, and I am
going to write some books, and I still cherish
the hope that either with my conjuh stories or
something else, I may come up to
your standard.*

Walter Hines Page

❦

February 13, 1897

Dear Sir:—

I am in receipt of yours of 10th inst. making the very gratifying announce-ment that you have accepted for the *Atlantic* two of the three contributions sent you by me.[1] "Po' Lonesome Ben" was left out, which makes his name only the more appropriate.[2] I fear, however, that he will have company before I get through corresponding with you.

I am very willing to adopt your suggestion to publish "The Wife of his Youth" and "The March of Progress" under a common heading. But if I had thought of that in advance, I should have sent you a third story, which is equally illustrative of the development of the colored race in this country, and which I take the liberty of enclosing herewith, under the title "A Matter of Principle." If it should be found available, and the exigencies of magazine space would permit, the three might be published under the general head, "Forward, Back, and Cross Over," adapting one of the figures in a quadrille— "The March of Progress" coming first, "The Wife of His Youth" next, and "A Matter of Principle" for the "cross over."[3]

Or, if "A Matter of Principle" could be used, it might be published with the "Wife of His Youth" under the general heading "The Blue Veins."

Or, if "A Matter of Principle" is not accepted, or whether accepted or not, if you wish to publish "The March of Progress" and "The Wife of His Youth" together as proposed, I would suggest the general head, "Forward and Back," or "The Warp and the Woof," whichever may commend itself to you, and if neither strikes your fancy I can try again.

I send you under this same cover the MS. of the long story you have kindly consented to read, entitled "Mandy Oxendine." I suppose that it will run about 50,000 words instead of 60,000. If it should be found available gener-ally, but not up to the mark in any particular respect, I should be glad to have the benefit of any advice or suggestion that would help to make it go. For I expect to write many stories, and do not know of any better place to make a literary reputation than the columns of the *Atlantic*.

If "Mandy Oxendine" is not available for magazine publication, I would like to know, since it must be read anyway, whether Messrs. Houghton, Mifflin & Co. would consider bringing it out in book form; and if they think it worth publishing, whether they would advise doing so now or waiting for a while?[4]

I hope that you may not think my letter too long, or that I am imposing on your patience by sending so much MS. along. I can say by way of extenuation that I have not sent you all the MSS. I have on hand.

Very truly yours,

TCU: TNF

[1] Walter Hines Page (1855–1918) was a progressive North Carolinian sympathetic to the plight of African Americans. After editing the Raleigh *State Chronicle*, and writing for the *New York Post*, and having remarkable success as the editor of *Forum*, he succeeded Thomas Bailey Aldrich as the editor of *Atlantic Monthly* in August 1895. He became Chesnutt's principal advocate at Houghton, Mifflin. Leaving Boston in the summer of 1899 to work for S. S. McClure, he soon became a partner of a new firm, Doubleday, Page & Co. Page would, paradoxically, facilitate the publication of the anti–African-American novels written by Thomas Dixon after the turn of the century as well as publish Chesnutt's third novel, *The Colonel's Dream* (1905).

[2] On 10 February 1897 (MH:P), Page accepted two short stories for *Atlantic Monthly*, "The Wife of His Youth" and "The March of Progress"; he returned "Po' Lonesome Ben," which was subsequently published as "Lonesome Ben" in *Southern Workman* 29 (March 1900), 137–45.

[3] Page's suggestion in his 10 February letter was that the two stories he accepted be published together: "They both illustrate interesting phases of the development of the negro race, and it has occurred to us that if they be put together under a common heading they would produce a better effort than if published separately. If this plan commends itself to you could you not suggest a general head under which they might appear, each with its own head?" Neither Page's plan nor Chesnutt's was realized. "Wife" was published in *Atlantic Monthly* 82 (July 1898), 55–61; "The March of Progress" appeared in *Century* 61 (January 1901), 422–28; "A Matter of Principle" was returned by Page on 12 March and first saw print in *The Wife of His Youth and Other Stories of the Color Line* (1899). These three stories "illustrative of the development of the colored race in this country" deal with the following topics: the existence of a sophisticated upper-middle-class community and the moral excellence of which the African American is capable ("Wife"); the gratitude felt for Caucasians who have labored to elevate former slaves and their children ("March"); and the snobbery of "Blue Vein" mulattoes who view more obviously negroid African Americans as inferior ("Matter").

[4] On 26 March 1897, Houghton, Mifflin rejected "Mandy Oxendine"—as both an *Atlantic Monthly* serial and a book.

George Washington Cable

❧

February 20, 1897

Dear Mr. Cable:

I have thought it might interest you to know that the *Atlantic Monthly* has accepted for early publication two of three stories that I sent them recently. One is "The Wife of His Youth," which I read to you last Winter;[1] it has an additional character, however, in connection with which I found the life-giving touch which I suspect made the story go.[2] The other I did not mention to you, but I am sure you will like it.[3] The editor has suggested their publication together, and they may appear under a common head. They have several others of my MSS., the fate of which is yet uncertain.

You have never sent me the copy of your publication.[4] I suspect you thought it would be seed sown on stony ground. But I should like to see and subscribe to it, if I didn't find time to do anything more.

I made the trip across the water, of which I spoke to you, and enjoyed it very much, visiting England, Scotland, Belgium, Germany, Switzerland, and France.

I see from the paper that you are contemplating a business visit to England. Permit me to wish that it may be as successful as you hope, and that the English people may greet you with the same warm appreciation that your American readers and friends have always exhibited.[5]

My wife and family join me in regards to you and yours, and a line from you at any time would be welcomed, and placed among the things we like to keep.

Cordially yours,
Chas. W. Chesnutt.

ADS: TNF

[1] When and where Chesnutt met with Cable during the winter of 1895–1896 are not known.

[2] "The Wife of His Youth" deals with a contemporary mulatto character, Mr. Ryder, who publicly acknowledges the considerably more negroid wife whom he has not seen since before the Civil War and whom he thought dead. The noble gesture comes at a high price, since he prides himself as superior to unlettered rural Southern blacks such as she. Chesnutt apparently added to his story the character of the widow, Mrs. Dixon, with whom Mr. Ryder is planning to become engaged. Mr. Ryder thus not only overcomes his pride (as in the version Cable heard) but sacrifices the pleasure of wedding the attractive, fair-skinned widow. (See Max Bennett Thrasher's interview "Mr. Chesnutt at Work," *Boston Evening Transcript*, 4 September 1901, 13; Chesnutt there explains that, without the widow, the "story lacked the element of conflicting interest.")

[3] "The March of Progress."

[4] In October 1896 Cable began publishing *The Symposium*, an illustrated literary magazine; after its December 1896 issue, it was absorbed by *The Book-Buyer*, a magazine published by Scribner's.

[5] Cable did not begin his reading tour of Great Britain until April 1898. Chesnutt visited Europe during the summer of 1896.

Albion W. Tourgée

◆

May 24, 1897

Dear Sir:—

I learn from the newspapers that you have been appointed U.S. Consul to Bordeaux, France. While it is not what I understood you had made application for,[1] I have no doubt, from what I know personally of Glasgow, that so far as climate and natural surroundings are concerned, you will find Bordeaux a much pleasanter place to live in; for Glasgow, even in midsummer, is in appearance as sordid and depressing a place as I ever saw. I suspect, too, that your daughter, if she accompanies you, will like it better; and no doubt we will have in the course of time some Franco-American literature from the family.

With cordial congratulations, I remain,

Sincerely yours,
Chas. W. Chesnutt.

TLS: NWefHi

[1] On 22 February, Tourgée's daughter Aimée wrote Chesnutt, soliciting a letter of support for her father's appointment to Glasgow and relating that other African Americans such as Harry C. Smith were organizing the writing of endorsements.

Walter Hines Page

꧁

October 22nd, 1897

Dear Mr. Page:—

I was duly in receipt of your favor of October 20th, and I do not know of any better time than the present to act upon it.[1] I have to-day forwarded to Messrs. Houghton, Mifflin & Co. by express copies of twenty stories, including published and unpublished stories, from which I trust your readers will be able to select enough to make a book. There is enough of them in quantity to make several books—quality is another consideration.

I think these stories will fall naturally into two or three groups, which will of course suggest themselves at once to the reader. This list is by no means complete without the two stories which you have on hand for the *Atlantic*,[2] as I consider them two of the best I have written, and I presume their publication in the *Atlantic* will help any book that might subsequently reproduce them. If I had to choose between having them printed in a book and having them appear in the *Atlantic*, I should prefer the latter, but I presume you would use them in both.

Among the stories I send a few earlier stories and sketches; I do not know that they have much value, but the longer of them, "Uncle Peter's House," has some elements of strength, though it is not so well written as the later stories.[3] It is quite likely, when a selection has been made, if such be the outcome of your examination, that I might want to re-touch a few of the stories selected before they are put into type.

There is one little story in the number entitled "The Fabric of a Vision," a sort of study in unconscious cerebration, if I use the term correctly, which I thought you might possibly find available for the *Atlantic*. It is entirely outside of the distinctive line of stories from which a selection will probably be made.

I am under the impression that for one of the stories sent you, "A Deep Sleeper," Mr. Arthur Ware of your city, the publisher of *Two Tales*, holds an assignment of the copyright. I presume it can be obtained from him without difficulty. I suppose also that courtesy would require me to request permission of the publishers of any other printed stories that might be selected; I do not just know what the law of the case is.

Thanking you for your promptness in answering my letter and for your personal interest in this matter, and trusting that a favorable report may be made, I remain,

Sincerely yours,

TCU: TNF

[1] In an unlocated letter of 18 October 1897, Chesnutt described to Page the short stories he had on hand that might be collected in a book. He was responding to one of the most important developments in his literary career, which occurred when Page wrote him on 2 October. Page rejected "The Dumb Witness" and "The Bouquet," explaining that "I should keep one of them, most likely both, but for the reason that we have had such hard luck in making room for" Chesnutt's two stories already accepted for publication in *Atlantic Monthly*. He then broached the possibility of working with Chesnutt to produce a book of short stories: "I have thought . . . that a skillfully selected list of your short stories might make a book. Whenever you are in the humor to talk about these things let me hear from you." On 20 October, Page replied to the proposal Chesnutt made: "I like the frankness and spontaneity with which you write and the full explanation that you give of the stories." Asking him not to forward the story "that contains 54000 words and the other one that contains 29000," Page requested all of the others, "both published and unpublished." He then promised that the Houghton, Mifflin readers would "see whether by selecting judiciously from them a selection can be made which seems likely to make a book of sufficient unity to put upon the market." The 54,000-word work may have been "Mandy Oxendine" and that of 29,000 words "Rena Walden," both of which had been previously rejected there; one of the two, however, may have been a version of "A Business Career," submitted by Chesnutt in late 1897 or early 1898.

[2] "The Wife of His Youth" and "The March of Progress."

[3] "Uncle Peter's House" was previously published in Cleveland's *News and Herald* in December 1885, date and pagination unknown.

John P. Green

༄

December 7th, 1897

My dear John:—

I received your letter of several days ago and was very glad to hear from you.[1] Sorry to hear that Mrs. Green is not as well as she might be, but have no doubt that she will become acclimated in due time.

I see that your friend Mr. Bruce got the persimmon—I presume because he had the longest pole, or the strongest pull.[2] I have no doubt that he owes something to you in that connection, and I hope that he will show himself properly appreciative of your efforts in his behalf. I met H. C. Smith on the street the other day. He said that the appointment was the worst one from the point of practical politics that could possibly have been made. He went on to say that the methods by which Bruce had secured his appointment and by which you had secured yours were altogether wrong—I violate no confidence in saying this because it was all repeated in the issue of his paper the next day. I smiled and said that your methods and Mr. Bruce's had been successful, and if they had enabled you to get what you wanted I really did not see how they could have been improved upon "practically." Poor Smith is neither a prophet nor the son of a prophet, and from present indications, he will ere long have difficulty in making any number of people believe that he is. The

Negro Protective Party I understand polled about 400 votes out of 40,000; I should think that would discourage even Smith.[3]

We miss you and Mrs. Green from our social gatherings, but we trust you are enjoying yourself. I see that you are getting to the meat of "Sambo"; you will find it interesting, and easy French.[4] I see your son William around almost everywhere.

Mrs. Chesnutt joins me in regards to yourself and Mrs. Green. We hope to see you occasionally and hear from you often. Wishing you both a Merry Christmas, I remain,

Sincerely yours,

Chas. W. Chesnutt.

TLS: OClWHi

[1] John Patterson Green (1845–1940), was born in North Carolina and was Chesnutt's cousin. He migrated to Cleveland in 1857, and after a brief return to North Carolina, where he became an attorney in 1870, he established his offices in Cleveland. An active Republican, he served in the Ohio House of Representatives and as a state senator. In July 1897, President McKinley appointed him U.S. Postage Stamp Agent in the District of Columbia. Signing himself "Carpetbagger," he was the author of Recollections of the Inhabitants, Localities, Superstitions and Kuklux Outrages of the Carolinas (1880).

[2] Blanche Kelso Bruce (1841–1898) was a runaway slave who became a teacher, financially successful planter, adroit politician, and the second African-American Mississippian to serve in the U.S. Senate (1875–1881). He won election as a Republican only a year before Democrats assumed control of state politics, and was thus "swept" out of office as the effects of the Reconstruction were being effaced. He subsequently enjoyed handsome political appointments: Register of the Treasury (1881–1885), Recorder of Deeds in the District of Columbia (1889–1893), and again Register of the Treasury in 1897.

[3] Harry C. Smith, editor of the Cleveland Gazette, had alienated himself from the Republican party and its black leadership in Ohio, and, as a consequence, he was no longer eligible for patronage of the kind enjoyed by Bruce and Green. The N.P.P. was a political organization formed shortly before the 1897 state elections by black Democrats and Independents, for the purpose of undercutting African-American support for the Republicans. Like Smith, their candidates for state office found themselves outside the circle of power when the votes were counted.

[4] This work has not been identified.

Walter Hines Page

❧

December 7th, 1897.

Dear Mr. Page:—

I felt in a somewhat effusive mood the other day, and I sat down to write a long letter, in which I was going to tell you something about my literary plans, how long I had cherished them, the preparation I had made for them by study in our own and other languages, by travel in our own country and in Europe; how I had in a measure restrained myself from writing until I should have something worth saying, and should be able to say it clearly and temperately, and until an opportune time should have come for saying it; how I had intended, for reasons which were obvious, and had in a measure paved the way financially, to make my literary *debut* on the other side of the Atlantic, and follow it up immediately by devoting my whole time to the literary life—etc.

But it occurred to me that you were a busy man, and that anything I might say to you as an editor might be better said by what I should write for publication; that all my preparations and my hopes would be of no use to me and of no interest to you unless I followed them up with something like adequate performance; and that it would be in better taste to reserve personal confidences until I might have gained your friendship and your interest by having accomplished some worthy thing. So I concluded that I would write you a simple business letter, and say that I sincerely hope your house will see its way to publish that volume of stories for me. I feel confident that they have sufficient originality to secure a hearing, and that their chance of doing so will be very much enhanced if they are brought out by a concern of Houghton, Mifflin & Co.'s standing. It is not difficult to find a publisher of some kind, on some terms,—but there are publishers and publishers.

I am prepared to follow up a volume of stories by a novel.[1] I have completed the first draft of a long story which I mentioned to you when I saw you in Boston,[2] and have started on the revision; in a month or two I hope to have it completed. It deals with no race problems, but mainly with a very noble order of human nature, more or less modified by circumstances.[3] I have also the raw material, partly digested, of a story on the order of what you suggested might be written along the line of my shorter stories.[4] When I get this other out of the way I shall attack it seriously.

You may remember that you said to me that you hoped to get at least one of the two short stories you have for the *Atlantic*, in either the December or the January number.[5] If that is not feasible for the January number I am sure you will do the best you can for them.

I write to you thus fully—for I see I have written a long letter, in spite of my disclaimer—because I do not want you to forget me. I know you have a great many people on the ground, near at hand, and that distance puts me at a disadvantage with the relays of people waiting in the outer room to see you. I wish to secure your interest and your friendship as well in furtherance of my literary aims, and I do not think you will find it amiss that I write and tell you so, and tell you why.

Permit me to say in closing that I thought the book reviews in the December *Atlantic* exceedingly good, and that I remain,

Sincerely yours,

TCU: TNF

[1] Page replied on 15 December 1897 that Chesnutt's short stories were being read "by our whole staff" and that the "practical trouble presented is the miscellaneous quality" of the group. He

promised to report the firm's decision shortly. He also related that he was "delighted" that Chesnutt was making progress on "a long novel" which would prove "a much more important step in your literary career than the book publication of any short stories whatever."

[2] The date of Chesnutt's visit to Boston, made at some time after his 22 October letter to Page, is not known.

[3] "A Business Career," identified in the next letter to Page.

[4] What Page suggested to Chesnutt is not known, though he most likely was interested in a work with the qualities of the "conjure woman" stories—imaginative, humorous, suffused with local color, and providing an engaging view of African-American folkways in the South (as in "The Goophered Grapevine"). Or, he advised Chesnutt to focus on the mores and manners of those African Americans who had settled in the North (as in "The Wife of His Youth").

[5] "The Wife of His Youth" and "The March of Progress."

Walter Hines Page

[*Circa* 23 February 1898]

Dear Mr. Page:—

I have written to you before about a long story I have been writing. I have finished it—at least I am going to stop working on it for the time being—and take the liberty of sending it to you herewith. I have entitled it "A Business Career."[1] I think it has some of the elements of a good story, and I would like to have your house consider it with that end in view. It would certainly strike a considerable class of people in large cities, if brought to their attention. I do not know whether in form or subject you would consider it suitable for the *Atlantic*; if so I should be glad to see it there.

Any information as to my collected stories that you have been considering[2] or any information as to when you will be able to use the stories accepted for the *Atlantic*[3] will be very much appreciated.

In the meantime, I remain

Cordially,

TCU: TNF

[1] A notice of the receipt of the "Business Career" manuscript by Houghton, Mifflin is dated in Chesnutt's hand 26 February 1898; and thus the present letter was very likely sent to Page during the previous week. "Career" was declined by Page on 30 March 1898.

[2] On 30 March 1898, Page informed Chesnutt that the publication of a volume of short stories derived from the collection sent him would not be possible.

[3] On 30 March 1898, Page informed Chesnutt that he would soon receive "a proof of the two stories" that *Atlantic Monthly* had accepted. "The Wife of His Youth" appeared in July; "The March of Progress" never appeared in *Atlantic Monthly* despite the promise of proof for it (see 27 September 1898 to Page, n. 8, regarding its final disposition).

Walter Hines Page

ᴥ

May 20, 1898

My dear Mr. Page:

I enclose you herewith the six "conjure" stories you suggested that I write with a view to magazine and book publication. They are entitled respectively: "A Victim of Heredity," "The Gray Wolf's Ha'nt," "Mars Jeems's Nightmare," "Sis' Becky's Pickaninny," "Tobe's Tribulations" and "Hot-foot Hannibal" or "The Long Road." In writing them, I have followed in general the lines of the conjure stories you have read already, and I imagine the tales in this batch are similar enough and yet unlike enough, to make a book.[1]

In one of them, "Hot-foot Hannibal," the outside and inside stories are both strong, and I have given an alternative title, "The Long Road," so that there is room for editorial choice, one name being taken from the conjure story, and the other from the outside story.[2]

In the case of "Mars Jeems's Nightmare" the transformation suggested is not entirely a novel one, but the treatment of it is, so far as I know. I have thought a good title for the story would be "De Noo Nigger," but I don't care to dignify a doubtful word quite so much; it is all right for Julius, but it might leave me under the suspicion of bad taste—unless perchance the whole title's being in dialect should redeem it.[3]

Speaking of dialect, it is almost a despairing task to write it. What to do with the troublesome *r*, and the obvious inconsistency of leaving it out where it would be in good English, and putting it in where correct speech would leave it out, how to express such words as "here" and "hear" and "year" and "other" and "another," "either" and "neither," and so on, is a "'stractin'" task. The fact is, of course, that there is no such thing as a Negro dialect; that what we call by that name is the attempt to express, with such a degree of phonetic correctness as to suggest the sound, English pronounced as an ignorant old southern Negro would be supposed to speak it,[4] and at the same time to preserve a sufficient approximation to the correct spelling to make it easy reading. I have taken the bull by the horns in the case of the word "you." To spell it "yer" all the time would not be as it would be spoken, and to avoid apparent inconsistency I have spelled it "you" all the way through. I do not imagine I have got my dialect, even now, any more uniform than other writers of the same sort of matter. If you find these stories available, I shall be glad to receive any suggestions in the matter of the dialect or anything else.

I hope you will like the stories and that you may find it possible to use them, or some of them, for the magazine, as well as for book publication, within the current year, if possible.

Of the three conjure stories heretofore written by me and published, one, "The Conjurer's Revenge," which appeared in the *Overland Monthly*, the mule transformation story, has a good deal of extraneous matter in it, and is a trifle coarse here and there. I shall rewrite it at once,[5] as I think it was checked by your house as suitable for book publication.

Hoping that these stories may meet with favorable consideration, which I know you will be glad to find them worthy of, I remain,

Sincerely yours,

TCU: TNF

[1] Although, on 30 March, Page announced that his firm would not be publishing a book made from the short stories Chesnutt had sent him, he related that there was still a chance for a collection of stories "if you had enough 'cunjure' stories to make a book, even a small one." Three of those that Chesnutt had sent him were appropriate: "The Goophered Grapevine," "Po' Sandy," and "The Conjurer's Revenge." If Chesnutt "could produce five or six more" like them, there "would be no doubt" about the outcome. In response to an unlocated letter from Chesnutt, Page again encouraged him on 8 April: "I am especially gratified to hear that you will write more 'cunjure' stories. If you will write half a dozen or so as good as the best of those you have already written, and will send us the whole group, I am frank to say, as I said in my other letter, that I shall have great hope of the house's willingness to bring them out."

[2] Chesnutt is describing "framed" stories: each begins with a Caucasian named John relating the circumstances under which Uncle Julius McAdoo begins to spin a yarn; within that frame of reference, the former slave tells his story, assuming total narrative control; each then ends with a return to the "outside story" as John reacts to or describes the effect of Uncle Julius' storytelling. In short, the structure is that of a story within a story.

[3] The tale concerns a slave owner who is transformed into a slave. This is not the only occasion on which Chesnutt was willing to exploit the potential of racist imagery; while he did not use the title given here, he did go ahead with another of the kind when, in 1900, he published "A Victim of Heredity; or Why the Darkey Loves Chicken," *Self Culture Magazine* 11 (July 1900), 404–9.

[4] By the time that Chesnutt finished his revision of the stories in question, such a description of Uncle Julius was no longer appropriate. In the new version of "The Goophered Grapevine," Uncle Julius was characterized not as an "old southern Negro," as Chesnutt here uses the term, but as a mulatto displaying a "shrewdness" that was "not altogether African."

[5] Like "The Goophered Grapevine," "Revenge" was given extensive revision by Chesnutt.

Walter Hines Page

✥

[20 May 1898]

My dear Mr. Page:

I have written you a business letter today, and sent it to you with some stories, under another cover.[1] As this letter is rather of a personal nature, I enclose it separately.

A friend of yours, Mr. Keatinge, of New York, with whom I have had more or less business for several years in connection with a railroad receivership out here, was in my office a few weeks ago. In the course of our conversation the *Atlantic* was referred to whereupon Mr. Keatinge said that one of his best friends edited the magazine, and mentioned your name, also the fact that you were a North Carolinian by birth and breeding, and a member of the old Virginia family of the same name.

Of course I ought to have known all this before, but when one lives far from literary centers and is not in touch with literary people, there are lots of interesting things one doesn't learn. I had even read some of your papers on the South, and know of your editorial work in North Carolina;[2] but when I met you in Boston I did not at the time connect you with them.[3] I calmly assumed, as nine people out of ten would offhand, that an editor of the *Atlantic* was, of course, a New Englander by birth and breeding. But when Keatinge enlightened me on the subject, I immediately proceeded to correct my impressions by reference to a biographical dictionary. You may imagine my surprise, and it was an agreeable one, I assure you, to find that you were "bawn en raise'" within 50 or 60 miles of the town where I spent my own boyhood and early manhood, and where my own forbears have lived and died and laid their bones.[4]

I hope you will find time to read my "cunjah" stories, and that you may like them.[5] They are made out of whole cloth, but are true I think, to the general "doctrine" on conjuration, and do not stray very far beyond the borders of what an old Southern Negro *might* talk about.

I am going to work on the novel I have been speaking of; it is a North Carolina story.[6] With your permission I shall sometime soon write you a note briefly outlining the plot & general movement, and ask you whether there is anything in the subject that would make it unavailable for your house. I am not easily discouraged, and I am going to write some books, and I still cherish the hope that either with my conjuh stories or something else, I may come up to your standard.

In the meantime, I remain   Cordially yours,

TDU: TNF

[1] See the previous letter to Page.

[2] In 1881, Page made an extended tour of the South and his articles on the conditions he observed were given syndicated distribution in American newspapers. Page's "editorial work in North Carolina" followed his departure from the staff of the New York *World* in 1883: he acquired control of the Raleigh *State Chronicle*, and in its editorials he bluntly argued for an end to the worst features of the Old South and promoted the concept of a new, more egalitarian and progressive state. His audacity was, in part, responsible for his lack of financial success with this newspaper. In 1885 he moved to New York City and took a position with *Forum*. It is likely that Chesnutt read Page's "A New Problem in the Education of the Freedman," *Independent* 41 (29 August 1889), 5, since Chesnutt was then George W. Cable's protégé and it appeared in a symposium with Cable's "The Nation and the Illiteracy of the South," 2–3. If he did so, however, it is probable that he is not here recalling Page's point of view: therein Page reflected on how education may work to the detriment of African Americans since it tends to make them discontented with the "hard manual labor" in which their opportunities were to be found; he argued that they should instead be trained for skilled labor and encouraged not to take a negative view of unskilled work. Page even quoted Joel Chandler Harris's Uncle Remus to the effect that a spellingbook has ruined many a good plough hand.

[3] See 7 December 1897 to Page, n. 2.

[4] Canceled by Chesnutt in the typescript draft transcribed here was a continuation of this paragraph, in which he attempted to minimize the possible effects of a faux pas he thought he had committed: "I frankly confess that if I had known some of the things I have learned about you since I might have spared you, among other things, some of my rather free criticism of the Southern people. Good taste, to say the least, would have suggested a little more reticence. I thought I was imparting information, but I suspect you understand the subject quite as well as I do. . . . I admit that I would have to revise to some extent my express views of the Southerner, if you insist on being one of them." Before he canceled this passage, Chesnutt altered "my rather free criticism of the Southern people" to "the information I thought I was imparting to you about the Southern people."

[5] The draft of this letter included an extension of this paragraph and a different final paragraph. The extension read: "If these stories are not interesting to a N.C. reader, *caeteris paribus*, they would not attract anyone, and if they interest you I am frank to confess that the value of a favorable opinion at your hands would be enhanced in my eyes by the fact that you are a N.C. My daughter of seven years old finds them of absorbing interest. (For heaven's sake don't think I intend to institute a comparison there: but a story that interests a child I imagine has the vital dramatic element.)" The canceled final paragraph read: "I hope that you may find time to read the stories yourself, and shortly, and that you may find them worth using."

[6] Chesnutt may possibly be referring to "The Rainbow Chasers"; see [April 1900] to Johnson, n. 2. More likely, though, the reference is to "Rena Walden"; he submitted a new, expanded version to Page in late August or early September 1898.

Walter Hines Page

[29 June 1898]

My dear Mr. Page:

I have your kind note with reference to the appearance of "The Wife of His Youth" in the July *Atlantic*.[1] I am glad you think it adds some interest to the number. It will be widely and appreciatively read in Cleveland, I can assure you; I have already received many compliments on it. I also received the very handsome check sent by Messrs. Houghton, Mifflin & Co.[2]

I must thank you for putting me in such good company, for the table of contents shows a notable list of scholars and literary celebrities. The unsigned article on Gladstone is very fine.[3]

I wish to thank you also for the assurance that the other story will follow soon,[4] and that I shall soon hear from the conjure stories, in the fate of which I am of course very much interested.

Yours very truly,

ADU: TNF

[1] 82 (July 1898), 55–61. In his "note" of 1 June, Page explained that "Wife" was scheduled to appear in the June *Atlantic Monthly* but had to be moved to the July issue. He also acknowledged receipt of the "new 'conjure' stories" to be considered for book publication.

[2] A check for $55.00 was sent to Chesnutt on 25 June.

[3] The unsigned essay on "Gladstone," 1–22, described the life and career of England's prime minister William Ewart Gladstone (1809–1898), touching upon his recognition of the Confederate government in 1862 as well as his various attempts to improve conditions in Ireland. Chesnutt may have found the latter of interest since the political situation of the Irish was frequently cited at this time in discussions of the denial of civil rights to African Americans.

[4] "The March of Progress."

Walter Hines Page

՟∾՟

[29 June 1898]

Dear Mr. Page:

I had written the other letter that I send you herewith, and it was lying on my desk, when I received your favor, enclosing Mr. Allen's letter.[1] It is needless for me to say that I experienced genuine emotion at so spontaneous and full an expression of approval from one who speaks with authority, as one of the scribes. If there is any quality that could be desired in such a story that Mr. Allen has not found in it, I am unable to figure out what it is. His letter has given me unfeigned delight, for I have read his books and know how to value his opinion. If you will be good enough to let him know that his praise and his good wishes are both a joy and an inspiration to me, I shall be obliged to you. You don't say anything about my returning Mr. Allen's letter. Of course, I should like to keep it, but if you think it would not be right to let me do so, I will content myself with a copy, which you will doubtless permit me to retain, in confidence, of course. In the meantime, I will keep the original until I hear from you again.

TCU: TNF

[1] James Lane Allen (1849–1925) was a widely acclaimed short-story writer and novelist who, in 1898, was at the apex of his career. In a 27 June letter to Page, Allen praised "The Wife of His Youth" thus: "I went through it without drawing breath—except to laugh but two or three times. It is the freshest, finest, most admirably held in & wrought out little story that has gladdened— and moistened—my eyes in many months."

Walter Hines Page

՟∾՟

[early August 1898]

My dear Mr. Page:—

You are certainly doing the handsome thing by me in the way of advertising. I have noticed the announcements in the August *Atlantic*, and I more than imagine that the information for the very fine notice in the *Bookman* came from you. Permit me to thank you, if I am correct in the latter assumption, for the graceful and tactful way of alluding to my connection with the colored race, by which it is made an element of strength instead of a source of weakness.[1]

I can easily imagine a person of less discernment & delicacy stating the same fact in a vastly different way. What has been said about this one story seems to stake out my field and warn others off, and it looks as though you and the other people who make literary reputations are going to give me an opportunity, to which I only hope that I may prove equal. I shall certainly try to do so.

I note what you say about the conjure stories.[2] I can only repeat that I hope you may be able to use them; I suspect you have a good many publishing problems to solve, and I trust you may find this one not too difficult. I rather inferred, from the announcement under the head of "Forthcoming Articles" in the August *Atlantic*, that you meant to use some of the conjure stories in the magazine.

This is my dull season & I have a month or two of comparative leisure before me, in which I hope to do something at least approximating the standard set for me. I think you have not yet seen the best story I have written.

I hope the September story[3] will clinch the good impression made by the first one. It ought to appeal to a wider circle of readers. You don't say anything about my returning Mr. Allen's letter. Of course, I should like to keep it, but if you think it would not be right to let me to do so, I will content myself with a copy, which you will doubtless permit me to retain, in confidence, of course. In the meantime I will keep the original until I hear from you again.[4]

Appreciatively yours,
Chas. W. Chesnutt

ADS: TNF

[1] *Atlantic Monthly* had announced as forthcoming "The March of Progress" and other stories of his that would appear in future issues. "Chronicle and Comment," *Bookman* 7 (August 1898), 452, made the initial disclosure to the national readership that Chesnutt was African-American: "Mr. Charles W. Chesnutt, whose touching story, 'The Wife of His Youth' . . . has, perhaps, caused more favourable comment than any other story of the month, is more than a promising new writer in a new field. Mr. Chesnutt has a firmer grasp than any preceding author has shown in handling the delicate relations between the white man and the negro from the point of view of the mingling of the races. Perhaps the most tragic situation in fiction that has ever been conceived in this country is that in which a mulatto finds himself with all the qualities of the white race in a position where he must suffer from the disadvantages of the coloured race. Mr. Chesnutt has for several years treated this subject in a capable and artistic manner, and has proved himself not only the most cultivated but also the most philosophical story writer that his race has as yet produced; for, strange to relate, he is himself a coloured man of very light complexion."

[2] On 25 June, Page gave the reason for a delay in his report on the stories being considered for book publication: "your 'conjure' stories take more time, because they arouse a very grave practical problem of publishing, than I had any idea they would take, but you shall hear from them now within a very brief period."

[3] "The March of Progress."

[4] Chesnutt originally wrote in his draft that, since he was in doubt about whether he ought to

ask for the privilege of keeping the letter, he was returning it to Page. This was canceled, and the decision to keep it was instead announced. For some reason, Chesnutt did not register Page's 6 July declaration that he should keep Allen's letter.

George Washington Cable

❧

August 5th, 1898

Dear Mr. Cable:—

I see it announced that you have returned from your very pleasant and I trust profitable visit to England, of which I have read much here and there.[1] Your reception was a well-earned tribute to a rare order of genius as well as to a representative American author.

When I saw you a year ago I told you, I believe, of several stories which the *Atlantic* had accepted for publication.[2] One of them appeared in the July number, and made a very good impression, bringing a letter of praise from a very distinguished author, whose name I am forbidden to mention just at present,[3] and drawing out a column notice in the August *Bookman*, as well as other letters from critics, newspapers and readers. The August *Atlantic* announces in a very flattering way another story for September,[4] and others still to follow;[5] and I have other publication schemes on foot of which I can not yet speak positively, and therefore will not specify. I hope to follow up the good impression made by this story, and if I can accomplish anything of permanent value in literature, I shall attribute no small part of it to the inspiration of your friendship and recognition, which, though our meetings have been rare, I have always cherished as one of the pleasantest things of a life which has not been altogether pleasant.

My daughters were much improved by their year at Smith, and will return next month. They had hoped to get on the campus, but the nearest they could come to it was Stone House, which I understand is a very nice place.[6]

I shall be glad if you will give my regards to Mrs. Cable, and believe me,

Respectfully and cordially yours,
Chas. W. Chesnutt.

TLS: LNHT

[1] See, for example, "Mr. Cable in England," *Critic* 32 (11 June 1898), 387. Cable's widely celebrated lecture tour, during which he successfully cultivated Andrew Carnegie as a benefactor of his Home Culture Club projects, extended from April through July 1898.

[2] When and where Cable met with Chesnutt in 1897 is not known. In his 20 February 1897 letter to Cable, he announced the acceptance by *Atlantic Monthly* of "The Wife of His Youth" and "The March of Progress."

[3] James Lane Allen; see the second [29 June 1898] letter to Page.

[4] "The March of Progress"; see 27 September 1898 to Page, n. 8.

[5] Although no short story appeared in September, one of the new ones written at Page's request, "Hot-Foot Hannibal," was published four months later in *Atlantic Monthly*.

[6] Ethel and Helen Chesnutt began their studies at Smith College in Cable's hometown, Northampton, Mass., in the autumn of 1897. In an 11 August 1898 letter to Chesnutt, Cable, after celebrating Chesnutt's success, wrote: "We did not pay your daughters as much attention as we should have liked to do, last season, I being away so much and Mrs. Cable not well. I hope we shall see more of them this year."

Walter Hines Page

⌒

[14 August 1898]

Dear Mr. Page:—

I have been hearing from my story every day since its publication. Editors kindly send me marked copies of magazines & papers containing approving notices. I get compliments right & left from the best people in Cleveland on the ethics, the English, and the interest of "The Wife of His Youth." I have had letters from my friends & notices in all the local papers. My autograph has been called for from "down East," a local publisher wants to talk to me about a book, a clipping bureau would like to send me clippings; and taking it all in all, I have had a slight glimpse of what it means, I imagine, to be a successful author. It has been very pleasant, and might have turned a vain man's head. I thank you for the pleasure, and shall guard against the other myself. I know it a long way from a successful story—its success partly due to its novelty—to a successful literary life based on an enduring popularity. I shall enjoy the one and hope for the other.

I am going to take a brief vacation within the next 30 days, and shall probably turn my footsteps eastward and be in Boston a few days, if I can hope to meet you there. There are some matters I should like to talk to you about, and if you will be good enough to let me know whether you will be in Boston from now on, or if not, during what time you will be absent, so that I may time my visit to catch you, I shall esteem it a very great favor.

I would like to send you along, a week or two in advance of my visit, a couple of stories I would like to have you read. One of them is a story of North Carolina life, just after the war;[1] the other more on the order of "The Wife of His Youth."[2] I would like to have you read them as a friend, if you have the time, and tell me whether I have made the most of the longer one.

I am looking for the appearance of "The March of Progress" with pleasurable anticipations, and I hope to learn, when I see you, if not sooner, the fate of the "conjure stories."

In the meantime I am ever   Cordially yours,

ADU: TNF

[1] The North Carolina story appears to have been "Rena Walden." Although Chesnutt, on 25 July 1890, told Cable that he did not have the temerity to resubmit a revised "Rena Walden" to *Century*, he was more persistent with Houghton, Mifflin. "Rena," in its most recent incarnation, made its way to Page in late August or early September, despite its rejection both as a part of a book

(see 8 September 1891 to Houghton, Mifflin) and as a short story for *Atlantic Monthly* (see 22 September 1890 to Cable).

[2] Chesnutt is very likely referring to "Her Virginia Mammy," in which a black woman keeps the secret of the apparently Caucasian heroine's African-American racial background. Page appears to have advised Chesnutt to submit it to another magazine. When *Century* declined it and editor Henry M. Alden of *Harper's Monthly* discouraged Chesnutt from even submitting it, Chesnutt wrote to Page on 27 September, "I shall probably have to send it back to you."

Houghton, Mifflin & Co.

ᎣᏊ

Sept. 19th. [1898]

Dear Sirs:—

I was duly in receipt of your favor of the 9th inst., notifying me of your decision to publish the book of conjure stories for me. Permit me to assure you that I appreciate the privilege of "coming out" under the auspices of your House, and I thank you for the complimentary terms in which you announce your decision.[1]

With regard to the financial success of the book, I am only solicitous that you may not lose by the experiment, and I am sure we would all be glad to see it turn out a pronounced success. I return the manuscript herewith. I have slightly enlarged the introduction to the first story, have revised the introduction to the others so as to avoid unnecessary repetition and have arranged the stories in what I think good order. The "Goophered Grapevine" cannot well be anything but the first story, "Po' Sandy" is a good second, and "Hotfoot Hannibal" winds them up well and leaves a good taste in the mouth. Barring the first one, however, and perhaps the second, the order is not essential. I have left out the two stories "Tobe's Tribulations" and "A Victim of Heredity." They are not, I will admit, as good as the others, and unless you think the book too small without them, I am content to leave them out. I have no idea, of course, of the form in which you think of bringing out the book, but should like to have it as dignified as the quantity of matter and the outlay you contemplate will permit.

I have written to the *Overland Monthly*, as suggested to me when in Boston,[2] asking leave to republish "The Conjurer's Revenge," included in the manuscript submitted. You speak in your letter of a better title for the book than "Conjure Stories." I send with the MS. a list of suggested and most of them "suggestive" titles. I would be glad to have your views on the subject, or to have you select a title from this list or independent of it.[3]

The customary royalty of ten per cent on the retail price of all copies sold will be quite satisfactory to me, and I shall be very glad to close the transaction formally by signing a contract in regular form.[4] I presume I ought to have the book copyrighted when a title is decided upon, though I suppose the contract will cover all questions about that.

With sincere thanks for the interest and confidence you manifest in my work, which could not be better shown than by your decision in the case of this book, and with the sincere hope that the outcome may be satisfactory to us both, and that this may be but the beginning of a connection which I am very proud to have made, I remain   Yours very sincerely,

TCU: TNF

[1] Page related in a personal letter of 6 September that the decision was unanimously made that day; on 9 September he more formally announced that "we feel disposed to publish for you your collection of short stories." Page suggested in the latter that Chesnutt consider the title it should be given; advised him that "we cannot help regarding with some doubt as to any great financial success"; and opined that "whether the present interest in this side of the negro character is suffi-cient to carry the book to the success we hope for can be determined only by experiment." (The record of printing orders [MH:P] indicates clearly the consequence: a first printing of only 1,500 copies was ordered on 24 January 1899; and, due to an overage of printed sheets, 1,528 copies in the trade binding were actually produced.) Page returned under separate cover the whole lot of stories considered, asking for revision of those "conjure stories" to be in the book. "We have this practical suggestion to make—since the stories were written each for separate publication, they each have a sort of independent preface or introduction . . . wherein you explain how you hap-pened to be in North Carolina and how you happened to meet Uncle Julius. . . . Now when the stories appear in book form of course one such explanation will do for the whole volume. We think, therefore, that you might possibly wish to change or to abbreviate the introductions of some of the stories that will appear in the book after the one that shall take the first place." Explaining that "Tobe's Tribulations" and "A Victim of Heredity" were not selected by the readers for inclu-sion, Page asked Chesnutt to "have the manuscript ready at [his] earliest convenience." "A Victim of Heredity" was published in *Self Culture Magazine* 11 (July 1900), 404–9, after being declined along with "The Bouquet" by *Scribner's Magazine* on 24 May 1899. "Tobe's Tribulations" was pub-lished in *Southern Workman* 29 (November 1900), 656–64.

[2] Chesnutt visited Page at some time after 14 August, when he announced his plan to be in Boston within thirty days and that he would send Page a North Carolina story ("Rena") and some short stories that they might discuss. In late August or early September, then, he discussed with Page not only the matter of copyright regarding "The Conjurer's Revenge" but how "Rena" might be made suitable for publication. See 27 September 1898 to Page, where Chesnutt refers to revi-sions of "Rena" made in light of Page's suggestions.

[3] This list has not been located. Whether Page or Chesnutt originated the title, *The Conjure Woman,* is not known.

[4] The contract for *The Conjure Woman* is dated 8 October 1898, specifying a royalty of 10 percent of the retail price and 5 percent when sold at a reduced price for export.

Walter Hines Page

୵ଊ·

Sept. 27, 1898

Dear Mr. Page:—

I wrote the *Overland Monthly* asking permission to republish the story "The Conjurer's Revenge," and received a reply waiving the copyright, which reply I attach hereto.

I received a letter from Mr. Allen the other day,[1] which had been addressed to your office & kindly forwarded to me, in which he explained why we had missed each other when I was in New York,[2] and still expressed a desire to meet me. It is a pleasure I hope to give myself in the future.

I am getting along swimmingly with the novel. The development along the lines we talked about has opened up new vistas of action, and emotion, and dramatic situations.[3] This of course throws some other parts a little out of proportion. I hope to be able to complete it in a very few months, as I am figuring so as to get plenty of time to work on it.

I left "Her Virginia Mammy" with Mr. Gilder.[4] He returned it with the statement that they didn't quite take to it, that he thinks "perhaps, somehow, it seems to lack something in the way of charm and mellowness, but it is not badly built either." He says further: "I read the *Atlantic* story that you asked me to read.[5] It is certainly very striking, but somehow it seems as though that poor fellow was entitled to a compromise of some sort. I don't know just what it would be, but the precise outcome hardly seems humanly right." It is surprising what a number of people who have done me the honor to read that story, do not seem to imagine that the old woman was entitled to any consideration whatever, and yet I don't know that it is so astonishing either, in the light of history.[6] I find, on looking over my memorandum book, that "The Wife of His Youth" was sent to the *Century* before it went to the *Atlantic*; so I do not therefore worry about the rejection of "Her Virginia Mammy." I hardly think it worthwhile to send it to *Harper's*, in view of a conversation I had with Mr. Alden.[7] I shall probably have to send it back to you, but I'll try it at one place more. If it were located in New Orleans, fifty years ago, it would be more likely to have "mellowness"; but I guess it is too nearly up-to-date to suit Mr. Alden or Mr. Gilder.

I hope you may see your way to get "The March of Progress" in the November number, as you thought you could when I saw you. The October number hasn't reached Cleveland yet, but I suppose will be out today. I know of several people who are looking for that story.[8]

Trusting that you have had time to read to the end of this long letter, I remain,   Sincerely yours,

ADU: TNF

[1] Novelist James Lane Allen, who had praised "The Wife of His Youth"; see the second [29 June 1898] letter to Page.

[2] Chesnutt was in New York City in late August or early September.

[3] The reference is to "Rena," which he discussed with Page in Boston before he went to New York City and met with Richard Watson Gilder and Henry Mills Alden (see n. 7).

[4] Editor of *Century*.

[5] "The Wife of His Youth."

[6] The old woman in question is an illiterate rural black for whom whites such as Gilder, Chesnutt implies, would normally have little sympathy.

[7] Henry Mills Alden (1836–1919), was the editor of *Harper's Monthly*. The particulars of this

conversation are not known, but Alden was committed to the ideal of publishing works that could be read aloud in the home to all family members; "Mammy" focuses upon an impending interracial marriage.

[8] On 22 November 1898, Page asked for Chesnutt's permission to publish "Hot-Foot Hannibal" instead of "The March of Progress," and the manuscript was returned to Chesnutt.

Walter Hines Page

⋴◌⋼

Nov. 11, 1898[1]

Dear Mr. Page:—

I am deeply concerned and very much depressed at the condition of affairs in North Carolina during the recent campaign.[2] I have been for a long time praising the State for its superior fairness and liberality in the treatment of race questions, but I find myself obliged to revise some of my judgments. There is absolutely no excuse for the state of things there, for the State has a very large white majority. It is an outbreak of pure, malignant and altogether indefensible race prejudice, which makes me feel personally humiliated, and ashamed for the country and the State. The United States Government is apparently powerless, and the recent occurrences in Illinois in connection with the miners' strike seem to emphasize its weakness.[3]

But I would not inflict my views on you in this matter, except for a circumstance you may find interesting. The colored people's newspaper *The Daily Record*, the office of which was burned yesterday by a mob of the "best citizens" of Wilmington, numbering in their ranks many "ministers of the gospel," and the editor of which has been compelled to flee for his life,[4] republished "The Wife of His Youth" in installments running over about a week, sometime ago, and somebody sent me several copies of the paper. It gave credit to the *Atlantic*, but I rather doubted whether it had obtained your permission to copy the story. If I had the heart to joke on a subject that seems to me very seriously and hopelessly tragical, I might say that the misfortunes of the newspaper were a sort of divine retribution, or poetic justice for a violation of copyright.[5]

I am making rapid progress on the novel,[6] and will have it ready to submit to you by the end of the year or sooner, I believe.[7]

Sorrowfully,

ADU: TNF

[1] Misdated 10 November by Chesnutt, who refers below to events transpiring on that date as having occurred "yesterday."

[2] During the North Carolina elections of both 1898 and 1900, Negrophobic demagoguery was widespread, and Democrats thus wrenched power away from the Populist-Republican "fusion" officeholders who had prevailed in 1894 and 1896. Fusionists were accused of having facilitated

"Negro domination," particularly in Wilmington. Chesnutt below describes one of the sensational events triggering the race riot of 10 November 1898, for which both blacks and whites had armed themselves. Chesnutt would later exploit the situation in *The Marrow of Tradition* (1901): for example, he included the destruction of the offices of Wilmington's *Record*, the black newspaper; and the fictional character Josh Green, who kills white racist Captain McBane in the novel, is related to Wilmington's coal and wood dealer Josh Green, who was involved in the events leading up to the riot. Chesnutt's former adversary in the forum provided by George Washington Cable's "Open Letter Club," Alfred M. Waddell, played a significant role in local politics then and was a primary spokesperson for the white supremacist point of view at the time of the elections (see 14 November 1889 to Moffat).

[3] See "Industrial War in Illinois: Miners' Strike at Pana and Virden," *Review of Reviews* 18 (November 1898), 512–13. Chesnutt associates labor unions with the African-American community, both of which needed federal protection.

[4] In a 14 December 1899 letter to Houghton, Mifflin, Chesnutt identifies the newspaper editor as Alex Manly, who had since established a new newspaper in the District of Columbia, the *Washington Daily Record*. The major reason that Manly became the target of the white supremacist Democrats during the 1898 election campaign was that his paper printed a response to characterizations of African-American males as a sexual threat to white womanhood; it argued that rural white females invited such attention. That he had impugned North Carolina womanhood became an inflammatory theme of Democratic speechmakers. Immediately before the riot began, it was made clear by the Wilmington's white citizens' committee that Manly was to be exiled.

[5] Chesnutt originally ended the draft here: he cancelled his closing, "Yours sincerely & sorrowfully,"; his signature; and "P.S." before the next paragraph; then he put "stet" marks above and below "sorrowfully," indicating to his typist that this was to be the closing.

[6] The manuscript is that of "Rena," which Chesnutt was revising in light of the discussion of it with Page, to which he referred in 27 September 1898 to Page.

[7] Page replied on 14 November, "I am glad to have your letter about things in North Carolina, for occurrences there have given me also very deep concern." He observed that Manly had no right to publish "Wife" in his newspaper but concluded that it was best to let the matter drop: "the *Atlantic* can very well afford to forgive him." As he did in all of his recent letters to Chesnutt, Page once more indicated that he was interested in seeing the novel being finished—in this instance "Rena."

Walter Hines Page

੭·

[27 December 1898]

Dear Mr. Page:

In am in receipt of a copy of the January *Atlantic*, and also of Messrs. Houghton, Mifflin & Co.'s offer for sixty-five dollars ($65.00), for which please let this serve as an acknowledgement.[1] The number is a fine one and I find myself in excellent company. The sketch of Mr. Du Bois has a charm and simplicity that at times is very touching.[2] The lines seem to be drawn pretty tight for the colored race just at present, and it ought to be a source of great satisfaction to them that there is certainly one high forum from which they can speak for themselves.

I have stopped work for the present upon the novel, and send it to you herewith, with the hope that you may find it, at least in part, what you thought I might make of it. I have put in more of the old town, and its people. I have tried to draw, in Rena's character, a fine character forced inevitably into a false position. The heroine, instead of being the interesting lay figure of the story as you read it before, I have tried to make a living, loving, suffering, *human* woman.

I have no doubt that the story has its weak spots and that a lynx-eyed reader will find much to criticize. I have not tried to dodge the hard places, though I may not always have made the most of them.

Personally, I believe in the story. It is true, I think, to nature, and there is scarcely an incident related in it that has not been parallel in real life to my actual knowledge. I enclose a newspaper clipping from last week's paper that suggests the main situation.[3]

I hope you may like the story, and that your house may see fit to bring it out. I would like to hope, if I dared, that you might find it available for serial publication in the *Atlantic*. If I have improved at all upon the story as you read it last fall,[4] I am glad to acknowledge the incentive thereto, your kindly advice and criticism, and if I have not bettered it, it is my own fault, and I can keep on working at it.[5]

I am getting the proof sheets from day to day of *The Conjure Woman*, and I imagine it will make a very pretty book.[6]

With greetings of the season and warm acknowledgement of your many favors, I remain   Sincerely yours,

ADU: TNF

[1] The issue included "Hot-Foot Hannibal," for which Chesnutt was paid $65.00.

[2] W. E. Burghardt Du Bois (1868–1963) was, by 1903 when *The Souls of Black Folk* appeared, a prominent spokesperson for the African-American cause. Having received a Ph.D. in 1895, he taught at Atlanta University from 1897 to 1910, played a major role in the organization of the National Association for the Advancement of Colored People, edited its magazine *The Crisis* (1910–1934), and was a novelist as well. Chesnutt is here referring to his "A Negro Schoolmaster in the New South," *Atlantic Monthly* 83 (January 1899), 99–104.

[3] The clipping has not been identified.

[4] Page read the previous version of "Rena" in late August or early September; see 19 September [1898] to Page, n. 2.

[5] Page acknowledged receipt of "Rena" on 28 December. On 12 January 1899, he acted in a way that Chesnutt, expecting only Page's personal consideration of the manuscript, did not anticipate: Page informed him that "Rena" had been put in the hands of the house readers.

[6] On 17 December 1898, Garrison sent editorially marked proofs of the first forty-two pages to Chesnutt; the dates on which other batches were sent are not known.

Walter Hines Page

‹◦›

[30 January 1899]

My dear Mr. Page:—

A number of my friends have called my attention to the very complimentary leaflet sent out by the *Atlantic* last week, in reference to my writings. I hope it may be of some value to the magazine and know it will promote the success of *The Conjure Woman*.[1]

I am desirous that the book should go well, because, for one reason, I want to stand well with the publishers, and I need the encouragement that even a very moderate success would give me. I am doing what I can in that direction. I have given several readings recently to audiences of the "best people" of the city & am asked to give another soon.[2] I am not ambitious just now to become a public reader, but I have responded to these calls for the sake of the advertising, the people I have read to being of the class who read and buy books, and who look upon the *Atlantic's* approval as the hall-mark of literary excellence.

If I had known just the form of circular you contemplated sending out, I could have supplemented the list of names Mr. Beacom sent you by some other good ones.[3] I have made out an additional list, and one of my friends, the principal of a fashionable preparatory school for young ladies, is to send me in a day or two a list of her patrons & friends, and, in return for my having read for her reception, is to work for the success of my book. A number of leading ladies, some of whom dabble in letters are taking an interest in my work, and I am encouraging their interest, judiciously, I hope, for I have observed that women play a large part in making literary reputations. I will send you these lists in a day or two, and if you think it advisable you might send them copies of the little circular; if it is followed pretty closely by the book it will help it along.

I shall be obliged if you will send me a few of the circulars you have had printed, if you have any of them on hand yet.[4]

I hope your readers will like "Rena." Personally, I have great confidence in it. I have discovered one thing about my stories, which I think I can say to you without risking the imputation of vanity,—that those who read them remember them; and the back numbers of the *Atlantic* and other periodicals containing them have been looked up and read over quite diligently here in Cleveland recently.

ADU: TNF

[1] The unlocated circular appears to have focused on the January publication of "Hot-Foot Hannibal" in *Atlantic Monthly* and the forthcoming publication of *The Conjure Woman* in March.

[2] Here and in later letters Chesnutt alludes to readings before small groups but refrains from citing the particulars. In a 27 January 1899 letter to Chesnutt, however, Mrs. A. N. Elliot, corresponding secretary of The Woman's Home Missionary Society of Cleveland, refers to

Mrs. E. C. Higbee, president, having heard Chesnutt read at the Hathaway-Brown School a short while ago. (He read "The March of Progress" there on 21 January.) She invited Chesnutt to the "young people's Missionary rally" to be held on 5 April at the Bolton Avenue Presbyterian Church in Cleveland. At this event, he read "The Fabric of a Vision," and on 12 May she thanked him.

³ One of many individuals who assisted Chesnutt in selling his books outside the conventional channels of the book trade (see 21 October 1899 to Love, n. 2), Madison W. Beacom was a Cleveland attorney with an office in the Society for Savings Building, to which Chesnutt moved his office by 1892. He was one of the founding members of the local bibliophile society, the Rowfant Club. He arranged subscription sales to club members and Cleveland attorneys of a special "Large-Paper Edition" of *The Conjure Woman*, 150 copies of which Houghton, Mifflin manufactured after it produced the first "trade" printing on less expensive paper.

⁴ On 1 February, the Publishing Department of Houghton, Mifflin replied that it would cooperate fully to insure widespread distribution of advertising circulars. Thus began Chesnutt's energetic promotion of all of his books among editors, book reviewers, politicians and political appointees, fellow authors, friends, relatives—all those, in short, who might purchase copies, ensure publicity, or effect greater sales to the public. How indefatigable he was in this is reflected not only in his own surviving letters but in numerous replies from his publishers to unlocated ones.

Walter Hines Page

⌒

[22 March 1899]

My dear Mr. Page:

I have been reading the March *Atlantic*, and haven't found a dull line in it. The contrast between slavery struggling for existence in an essentially free democracy, and liberty struggling vainly for life in a despotism, is strongly marked in Mrs. Howe's "Reminiscences" and Prince Kropotkin's autobiography. The dialect story is one of the sort of Southern stories that make me feel it my duty to try to write a different sort, and yet I did not lay it down without a tear of genuine emotion.¹ The advertising pages were interesting for two reasons—because of the very handsome characterization of my book, and the announcement that you are going to write an essay on the race problem.

I have known for some days that you were in the South, and I guessed that you had gone down there to see if you could help pour oil on the troubled waters in North Carolina.² I hope your labors have not been in vain. Others have been trying to do something in the same line. I have a letter in my pocket from a colored man who holds a minor office at Washington, but who is an influential citizen at his home in North Carolina, and a member of the board of directors of an Agricultural and Mechanical College. He has been down there four times since Christmas, "where I spent some time," he says, "dealing with that d_____ wild legislature. Of course, I am not *compelled* to go back there to live, but feel that it is my duty to do anything I can for those poor Negroes who cannot help themselves."

I read the other day a letter from a colored woman, a North Carolinian who lives in Washington. In it she says: "I have no further use for North Carolina. Never again will I sing her praises. She has fallen so low that she can never be redeemed in my estimation. C_____ expresses the hope that the cooler judgment of wiser heads will prevail and that there will not be legislation against the Negro which will be hurtful to him. But I entertain no such hope. I believe they are capable of anything which will humiliate self-respecting colored people."

This letter was written exactly three months ago and subsequent events have justified the writer's intuitions.[3]

In another letter received yesterday, from Wilmington, the writer characterizes the town as a place "where no Negro can enjoy the blessed privilege of free speech and a free press, and where every organization, whether social, political, or industrial, undertaken by our race, must needs meet with opposition from the whites, incited by jealousy and envy. If we did not read of 'better times in other climes' we would indeed be enduring a living death."

It would be a great privilege for me to talk with you about what you heard and saw there, and I hope to have it ere many months. I know your views in general on these subjects and have no doubt that you have heard both sides of the matter—if there can be two sides to it. There never will be any final or peaceable settlement of the race question as long as the two subjoined gems of thought[4] represent the attitude of the great majority of Southern white people towards the colored race.

With these sentiments controlling the South, and the South trying to force them on the North and with the colored race in spite of them moving steadily, though slowly upward, there will grow up a state of feeling between the two classes that is not conducive to good government. Oppressive, discriminating and degrading legislation is the logical outcome of such promises; and from present indications it seems that such is to be the order of the day for some time to come. It is difficult to conceive of a more outrageously unjust and unconstitutional law than the franchise amendment proposed in North Carolina.[5] But I could write on the subject for a week, and I therefore refrain; and I am really wasting time, for I know that whatever personal or editorial influence you may have will be thrown in on the side of justice and equity. I will say, however, that the Supreme Court of the United States is a dangerous place for a colored man to seek justice. He may go there with maimed rights; he is apt to come away with none at all, and with an adverse decision shutting out even the hope of any future protection there; for the doctrine of *stare decisis* is as strongly intrenched there as the hopeless superiority of the Anglo-Saxon is in the Southern States.

Your house has turned down my novel "Rena" in great shape. They have condemned the plot, its development, find the distinctions on which it is based unimportant, and have predicted for it nothing but failure.[6] I have not slept with that story for ten years without falling in love with it, and believing in it, and I should feel very unhappy about it if it came back without your having read it, if you have not already.[7] The fact that it met with your approval in the rough, was my chief incentive in rewriting it. Whether I took the wrong tack in my revision I don't know; perhaps I did; but if you find time, I should like you to read it—even if it is already disposed of—in order that I may be able to discuss it with you when I see you again. If the distinctions on which that story is based are so unimportant as to foredoom to failure any story based on them, then I have yet to find my *metier* as a story writer, for they are my strong cord, I firmly believe.

I see an *Atlantic* ad, running in the *New York Age*; the editor is a manly man, and not afraid to speak out what he has to say if sometimes a little intemperately.[8] The people he represents so well are finding eyes as well as voices, and they have only to use them to see that in the *Atlantic* they have a staunch friend at a time when they need a friend badly.[9]

Sincerely yours,

ADU: TNF

[1] Julia Ward Howe (1819–1910) was a social reformer and the abolitionist author of "The Battle Hymn of the Republic" (1862). "Reminiscences of Julia Ward Howe" ran serially in *Atlantic Monthly* 82 (December 1898) through 83 (May 1899); the March installment appeared on pages 330–42. Prince Peter Kropotkin (1842–1921) was a Russian aristocrat, explorer, scientist, and political reformer who embraced anarchist principles in response to the reactionary nature of government his Tsarist homeland. His "Autobiography of a Revolutionist" was also being serialized: 82 (September-October, December 1898), 83 (January-March, May-June 1899), and 84 (July-September 1899); the March installment appeared on pages 382–98. The sentimental story featuring African-American dialect to which Chesnutt alludes is "Chief" by James B. Hodgkin, 83 (March 1899), 374–82: Chief's mother lived on a plantation being sold; his master mortgaged his own property to purchase her and reunite the mother with her son; and, years later, the grateful ex-slave saves his former master's impoverished widow by buying the plantation and returning the deed to her.

[2] Page left Boston in February, making a six-week trip through the South, where he planned to investigate the racial situation, largely duplicating his 1881 journalistic study of the region. In his 30 March reply, Page briefly outlined the itinerary of his Southern tour: "I need not tell you that I had a very delightful time in my journey through Tennessee, Mississippi, Louisiana, and thence through all the states back to North Carolina, and I hope to have something to say about what I saw a little later."

[3] Since the November 1898 state election and the Wilmington riot on the 10th, the victorious Democrats had proceeded to dismantle the voting rights legislation benefitting blacks that the Republican-Populist "Fusion" electees of 1894 and 1896 had passed.

[4] Chesnutt apparently enclosed two unlocated newspaper clippings ("gems") with his letter.

[5] "Mississippi, South Carolina and Louisiana, the three states which have already adopted suffrage restrictions practically disfranchising the Negroes, are presently to be joined by North Carolina and Alabama. . . . The North Carolina amendment follows closely the Louisiana precedent" ("Disfranchised," *Cleveland Gazette*, 4 March 1899, 1). That is, a registrant must convince a registrar that he possesses $300.00 in property and can read and write. Not subject to these requirements were those individuals who had the right to vote by 1 January 1867 and their descendants; blacks were subject to the requirements since they did not receive voting rights until the passage of the Fourteenth Amendment on 2 March 1867.

[6] Garrison noted Page's absence from Boston in a 16 February reply to Chesnutt's letter of the

13th (unlocated), and he then announced that "Rena Walden" had been rejected by Houghton, Mifflin. Garrison saw little in "Rena" that would appeal to a wide readership: "when it comes to the whole, the story is based on distinctions which are of but little interest to a great many readers." He further explained, "Rena" is, "in effect, a long short story, and though the simplicity of the plot gives unity to the book, it also makes a little more plain certain fundamental facts which will weaken the sympathy of the reader with the heroine, a sympathy which is indispensable. For it is borne in on the reader that the girl, wholly aware of the ineradicable prejudice against the negro strain, and testing her lover on the point, is weak enough to think to conceal the truth; and again, that with all her natural refinement and pure intuitions, she allows herself to drop into the position of the wife of a scoundrel of color. Would it be necessary that the evil of the second man should be demonstrated to a girl of the instinctive delicacy of Rena?"

[7] Although on 2 February Page related "I have not myself yet read it since it came back in this form," he told Chesnutt on 30 March that he did have a chance to do so before he left for the South. In the latter letter, Page attempted to mitigate Chesnutt's disappointment over the most recent failure of "Rena"; but he also felt that it was best to be frank about how Chesnutt "had not by any means . . . done [his] best work on it . . . or developed to the fullest extent the possibilities of the story." The rejection resulted from the judgments of several readers, but Page himself could not recommend its acceptance: "I believe that a year hence you . . . will agree with me that it is not even yet sufficiently elaborated and filled in with relieving incidents—not sufficiently mellowed— there is not sufficient atmosphere poured round it somehow—to make it a full-fledged novel." It was the consensus at Houghton, Mifflin, continued Page, that Chesnutt had not made the transition from short story writer to novelist, for a "novel is something of greater leisure and different and more elaborate structure, not simply a longer thing."

[8] T. Thomas Fortune (see 1 February 1896 to Haldeman, n. 7). The earliest known letter from Fortune to Chesnutt is dated 14 December 1898; in it he thanks Chesnutt for his "words of commendation" regarding his newspaper: "I am gratified when the friends can approve my course. We are at a very critical stage and I feel that we must speak out without fear or favor."

[9] On 24 March, Garrison acknowledged Chesnutt's 22 March request (unlocated) for five copies of the "edition de luxe" of *The Conjure Woman* (see [30 January 1899] to Page, n. 3). Chesnutt's first book—in both its "trade edition" and its "de luxe" printings—was published circa 24 March 1899.

Corresponding Editor, The Youth's Companion

April 17, 1899

Dear Sir:

Replying to your letter of recent date with reference to contributions to the *Youth's Companion,* I would say that I should like very much to find in it a medium for the publication of my stories.[1] I have not been a very prolific writer, owing to the absorption of my time by other interests, and I have not troubled many editors with my manuscripts. However, I shall be glad to submit contributions for your consideration.[2]

I do not know why I should not undertake to write a Labor Day story, if I can get at what you would like; and as your announcements for 1900 will not, I presume, be made for some time yet, I suppose I will be given ample time to see whether I can write it or not. Can you give me any more definite notion of what you want? Would you like a story about colored people? That is my specialty, though I have written outside of it. I had thought, vaguely, of a meeting held by the operatives in a mill or factory, to determine the momentous question whether a colored hand could take part in the Labor Day celebration, or procession, and of making the man do some act of bravery—saving the mill from burning, or preventing some accident that would have thrown them all out of employment, the result being that he becomes a hero in the mill and nothing is too good for him. This is merely an[3]

ADU (fragment): TNF

[1] Chesnutt is responding to a 6 April request for short stories like those that had appeared in *Atlantic Monthly*, preferably along the lines of "The Wife of His Youth" rather than "the tales which have a supernatural element"; one "appropriate for Labor Day" was suggested. The author of the request was most likely M. A. De Wolfe Howe (see [5 September 1899] to Howe, n. 1).

[2] On 22 April 1899, the magazine acknowledged Chesnutt's submission of two stories. On 4 May it accepted "Aunt Mimy's Son" and sent Chesnutt a check for $50 on 6 May; the story appeared in volume 74 (1 March 1900), 104–5. "The Bouquet" was rejected "less on account of its handling the difficult subject of race than because its quality is perhaps too delicate for an audience so large and varied as *The Companion's*."

[3] Although the remainder of this letter has not been located, what Chesnutt went on to say about his planned story may be inferred from the editor's 22 April reply to it: "the only possible objection to what you propose is that members of the labor organizations which pride themselves on drawing no color line might question the plausibility of your plot." Chesnutt also appears to have ruminated on the problem of the Southern reaction to such a story since the corresponding editor wrote, "What you say about the difficulty of treating questions of race for Southern readers shows me clearly that you understand the very motives which make *The Companion* most careful in such matters." *Companion* accepted the Labor Day story, "The Averted Strike," on 19 May and sent Chesnutt $50 on 28 July. On 28 April 1900, however, Chesnutt learned from a form letter that, due to a surplus of manuscripts, his story would not be published.

Walter Hines Page

❧

July 15, 1899

My dear Mr. Page:—

I am thinking of making a run down East in the near future, and as one of the objects of my visit would be to see you and talk with you, would you mind telling me whether you will be in Boston or anywhere near it for the next month or thereabouts?[1] I see you are slated for some lectures at Chautauqua, but I suppose they will come later in the Summer.

While I am writing to you, I will ask you, personally, what you think of the probability of Messrs. H. M. & Co.'s being willing to bring out for me, at a suitable time from the appearance of *The Conjure Woman*, a volume of stories along the line of "The Wife of His Youth?"[2]

ADU: TNF

[1] Chesnutt was in Boston by 1 August 1899 (see [5 September 1899] to Howe, n. 1). On 9 August he reached an agreement with Houghton, Mifflin concerning the publication of a second collection of short stories, to which he refers below. (Garrison cited this visit to the editorial offices in a formal confirmation letter dated 10 August). By 10 August, Chesnutt was at the Waldorf Astoria Hotel in New York City, where he received two letters from Page (HM:P): the first announced "arrangement satisfactory and heartily welcomed"; the second informed Chesnutt that Page was ending his relationship with Houghton, Mifflin. The "arrangement" to which Page referred may have been the contract for *The Wife of His Youth;* but it more likely concerned a speaking engagement at Eliot, Me., that Page arranged for Chesnutt (see 15 August 1899 to Page, n. 1). Chesnutt went to Eliot directly from New York City, and he stopped in Boston for only a few hours (see [5 September 1899] to Howe) on his way south to Washington, D.C. (see [August 1899] to Lewis H. Douglass, with a District of Columbia return address). By 19 August at the latest Chesnutt had returned to Cleveland: a 21 August letter from John S. Durham of Asbury Park, N.J., expressed regret that he had not known Chesnutt was in the East; Chesnutt would have had to inform him by mail of his itinerary and return to Cleveland. While in Boston, Chesnutt was interviewed by Pauline C. Bouvé, "An Aboriginal Author," *Boston Evening Transcript,* 23 August 1899, 16. Two novel points were made by her: she related that Chesnutt spoke of himself as "a descendant of three races," the third being determined by "Indian blood he inherits from an aboriginal ancestor"; and she was the first commentator to describe Chesnutt's attitude of "concentrated bitterness" toward white racism in the South.

[2] That Chesnutt secured a contract for this book on 9 August is a testimony to the commitment Houghton, Mifflin was disposed to make to him on other than strictly business principles: 6 May 1899 from Houghton, Mifflin made it clear that, since its publication in March, the firm's modest sales expectations for *The Conjure Woman* had been proven correct (see 19 September [1898] to Page, n. 1). The firm phrased its report on sales as positively as it could: "it has done, we think, quite as well as we anticipated. We have disposed of over 1,000 copies besides the copies sent to the press." By the time Chesnutt wrote the present letter, the first trade printing had been spent, and a new printing was ordered at some time between 14 and 20 July. Still, how little confidence Houghton, Mifflin had in *The Conjure Woman* was indicated by the size of the press run: the sheets for a mere 518 copies were sent to the bindery on 9 August 1899 (MH:P).

Walter Hines Page

∾

August 15, 1899

My dear Mr. Page:—

I reached Greenacre in good time, and found Miss Farmer an amiable woman, with high but somewhat vague ideals that have in a measure obscured the practical side of things.[1] I talked to quite an audience of highly intellectual people, or as I termed them in my remarks, "a choice band of enlightened spirits, seeking after truth in whatever guise"—and some of the guises are queer ones.[2] I had the close attention of the audience, and made a good impression, receiving quite as much applause as they could find any decent excuse for giving me. I frankly confessed my lack of skill as a platform speaker, but they were good enough to say I underestimated my effort, and that any lack of rhetorical graces was more than compensated by my evident knowledge of the subject and the interesting nature of what I said. The subject was a little large, and I am afraid I dwelt more on the political and civil status of the negroes in the South and didn't have time to properly consider the remedies. I did suggest education, however, as the most obvious and immediate palliative; but maintained that race troubles would never cease until the Constitutional amendments were strictly observed, in the spirit in which they were meant, the color line entirely wiped out before the law, and equal justice and equal opportunity extended to every man in every relation of life. This sentiment was vigorously applauded.

Miss Farmer expressed herself as entirely satisfied, and I was satisfactorily entertained. She also insisted on paying my fare from N.Y. to Boston, on my way to Greenacre. I presume she will write to you, and hope her[3]

ADU (fragment): TNF

[1] Miss Farmer was the founder and director of the Greenacre Conference, then in the midst of its sixth summer season at Eliot, Me., which extended from 1 July to 2 September. The Chautauqua-like nature of the series of lectures and discussions was characterized by a quotation of its 1899 program in "The Season at Greenacre," *Boston Evening Transcript*, 8 July 1899, 8: "Greenacre was born out of a life of unrest, impatient of control, to which the secret of peace had come. Once learned, this secret became a compelling force, reaching out to other lives with the assurance that 'all things work together for good.' The work was inaugurated as a gift of love and gratitude, and its success is due to the fact that many others who had learned the same secret came in joyfulness and offered time, strength, service and means for the establishment of the Ideal." The article went on to provide the schedule of lectures, identifying Page as slated to speak on "The Negro in the South" during the week of 6–12 August. Page secured Chesnutt's services as a replacement speaker on the same topic; the text of his address was summarized in detail in "The Greenacre Season," *Boston Evening Transcript*, 20 September 1899, 16.

[2] Noted in "The Season at Greenacre" was the exotic dress of many of the conference participants, e.g., the "flowing robes of bright fabrics" from "far away India, China, Japan"; contributing to the "picturesque" environment as well were the visages of those from Syria, the Philippines, Chile, and "the leading nations of Europe." Chesnutt, however, is undoubtedly alluding primarily to the motley group of enthusiasts seeking truth and ethicality via lectures on and discussions of spiritualism, the philosophies of German idealists, ethical materialism, non-Christian religious thought, the temperance and women's suffrage movements, and—of course—Emersonian transcendentalism.

[3] On 17 August 1899, Page—now employed by S. S. McClure in New York City—responded to Chesnutt's report with "Good! I congratulate myself on my substitute." He also assured Chesnutt, "You shall soon hear from me about Rena."

Houghton, Mifflin & Co.

⌒

[23 August 1899]

Dear Sirs:—

I have kept the MSS. of "The Wife of His Youth" &c. a few days, with a view to selecting and arranging them most effectively. I have made an arrangement, how effective I do not know, and if anyone there can suggest a better I shall cheerfully acquiesce. The total amount of matter is 65 to 70 thousand words.

Mr. Page suggested as a good title for the volume, *The Wife of His Youth, and Other Stories of the Color Line*.[1] I have not been able to think of any better title, and all the stories deal with that subject directly, except one which heads it I might say collaterally. So unless there is some good reason to the contrary, I rather think that name would very aptly characterize the volume; and I would like to hope that the stories, while written primarily as attempts at literary art,[2] might by depicting life as it is in certain aspects that no one has ever before attempted to adequately describe, throw a little light upon the great problem on which the stories are strung; for the backbone of this volume is not a character, like Uncle Julius in *The Conjure Woman*, but a subject, as indicated in the title—the Color Line.

The story "The Sheriff's Children" was published in the *Independent*, and I have the permission of that paper to reproduce it, but they would like to have their courtesy acknowledged in the book, if feasible, and I suppose it is entirely so. Mr. Page left a note on his desk for Prof. Perry, suggesting that he look over the unpublished stories, and see if there is one suitable for the *Atlantic*. I have addressed a separate note to Mr. Perry, and have no doubt he will give the matter attention, and do whatever he finds best in the matter.[3]

I enclose your copy of the contract, which is entirely satisfactory, with the change of name suggested above, if that is agreeable to you.

TDU: TNF

[1] The contract for *The Wife of His Youth and Other Stories* was dated 10 August 1899; Chesnutt's royalty was 15 percent of the retail price and 7½ percent on copies sold at a reduced price for export. In his 10 August cover letter to Chesnutt, Garrison closed by relating that he would be "happy to take up and push the typesetting of the book as soon as the stories have been selected and arranged." The new title that Page suggested and Chesnutt approved was adopted.

[2] Wording that Chesnutt revised in the remainder of this sentence reveals initial impulses toward describing the volume as having a more overt social-reform purpose: "might by depicting life" originally read "might contribute something to the discussion," and "throw a little light upon the" originally read "may contribute a little toward the settlement of the." See [10 December 1899] to Houghton, Mifflin, where Chesnutt responds to the reformist personality of editor Harry D. Robins by not only admitting but emphasizing the sermon-like character of his stories.

[3] Bliss Perry (1860–1954) taught at Williams College and Princeton University before replacing Page as the editor of *Atlantic Monthly*. A "genteel" writer like Chesnutt in the *Wife* pieces, Perry published his own most significant collection of short stories in 1899, *The Powers at Play*.

Lewis H. Douglass

·◌·

N.W. Cor. 18th & U Sts.
Wash. D.C.
[August 1899]

My dear Mr. Douglass:—

I have accepted a commission from Small, Maynard & Co. of Boston, to write for their Beacon Series of Biographies of Eminent Americans, a volume on your illustrious father.[1] It is to be a small book—really a sort of extended sketch; it would be presumptuous in me to undertake anything more important without long and careful preparation. The subject is one that appeals to me, and there is abundance of material, that is, as to the public portion of his life; for the facts of his early life there is practically only one source—his various autobiographies. I hope with the material on hand to be able to construct, in even the limited time at my disposal, a dignified and appreciative sketch—a birdseye view as it were—of the life of our most distinguished citizen of African descent.

The immediate object of my writing to you, however, is to ask if you can tell me where I can get the best photograph of your father, or two or three from which a choice can be made, and which I can procure permission to use, in the form of a small frontispiece. It seems to me I have heard somewhere that there is a particular photograph that the family prefer. I will very willingly pay for what I want, if the photo. is purchasable. I want a photograph if possible, and not an engraving.

My little book will contain a Chronology showing the principal events of Mr. Douglass's life. These are matters of history mainly, but I would particularly desire to get straight the various honors that were shown your father— the bust at Rochester, and the subsequent monument, and things of that kind. I do not venture to intrude upon a busy man's time, but if you have any printed matter in the way of newspaper clippings that would give dates and names of participants in the meetings to honor Mr. Douglass, or with reference to his funeral & burial place, I would esteem it a favor to have the privilege of looking at them. It is my sincere desire to honor the memory, as adequately as the scope of this little work will permit, of one whom the world delighted to honor for so many years.

If you will kindly advise me about the photo. I shall be obliged.[2] Mrs. Chesnutt has spoken to me of meeting you last Spring, and has repeated some pleasant things you said about *The Conjure Woman*, for which I thank you.

Sincerely yours,

ADU: TNF

[1] Lewis Henry Douglass (1840–?) was the second child of Frederick and Anna Douglass. Trained in journalism at the editorial offices of his father's newspaper, *The North Star*, he was the

senior editor of *New National Era*. See [5 September 1899] to Howe, n. 1, regarding the commission from Small, Maynard.

[2] On 12 September, Douglass directed Chesnutt to Kent Photographer, State Street, Rochester, N.Y., for a photograph of his father. He informed Chesnutt that he had no clippings.

M. A. De Wolfe Howe

·◦·

[5 September 1899]

My dear Mr. Howe,

I am in receipt of your kind favor of August 29th.[1] I am back in Cleveland and working away at the Douglass Biography, and making, as I think, very fair headway. It is a new line for me, but I am not at all appalled by it, and shall I think do very well with it.

I will send you the Chronology, Bibliography and Portrait first, and I think very soon now.[2]

I passed through Boston again after seeing you, on my way back from Greenacre, Me., where I spoke on the "Race Problem in the South," to an interested and appreciative audience; but I only remained in Boston a few hours, and therefore had to forego the pleasure of seeing you again.

Sincerely yours,

Chas. W. Chesnutt

ADS: TNF

[1] Mark Anthony De Wolfe Howe (1864–1960) was a professional editor as well as a poet and an author of numerous works dealing with New England culture and its historically significant figures. Chesnutt appears to have first made his acquaintance when he began correspondence with *Youth's Companion*; see 17 April 1899 to the Corresponding Editor of that magazine. Howe was also employed as editor by the book-publishing firm of Small, Maynard & Co. On 1 August 1899, Chesnutt met with Howe, and they discussed the possibility of a Douglass volume in the firm's Beacon Biographies series. Later that day, Howe wrote to him, offering a 10 percent royalty and asking to see him the same evening. The contract is dated 4 August 1899 and specifies a royalty rate of 10 percent of the retail price or of the price offered canvassers and others receiving more than the normal discount.

[2] On 29 August, Howe suggested that Chesnutt forward these three sections so that they might be processed for printing "before the body of the book comes to us." On 14 September, Howe acknowledged their receipt, noting that the bibliography would have to be put into chronological order and perhaps shortened (see 31 October 1899 to Howe regarding the receipt of galley proof).

PART IV
THE PROFESSIONAL NOVELIST
OF 1899–1902

❧

Pursuit of the Dream

❧

I thank you for the comparison with
Uncle Tom's Cabin; if I could write a book
that would stir the waters in any appreciable
degree like that famous book, I would feel
that I had vindicated my right to live &
the right of a whole race.

Houghton, Mifflin & Co.

⌒

October 11, 1899.

Gentlemen:

I received the package of circulars you sent me,[1] and used some of them for distribution at a little reading I gave last night. I may ask you for more of them soon, as there are several ways in which I can use them to advantage. One of the large book stores would like to have some to send out with purchases they deliver, if you think the probable returns from that kind of advertising would justify the expense.

I am reading the proof-sheets of the new book. The stories read very well, but will read better I think when they have been corrected.[2] I am glad to know the book is to be out by November 11th, that will give it a chance at holiday trade. I sincerely hope it may make a good impression; that it has some good qualities I am quite confident.   Sincerely yours,

ADU: TNF

[1] On 28 August 1899, proof of a circular, most likely advertising *The Conjure Woman* and the forthcoming *Wife*, was sent to Chesnutt. In the interim, he had returned the proof and received a batch of circulars that Garrison, on 4 October, promised to put in the mail the next day. Houghton, Mifflin aided in the local promotion of the new book when its advertisement for the November issue of *Atlantic Monthly* appeared in the *Cleveland Leader*, 28 October 1899, 5: it announced that "The Bouquet," by Charles W. Chesnutt "of Cleveland," would be found in that issue.

[2] On 30 August, Garrison acknowledged receipt of the manuscript for *Wife* and related that Perry had selected one of the new stories for separate publication: "The Bouquet," *Atlantic Monthly* 84 (November 1899), 648–54. The manuscript for the book, he wrote, would first go to the illustrator so that he could make notes for the art work; then the typesetting would begin at once. Garrison promised that he would "endeavor to put it through rapidly." On 4 October, Garrison sent him the proof for the first sixteen pages. The remainder reached Chesnutt well before 24 October, when Chesnutt was informed that the firm was "much pressed for time" and that he needed to "return the proofs with all possible promptness."

Walter Hines Page

⌒

[*Circa* 11 October 1899][1]

My dear Mr. Page:

I have taken the step I contemplated when I saw you last, and have retired from business since October 1, with the intention of devoting my time henceforth to literary pursuits of one kind or another.[2] I have finished, and sent off yesterday the biography of Douglass I agreed to write for the Beacon Biographies, and have done a conscientious piece of work that I am not ashamed of. I am now reading the proof-sheets of *The Wife of His Youth*, etc. During the past week, I gave two readings from my stories to cultured and appreciative audiences, no money in them, but good practice and good advertising. People say I read my stories very effectively.

In the course of a few weeks, I want to lay out the plan of a novel,[3] and in the meantime, I would be very glad to know, if you have had time to read it yet, your opinion of my novel, "Rena." I should like to think you had read it, even if it should take more time for you to get around to it—for I realize that in your new position, you must find yourself a very busy man.[4]

I am going to write Mr. James Lane Allen a letter asking leave to use for advertising purposes an extract from that letter of his you sent me on the appearance of "The Wife of His Youth" in the *Atlantic* last year; and it has occurred to me that as Mr. Allen must be in New York by this time and you are likely to meet him often, you might render me a service, without any trouble on your part, by mentioning the subject to him casually, if you should chance to meet him and think of it. Don't burden your memory with it, but if it occurs to you and you don't mind it, I should be obliged; I shall write to him anyway.

I hope you are finding your new work agreeable, and I remain

Cordially yours

TDU: TNF

[1] Receipt of the manuscript of the narrative portion of *Frederick Douglass* was acknowledged by Herbert Small on 12 October (see 31 October 1899 to Howe, n. 1). Chesnutt's statement below that it was sent "yesterday" suggests that the present letter was written on 10 or 11 October.

[2] The extent to which Chesnutt actually withdrew from business is not clear, nor is it known how much capital he had accumulated before making his trial of authorship as a livelihood. When his wife decided to spend the summer of 1900 in a rented house at Willoughby, to the east of Cleveland, Chesnutt wrote on 12 May 1900 to his future son-in-law, Edward C. Williams, that he had to return to "vulgar toil . . . in an old matter downtown, to pay the rent for our summer cottage" (unlocated letter quoted by Helen Chesnutt, *Charles Waddell Chesnutt* [Chapel Hill: University of North Carolina Press, 1952], 148). With two daughters at Smith College and the amenities of an upper middle-class style of living to maintain, it is unlikely that Chesnutt was ever truly "retired." He maintained his listings as stenographer and attorney in the city directory through July 1900; and through August 1901 his business address as an attorney only was included. In the volume for September 1902 through August 1903, he advertised himself as attorney, stenographer, and notary; that is, by August 1902 he was again fully involved in his old occupation.

[3] Chesnutt is possibly referring to "The Rainbow Chasers," rejected by Houghton, Mifflin on 24 March 1900; see [April 1900] to Johnson, n. 3, for another rejection of it.

[4] On 10 November Page replied, describing the hectic pace of his life since joining S. S. McClure. McClure was in midst of an ultimately unsuccessful attempt to take over Harper & Brothers, whose Book Department he wanted Page to head despite an earlier indication that he would be involved in the editing of one of the four Harper magazines or *McClure's Magazine*. As vexed with McClure as Frank N. Doubleday of the Doubleday & McClure book-publishing company was, the two men announced the formation of Doubleday, Page & Co. on 18 December. Very busy with reading and editing manuscripts, and having recently passed through a series of illnesses, Page apologized for keeping the "Rena" manuscript for so long and for not yet having read it. He promised to give himself the pleasure of taking up the manuscript "as a part of my Sunday devotions."

John L. Love

◆

October 21, 1899

My dear Mr. Love:—

I have just been reading your pamphlet on the Disfranchisement of the Negro.[1] Such a paper ought to have been offered to some review or magazine, here or in England, before it was buried in a pamphlet—by which I simply mean it would have had a wider circulation and have attracted the attention it ought to command. You have put the whole case compactly, logically and dispassionately in a nutshell. If Booker Washington dared make a speech like that, it would create a sensation; but he very wisely refrains.

I have just written Tyson fully about our proposed reading, and have requested him to communicate with you.[2] I shall have to leave the matter largely in the hands of you gentlemen, as you are on the ground. I should prefer to kill the two birds with one stone,[3] if you think it worth while.[4]

Very sincerely yours,

TCU: TNF

[1] John L. Love was a teacher in Washington, D.C., and one of the founders of the American Negro Academy in 1897. The pamphlet to which Chesnutt refers is *The Disfranchisement of the Negro*, in the "American Negro Academy Occasional Papers" series, No. 6 (1899). In it Love explained the methods being used to disfranchise African Americans, focusing particularly on constitutional revisions in Mississippi, South Carolina, and Louisiana. Love was a fellow North Carolinian whom Chesnutt already knew when he wrote the present letter: this is made clear in a 26 September 1899 letter from Chesnutt's future son-in-law, Edward C. Williams, who described his meeting with Love to discuss Chesnutt's visit to Washington mentioned below.

[2] E. French Tyson was a relative who handled direct sales and distribution to vendors of Chesnutt's books among African Americans in the District of Columbia. See 16 August 1905 to Doubleday, Page, where Chesnutt proposes the same unconventional arrangement to his new publisher in order to maximize sales of *The Colonel's Dream*. Lewis H. Douglass related to Chesnutt on 5 January 1900 that he had purchased his copy of *Frederick Douglass* from "Frenchy Tyson." Chesnutt worked as well with other African Americans as he tried to boost the sales of his books: on 19 June 1889 he was billed for seven copies of *Conjure Woman* that were sent to Mrs. Catherine Perry (the maiden surname of Chesnutt's wife) in Fayetteville, N.C.; a Mrs. Sampson was, it appears, a New England relative (Anne Maria Sampson was Chesnutt's mother's maiden name) who took orders for *The Wife of His Youth* and *Frederick Douglass* in 1900 (noted in Garrison's 14 February 1900 letter to Chesnutt); and on 21 October 1899 Chesnutt asked Charles P. Lee of Rochester, N.Y., whether he would be interested in earning a commission for distributing copies of *Frederick Douglass* locally.

[3] The first "bird" was a 17 November reading of "Hot-Foot Hannibal" and "Uncle Wellington's Wives" for pastor F. J. Grimké at the 15th Street Presbyterian Church in the District of Columbia, described as "exceedingly entertaining" in "Entertainment for Sunday-school," *Washington Post*, 18 November 1899, 10. The second was a hoped-for appearance before the Bethel Literary and Historical Society, originally scheduled for 19 December. In an earlier, undated draft of a letter to Bethel President and Howard University lecturer on law William H. Richards, Chesnutt proposed four possible topics: "New Wine in Old Bottles," concerning "the difficulty of putting the new liberties of the colored race in the old forms of slavery [sic] race prejudice"; "The New American,"

a "discussion of the present make up of the American people and a prophecy as to the future"; "Progress and Retrogression," an "historical review of the general forward movement of the world with some references to certain reactions that had taken place"; and "Literature in its Relation to Life," dealing with "literature as a reflection of life as it is, as a warning of life as it should not be, and as an example and inspiration of life as it ought to be." On 21 November rather than 19 December, Chesnutt lectured on "Literature and Its Relation to Life."

[4] Chesnutt made a third appearance while in the District of Columbia. Attorney Robert H. Terrell wrote Tyson on 20 March 1899, thanking him for calling attention to "Hot-Foot Hannibal" in the *Atlantic Monthly*: "Mr. Chesnutt is a story writer of a very high order. My only regret is that the world will always take him for a white man—because he has a white man's intellect." As the Principal of the M High School, he wrote Chesnutt directly on 15 November, requesting that he "say a word to our pupils": "I should like to have our 700 students see and hear the man whose stories are doing so much to dignify Negro dialect." Chesnutt appeared there on 20 November.

M. A. De Wolfe Howe

⋅◌⋅

Oct. 31, 1899

My dear Mr. Howe,

I send you herewith last batch of the body of the Douglass Biog.[1] I have chopped it up some, but only as I thought I could improve it; sometimes a sentence has an insidious way of seeming to be right when it will not stand analysis. I have been a little bit particular, for I want these first books of mine to be as good as I can make them—though I do not mean to slight any later ones.

I shall go to work on the preface, Chronology & Bibliography and will forward them tomorrow or next day.[2]

Sincerely yours,
Chas. W. Chesnutt.

ALS: PSt

[1] Chesnutt is referring to the galley proof. On 12 October Herbert Small thanked Chesnutt for the manuscript; and on 15 October, Howe reported that the manuscript was more than satisfactory and would be sent directly to the typesetter. On 21 October, Howe informed Chesnutt that he had received his own proofs for galleys 1–8, referring to the fact that Chesnutt had been sent another set. On 26 October, he forwarded his marked galleys 1–8 for Chesnutt's approval, the next day mailing the remainder of the proof to him along with "suggestions" for changes. Howe closed by stating that, on second reading, the text was as impressive as it was when he first read it.

[2] That is, the proofs of them. On 27 November 1899, Small announced to Chesnutt the publication of *Frederick Douglass*. The copyright deposit copies were received at the Library of Congress on 28 November.

Houghton, Mifflin & Co.

&

Nov. 12th, 1899.

Dear Sirs:—

Replying to your favor of the 10th inst. I note what you say with reference to special advertising work in connection with my lectures. I am going to give you every opportunity to do as much as you are willing to stand, just as soon as I can get started at it; which will be very soon; in fact I am started now, to the extent that I have accepted all engagements offered me, but have not as yet actively sought any, even in Cleveland. I am, however, going to appear three or four times within the next month, in Cleveland and Washington. I have not troubled you about the Washington engagement, for it is being very thoroughly worked up by people there, and undoubtedly will result in considerable sale of books. The Cleveland end of it will also be well looked after, as the new book will keep me advertised here. I imagine *The Wife of His Youth* will sell very well here.

The circulars you have sent me have all been used at lectures, of which I have given three here and in the neighborhood during the past month—all but a few which I have left.[1] I shall be glad if you will send me the 100 others that you refer to, as I think I can use them in Washington the latter part of this week, as I am going to give a reading there on the 17th.[2] If you will kindly mail them to me at

2124 K. St., N.W., Washington, D.C.,

it will save me the trouble of carrying them there with me.

I think it much better to print a smaller number of *Wife of His Youth* circulars—say five hundred to start with, and include in it later such good notices as the book may elicit. I have already a number of excellent notices of the separate story "The Wife of His Youth."

I shall be glad to cooperate with Burrows Bros. Co. and The Helman-Taylor Co.,[3] in pushing my books, which I have every reason to suppose they are willing to do. The Helman-Taylor Company have displayed a great deal of interest in them from the start, though you know better than I do which has sold the most books—they or Burrows Bros.

As soon as the book is out and under way I shall put my name in the hands of some one or more lecture bureaus, and see if I can secure some engagements through them, and also get some myself in quarters that I know of. I hope that with our joint efforts we shall make the books go. Call me at any moment for anything I can do, and in the meantime believe me

Sincerely yours,

TCU: TNF

[1] One of the lectures occurred in Willoughby, Ohio, on 1 November, as indicated in a 27 October letter from Philip E. Ward, Superintendent of the Kirtland Public Schools.

[2] See 21 October 1899 to Love, n. 3.

[3] Two Cleveland book vendors.

Houghton, Mifflin & Co.

⌒

November 24, 1899.

Dear Sirs:—

During my recent visit to Washington I have been working up more or less interest in my books, and to a certain extent among a class of readers who are not ordinarily large buyers of works of fiction, but who can be very easily reached by a little personal attention.[1] I have made arrangements for some books to be sold there, acting on the assumption that you would bill them to me, as heretofore, at the trade discount, and that my royalties are figured on these sales the same as on sales to others. If I am correct in these assumptions, kindly forward to

Master E. French Tyson,
2124 K St., N.W., Washington, D.C.

the following books:—

15 copies *The Conjure Woman*,
15   " *The Wife of His Youth* (when published),[2]

and charge the same to my account. Please prepay the expressage. This order is independent of any complimentary copies of *The Wife of His Youth* which you may be good enough to send me.

A Mr. J. W. Patterson, of 407th St., N.W., Washington, D.C., having observed something of the interest aroused by my presence in Washington, called on me with reference to the sale of my writings. Mr. Patterson is a colored man, and I should judge from his appearance and manner that he could be quite a "hustler." He is a member of the bar, in a small way I imagine, and conducts as a side issue a book-selling agency, mainly of books that would appeal to colored readers. He sells them in all sorts of ways—for cash, on time, and on the installment plan, and reaches still another class of readers. He thinks that my books, both because they were written by me, and because they treat Negro life from a sympathetic standpoint, might sell well among his patrons. I was not able to look up Mr. Patterson's standing at all, but I referred him to you, with the suggestion that he write to you for rates, terms etc., and I stated that I would write to you about him. I know nothing about his financial responsibility, and I presume you know how to protect yourselves in such matters. I imagine he has written you, and that he might sell some books.[3]

Yours very truly,

TCU: TNF

[1] Chesnutt is referring to African Americans.

[2] On 25 November 1899, Garrison announced that he was sending Chesnutt an advance copy of *Wife* "by this mail" and that the "book will be published on Wednesday next, Nov. 29th."

[3] On 28 November, Houghton, Mifflin informed Chesnutt that it had not heard from Patterson.

Houghton, Mifflin & Co.

ᴄᴏ·

[10 December 1899]

Dear Sirs,

I am in receipt of your letter signed with the firm name & the initials H. D. R., with ref. to bringing *The Wife of His Youth* forward along the line of the sub-title, as a contribution to the discussion of the color line. I am entirely willing to have the book brought forward in any way that the greater experience of the house may deem wise, and I should welcome the thought that the book might be made to contribute in any degree to the "enlightened and civilized treatment" of a subject the handling of which has shown a tendency to lapse into unspeakable barbarism.[1]

I quite approve of your suggestion to make special effort in the cities named.[2] I do not see why Cincinnati might not be added to the list of Northern cities, and perhaps Chicago & Detroit; and Columbus, Ohio, if it is not too small a town. I should think other New England cities wouldn't be a bad field; for instance I have just received a splendid press notice from the Bridgeport, Conn., *Standard*, from which I quote as follows: "They [the stories] possess a very great and peculiar charm and are full of careful studies from life and to read and understand them is to know much about the heart of the important matter involved in the race issue, the settling of which will require almost limitless faith and patience and be made only through sacrifice and suffering."[3]

As to the Southern cities I am afraid my suggestions would not be very valuable. I expect the book to receive some adverse criticism—any discussion of the race problem from any but the ultra Southern point of view naturally would. One critic has already stamped me as a advocate of miscegenation, or at least as desiring a relaxation of the rigid attitude of the white race in this particular, says that the theme is unsavory, that I do not understand the "subtle relations" existing between the two races in the South, & that I have some resentful feeling left over from the carpet-bag era![4] I thought I had distinguished myself by Christian moderation. However, I anticipated such criticism, and imagine it is a healthy sign; it ought to help the book, in its character as a study of the color line. It is quite likely that people will buy a book they disapprove of, if the disapproval is strong enough, just to see what it is like; and to the Northern mind, the fact that the South criticizes severely a thing creates at least a suspicion that there may be something in it.

As to Washington, I imagine the point of view among the white people on the race question there is divided, the Southern predominating. Most of my work put in there recently was among the colored people, but I imagine the book will sell there among the whites—there is no city where the color line battle is more active, or more frequently discussed.[5]

The book was written with the distinct hope that it might have its influence in directing attention to certain aspects of the race question which are quite familiar to those on the unfortunate side of it; and I should be glad to have that view of it emphasized if in your opinion the book is strong enough to stand it; for a sermon that is labeled a sermon must be a good one to get a hearing. I have confidence in the book myself—but that might be an author's partiality.

The portion of your letter concerning Afro-American journals, I will[6] answer, in a day or two, under another cover.

I will also write again as to the half-dozen persons to whom books might be sent for an opinion. I have written Prof. W. E. B. Du Bois, Atlanta University, Atlanta, Ga., that I had suggested his name to you and requested you to send him a copy. I do not know him personally, tho we have had some slight correspondence;[7] his connection with your firm thro articles in the *Atlantic*, as well as his interest in the subject, ought to elicit a good opinion.

About Booker Washington I don't know. Anything he might say would doubtless be valuable, if he would venture to express himself favorably of a book supposed from the Southern standpoint to preach heretical doctrine. Perhaps one ought not to ask him, however, until the Southern reviews come in. Though, as I have reviewed his book on The F. of the A.N. for the *Saturday Ev. Post* and have been asked to write a signed article on it for the *Critic*, one good turn ought to deserve another.[8] I have written to a sort of personal representative of mine at Washington to speak on the subject to several prominent men there, including the sole remaining colored congressman,[9] and I will let you know in a few days whether or not to send them books; we may be able to get the opinions without, and in any event it would hardly be worth while to waste the books without results.

ADU: TNF

[1] H. D. R. was Harry Douglas Robins, who joined the Houghton, Mifflin staff in 1899 and who proved more overtly supportive of Chesnutt *qua* African American than Page or Garrison. Amidst a series of communications regarding the marketing of *Wife*, his 8 December 1899 letter to Chesnutt explained that the firm was thinking of emphasizing in its advertisements the racial content of *Wife*: "We having in mind getting out a card . . . reading instead of 'A Book Of Short Novels' in this wise: 'Stories of the Color Line'. With the recent coming forward of Mr. Washington, the publication of his book, the growing interest in Tuskegee, and the public notice attracted to the general subject of the colored people we believe it will be well worth while to bring the book forward in a number of places in the way indicated; that is, as a book of stories treating of a subject, which, (as a Southerner I may say gladly) is at last approaching a possibility of enlightened and civilized treatment." Chesnutt, then, is here replying to a white Southerner who has signaled his sympathy for African Americans and indicated that he too has found previous discussion of the race problem characterized by, as Chesnutt terms it, "barbarism."

[2] Robins had related that special advertising efforts were being considered for Boston, Washington, New York, Baltimore, Philadelphia, Atlanta, Louisville, and St. Louis. On the unlocated second page of his letter, he apparently requested the names of additional cities, which Chesnutt provided on 14 December 1899.

[3] The quotation from the review of *Wife*, intended to appear in the final version of the letter sent to Houghton, Mifflin, is not present in the sole surviving form of this letter, the holograph draft— although Chesnutt did write and cancel "They (the stories)" and thus indicated the concluding portion of the review that he directed his typist to copy. The review appeared in the no longer

extant 4 December 1899 issue of the *Bridgeport Standard*; the source is a clipping in one of Chesnutt's scrapbooks. The remainder of the review, less the listing of the titles of Chesnutt's stories, read: "No writer on kindred topics has made a greater impression on the discriminating public than has Mr. Chestnut [sic] and he fairly divides the honors of the literary situation with Thomas Nelson Page, Joel Chandler Harrs [sic], Paul Laurence Dunbar and Booker T. Washington. In his stories Mr. Chestnut [sic] not only manages to disclose the underlying facts and inevitable conditions of the race situation, but in so doing he felicitously presents the negro character in stories the literary merit of which is far above the average, and not one of all the writers upon 'the color line' has a truer sense of the picturesque and illustrative or a greater charm of manner. Indeed in the power of presentation of the pathetic side of the situation and the depicting of exceptional character Mr. Chestnut [sic] occasionally suggests the work of Mrs. Rebecca Harding Davis in *Waiting for the Verdict*, the greatest work thus far put forth upon the same subject. The stories of this collection have appeared in several high class periodicals, the first, 'The Wife of His Yough [sic],' being published in the *Atlantic Monthly* about a year ago, and their appearance in book form will be welcomed by a large number of appreciative admirers."

[4] Chesnutt is here referring to "For Literary Folks," *Nashville Banner*, 2 December 1899, 14. The critic claimed that the book is "a sore disappointment." He went on to assert: "Mr. Chestnut [sic] now appears as an advocate of miscegenation, or at least he intimates a desire for the relaxation of the rigid attitude of the white race in this particular. Southern feeling is so strong and so thoroughly rooted on questions relating to race admixture that no Southern criticisms of such ideas can escape the imputation of prejudice, but we don't believe that there is a very different sentiment on the part of the white people of the Teutonic races anywhere." He continued: "Other stories in the book [not dealing with the upper ten per cent of "colored society"] that treat of life in the South evince an utter misconception of the race relations in this section. It is a subtle relation which outsiders seem never able to learn or properly comprehend. One of these stories attempts a pathetic picture by representing a little negro girl shut out from a cemetery where she wished to attend the funeral of a white benefactor. Any Southerner of any color knows such a situation to be entirely impossible." The critic concluded: "Mr. Chestnut [sic], we believe, had some manner of experience in the South during the carpet-bag regime. None of that class will ever have other than resentful feeling toward Southern whites or cease to deem it their mission to bring about a status of race equality in this section."

[5] In his holograph draft, Chesnutt replaced his original ending of this sentence, which read "or the opposing forces more evenly balanced."

[6] Chesnutt originally began this sentence thus: "With reference to the"; and he here continued it with "say that I agree with you in thinking it a doubtful investment to ask reviews from the body of them. There are a few however that it might be worth while"; he then canceled the second, incomplete sentence and wrote "Their constituency as a class is illiterate, and books sold among them as a rule have to be sold by personal"—at which point he canceled "say . . . personal" and drew a pointed line from "will" to the next word printed above, "answer." In his 14 December 1899 letter to Houghton, Mifflin, Chesnutt did express his low opinion of African-American readers and most of the periodicals published for them; but he opined that it would pay to have reviews or advertisements appear in those periodicals.

[7] When Chesnutt and Du Bois began their correspondence has not been determined, but Du Bois, in 1898, identified Chesnutt to John Wesley Cromwell as one who should be invited to join the American Negro Academy; in a letter to Cromwell Chesnutt declined the honor on 29 March 1899. See Alfred A. Moss, *The American Negro Academy* (Baton Rouge: Louisiana State University Press, 1981), 76.

[8] Chesnutt's two reviews of *The Future of the American Negro* were: "On the Future of His People," *Saturday Evening Post* 172 (20 January 1900), 646; and "A Plea for the American Negro," *Critic* 36 (February 1900), 160–63.

[9] George H. White (1852–1918), a teacher and attorney, was elected to the U.S. House of Representatives from North Carolina in 1896.

Harry D. Robins

ᐧᐁᐧ

December 25, 1899.

My dear Mr. Robins,

Your recent favor was received, and I am very glad to make your acquaintance, which I shall consummate in person when I am next in Boston, which will be sometime this Winter.[1] I quite agree with you as to the provincialism and backwardness of the South, and in your view that a new country—of course not too new—is the place to look for the development of new men and new ideals.[2]

I called on your friend Mr. Blanchard, and spent a very pleasant half-hour with him. The question came up about what you were doing with H.M. & Co., and he said you were "selling Hopkinson Smith's books." I told him I thought you meant to take a whirl at mine before you got Smith's all sold.[3]

I thank you for the proof of the very handsome ad. that appeared in the *Transcript*, where I also saw it, as I did the ad. in the Cleveland papers.[4] I cannot complain of being a prophet without honor in my own country, for the papers here give me much space. The *Transcript* has treated me very handsomely indeed; as you have undoubtedly noticed, there have been three notices of the *Wife of His Youth* since its appearance, all complimentary, and all finding something more in the book than mere reading for amusement; in fact all the Boston papers that I have seen have commended the book.[5] The little biography that Small, Maynard & Co. have brought out for me is received with a unanimity of appreciation that is very gratifying, and which will do its part, I hope, to swell the little stream that I am hoping may grow into a current of popularity.

If you have not sent a copy of *The Wife of His Youth* to T. Thomas Fortune, care *The New York Age*, 4 Cedar Street, New York, I should be glad to have you do so; he has written me that he will with pleasure write an "appreciation" of the book.[6] I also mentioned in my former letter the name of W. E. B. Du Bois, Atlanta University, Atlanta, Ga., to whom I have written that I had asked you to send him a copy.

With reference to prominent colored men in Washington, of whom I wrote, I am informed that most of them have bought the book already, and that they will write something about it very willingly. My friend there attending to the matter is absent for the holidays but will return on the 28th, when he will look after it.

I hope the house is encouraged by the reception *The Wife of His Youth* is receiving, and that they will do what they can to give it prominence. I am told it is selling well here, in spite of the enormous Christmas trade in special gift books etc. Burrows Bros. are going to give it another window display. I have had several favorable notices from St. Louis, which might be a good city to put on your list.[7] I am also informed that Toledo, Ohio, is a city where books dealing with the same general subject sell well.

Permit me to extend the greetings of the season, and to say that I remain,

Very cordially yours,

TCU: TNF

[1] Robins wrote to Chesnutt on 12 December, introducing himself as the H. D. R. of previous letters, enclosing proof of an advertisement to appear in the Boston Evening Transcript, and suggesting that Chesnutt visit a friend of his in Cleveland, C. E. Blanchard.

[2] On 12 December, "Southerner" Robins (see [10 December 1899] to Houghton, Mifflin, n. 1) disclosed to Chesnutt that he was not really a Southerner by birth or disposition: he was born in Indiana; spent ten years in Kentucky, four years in Colorado and one in New York City; and then moved to Boston. He further explained that, although there were things in the South that he found attractive, its "detestably provincial atmosphere and . . . intolerance" caused him to prefer living in "some other place than 'Old Kentucky.'" His animus and idealism then revealed themselves in full, undoubtedly to Chesnutt's delight: "That's just the trouble—[it is] TOO old. . . . Down South (and lots of places up North, too,) 1900 is merely a calendar date. I like to think of myself as one who believes it the first year of a NEW century, as not a matter of Time but of Evolution of the soul in man: and, therefore, as a step in Time nearer a real Brotherhood." Robins' enthusiasm for assisting the African American is seen again in a 6 February 1900 letter, in which he asks Chesnutt to help a wealthy Californian, David Lubin, establish "a conservatory for music for colored people at Washington."

[3] Charles Elton Blanchard apologized on 3 September 1901 for not seeking Chesnutt's further acquaintance after this visit; the would-be novelist then asked Chesnutt if he would read a manuscript of his. F. Hopkinson Smith (1838–1915) was a popular author who, ironically, offered a positive image of Southern life.

[4] The advertisement in the Boston Evening Transcript for The Wife of His Youth and The Conjure Woman included flattering quotes from reviews in The Christian Register and the New York Mail and Express; in the 16 December 1899 Cleveland Leader, the ad for these same two books featured positive comments from the Portland Transcript (Oregon) and, again, the New York Mail and Express.

[5] The Boston Evening Transcript published brief notices of The Wife of His Youth in the 11 November 1899, 9 December 1899, and 16 December 1899 issues; acknowledged were the quality of writing in Chesnutt's stories and the author's "remarkable power of observing scientifically but not coldly" (9 December). Other periodicals in the Boston area that praised the book included the Boston Herald (6 December 1899), the Watchman (7 December 1899), The Christian Register (14 December 1899), the Cambridge Tribune (23 December 1899), and the Boston Times (24 December 1899).

[6] On 19 December, Fortune acknowledged Chesnutt's unlocated letter of the 14th, explaining that he had not yet obtained a copy of Wife but that he would be glad to read it "and write your publishers along the line you suggest." He had, however, read "The Bouquet," which appeared in Atlantic Monthly 84 (November 1899), 54–64; Fortune termed it "the best piece of literary work you have done."

[7] The "favorable notices" were in the St. Louis Republican (9 December 1899), the St. Louis Mirror (14 December 1899), and the St. Louis Globe (16 December 1899).

William Dean Howells

~

The Dalhousie
40 to 48 West 59th Street
[New York]
[3 February 1900]

Dear Mr. Howells,[1]

I was in Boston yesterday, & Messrs. Houghton, Mifflin & Co. suggested that I see you on my way thro New York.[2] This is an unconscionable hour to make a call, but I wanted to find out if I could see you this morning for a few minutes, if possible before 10 o'clock.[3]   Sincerely,

Chas. W Chesnutt

ALS: OFH

[1] William Dean Howells (1837–1920) was a novelist, social and literary critic, and America's preeminent man of letters. He encouraged promising young writers and promoted their work in his reviews in such prominent periodicals as *Harper's Monthly*, *Atlantic Monthly*, *Cosmopolitan*, and *North American Review*. At this time Howells and his family were living at The Dalhousie in an apartment they had occupied since 1892.

[2] W. B. Parker wrote to Howells on 5 February 1900 (MH:P), relating that Chesnutt was in Boston at Houghton, Mifflin on 2 February and that "he hoped to see you before going West." The reason for Chesnutt's interest in seeing Howells—whom he had not previously met—was that Howells had offered to *Atlantic Monthly* an essay on Chesnutt's three books. In the same letter to Howells, Parker told him "we'll be glad to have it." See [1 May 1900] to Howells, n. 2.

[3] That Howells met with Chesnutt is suggested in his essay, received by Houghton, Mifflin on 15 February (MH:P). Howells referred to Chesnutt's appearance therein, noting that, if Chesnutt himself did not disclose it, one would not think that he had "negro blood." Howells' reference to the "sixteenth part" of Chesnutt that was not Caucasian strongly suggests a conversation between the two. It is possible that they saw each other again the next month, for Howells referred on 25 October 1900 to the "pleasure of seeing you in the spring." See [April 1900] to Johnson, n. 2.

Booker T. Washington

~

February 24, 1900

My dear Mr. Washington,

I am in receipt of your favor acknowledging my reviews of your book.[1] It was very kind of you to write, for so many good things are said of you that they are no novelty. I am glad to add my weak voice to the chorus.

I also have your letter requesting copies of my books for the Tuskegee library. I have ordered *The Conjure Woman* and *The Wife of His Youth* sent to you, and will see that you get the other,—the life of Frederick Douglass. A visit to

Tuskegee at some time in the future is one of the pleasures to which I look forward.[2] I have met a number of gentlemen who have been there, and they all agree upon the wonderful results accomplished by your labors.

Sincerely yours,
Chas. W. Chesnutt.

ALS: DLC

[1] See [10 December 1899] to Houghton, Mifflin, n. 8.

[2] Chesnutt did not act upon the invitation to visit Tuskegee until February 1901.

Robert U. Johnson

[April 1900]

Dear Mr. Johnson:—

When I saw you in N.Y. several weeks ago you expressed a desire to read the MS. of a certain novel of which I was telling you, and suggested that you could give it a prompt reading, the period of two weeks being mentioned.[1] I send you the MS., entitled "The Rainbow Chasers," by Adams Express to-day.[2]

I am offering it for serial publication, preferring to retain the book & other rights. If you find it available, I shall be glad to comply with any suggestions you may have to make. I imagine the action is rapid enough for a quiet novel, and I should like to hope that it had, here and there some little charm of style. I do not know that I have divided the chapters so as to bring out the climaxes most effectively, but that may be a matter of editorial determination.[3]

I think I mentioned to you that H.M. & Co. are bringing out for me a novel in the Autumn,[4] and that Mr. Howells has written for the May *Atlantic* an "appreciation" of my work.[5]

ADU (fragment): TNF

[1] Robert Underwood Johnson (1853–1937) was the associate editor of *Century.*

[2] Chesnutt was in the East in March. Letters from Estelle Merrill of North Cambridge indicate that Chesnutt read before the Northeast Wheaton Seminary Club on the afternoon of 10 March; met with the Atlanta University Committee on 19 March and with the Northeast Women's Press Association on 21 March; and read at the Universalist Church on 22 March. Her 10 March letter also refers to a reading at Concord. A 16 March letter from Horace Bumstead of the Atlanta University Committee informed Chesnutt that he was free to visit Northampton on the 18th since their meeting at the home of Mrs. Thatcher Loring was on the 19th. Whether he met Cable there is not known. Chesnutt's daughters Ethel and Helen were attending Smith College in Northampton at this time. The meeting in New York City with Johnson occurred circa 24 March. On that date, "The Rainbow Chasers" was rejected by Houghton, Mifflin in a letter sent to Chesnutt "Care New York Office." Chesnutt reacted with dispatch by seeking another publisher.

[3] Johnson declined the work on 2 May 1900. Referring to Chesnutt's recollection of the assurance that a decision would take no more than two weeks to render, Johnson began his letter by stating that he was "ahead of my promise this time." This appears to indicate that Chesnutt's letter

and manuscript were sent to Johnson at the end of the third or beginning of the fourth week in April. "Rainbow Chasers" was described by Johnson as not having "the qualities necessary for availability as a serial for *The Century*, though it has striking good features for a book."

[4] On 24 March, the latest version of the "Rena" manuscript—now with the new title of "The House Behind the Cedars"—was accepted for publication as a novel by Houghton Mifflin, with one special condition specified: "that this shall be the only book of yours published this year." The contract was dated 30 March 1900, specifying a royalty of 15 percent of the retail price per copy and 7½ percent of the reduced price for export.

[5] Canceled at the end of the unsigned holograph draft of this letter was a continuation of this sentence: ". . . work, in which he predicts for me a literary future. I hope he may prove a true"; how Chesnutt actually concluded this letter to Johnson is moot.

William Dean Howells

⋅◌⋅

[1 May 1900][1]

My dear Mr. Howells,—

I want to thank you very cordially for your appreciative review of my books in the May *Atlantic*.[2] It would have been pleasant coming from any source, and it has a very great value coming from you. I thank you especially for the few words of frank criticism where you call attention to lapses in style, and to the occasional "look in the reader's direction." I think I appreciate the force of these suggestions and shall be able to profit by them in the future—there would be little hope for me as a literary artist if I could not. I shall try to keep in mind the heights to which you point me, both by precept and example, and shall hope to meet the conditions which you prescribe for my success. I may not confine my studies to the "paler shades",[3] but I shall endeavor always to depict life as I have known it,[4] or, if I wander from this path, as I think it ought to be. I am very grateful for your kindly notice and encouragement, after which I feel that I can safely subscribe myself a man of letters and hope for a worthy career in that field of effort. Permit me to count myself among your friends as I have numbered you with mine,[5] and believe me

Sincerely & cordially yours,

Chas. W. Chesnutt.

ALS: MH

[1] This letter was misdated April 31, 1900.

[2] "Mr. Charles W. Chesnutt's Stories," *Atlantic Monthly* 85 (May 1900), 699–701. This positive evaluation of Chesnutt's two collections of short stories by the major arbiter of literary taste of this time was the most significant benchmark of Chesnutt's success to date, and it promised a glowing future of widespread recognition.

[3] In his essay, Howells had referred thus to the mulattoes pictured in *Wife*.

[4] Here Chesnutt expresses a cardinal principle of Howells' aesthetic as a proponent of literary realism.

[5] Howells continued to show an interest in Chesnutt through at least November 1900. Chesnutt's letters to him have not been located, but on 25 October, Howells wrote in behalf of Harper

& Brothers, soliciting a novel about the color-line or "anything you thought good enough to offer." Chesnutt apparently proposed a work that might be serialized in *Harper's Monthly*, for Howells replied on 31 October that there "is no chance for your novel as a serial, . . . and I would rather wait for the color-line story which your brief suggestions greatly interests me in." Howells' first reference may be to "The Rainbow Chasers." "Mandy Oxendine" is very likely the "color-line story." Howells went on to request "the story of office-life" Chesnutt had mentioned: he was referring to "A Business Career." Howells' last known letter to Chesnutt is dated 12 November 1900; in it he wrote: "Do not wait to send me the Color Line story. Let me see the other, if you can, at once." If "the other" was "The Rainbow Chasers"—rejected by Doubleday, Page on 8 May 1900—the never-published novel was declined for the fourth time. However, what, if anything, Chesnutt sent Howells is not known.

Booker T. Washington

∽

May 16, 1900

My dear Mr. Washington,

I thank you for your kind words *apropos* of Mr. Howells's *Atlantic* article. I trust I may be able to write up to the standard he is good enough to set for me.

I appreciate your cordial invitation to visit Tuskegee some time in the future, and it is possible that I may avail myself of the privilege sometime during next Fall or Winter, as I hope to make a Southern trip within a year.[1]

I have read various newspaper reports of the Montgomery Conference, which I hope may be as fruitful of good results as you anticipated.[2] It has seemed to me that the thing most desired was the repeal of the Fifteenth Amendment. Cochran's argument that repeal should go because it had been "lynched" by the States, is scarcely more than to say that because Negroes, forsooth, had been lynched in the South, it were better to withdraw from them the protection of the Courts, and leave them to the tender goodwill of their neighbors, who would treat them well because they didn't have to! I should like very much to know where to write for a complete report of the proceedings, which I understand are to be published; the newspaper reports have been only fragmentary.

I feel just a little ashamed that your visit here was not productive of larger immediate results, but I trust it may prove seed sown upon good ground.[3] One thing is true about this city—it has apparently little enthusiasm for outside people—for the Negro in the abstract—but it gives those within its borders comparatively good opportunities to rise in the world. With best wishes,

Sincerely yours,

Chas. W. Chesnutt

ALS: DLC

[1] In 29 October 1900 to Washington, Chesnutt alludes to the research in the South made necessary by his plan to write *The Marrow of Tradition*; already, however, he seems to have conceptualized that work.

[2] A conference on the "Negro problem" was held in Montgomery, Ala., 8–10 May 1900, during which the African-American audience was separately seated in a gallery. Alfred M. Waddell spoke in behalf of limiting the franchise, in light of the demonstrated need for doing so in North Carolina. W. Bourke Cochran shared his point of view, addressing the more radical alternative of repealing the Fifteenth Amendment. W. A. McCorkle responded to Cochran, opposing its repeal. Washington's view of the conference was far more positive than Chesnutt's: he described it as a promising step toward the ultimate solution of the race problem ("Montgomery Race Conference," *Century* 60 [August 1900], 630–32). When reporting the conference, Isabel C. Barrows noted a development about which Chesnutt does not comment: one of his favorite themes in his nonfiction writings was enunciated by "one or two" speakers, that the "outcome in the far future would be amalgamation of the two races" ("The Montgomery Conference," *Outlook* 65 [19 May 1900], 160–62).

[3] An 11 March 1900 letter from Washington to Emmett J. Scott (DLC) indicates that Washington was to visit Chicago, Mississippi, and Arkansas in early April; return to Tuskegee; and then visit Cleveland, most probably in late April. The date and nature of his Cleveland visit, however, have not been determined.

Francis J. Garrison

June 2, 1900.

My dear Mr. Garrison:—

I received your letter a day or two ago, in which you made reference to the results of displays etc. of my books. I have no doubt you are doing the best you can for them, and am quite content to have the benefit of your well-tried methods.[1] I see a little ad. now and then in the N.Y. *Evening Post*, and I imagine you are keeping my books before the public quite as well as their sales justify.

I write this letter, however, to consult you about another matter. The editor of *The Self Culture Magazine* has just called on me, and made me an offer for the serial publication of "The House Behind the Cedars."[2] The magazine is doubtless known to you; it is thoroughly respectable, though not very prominent. It has been publishing during the last year from 40,000 to 50,000 copies. It has been published in Akron, Ohio, but is henceforth to be published in Cleveland. They want a serial, and are pleased to think that one from my pen would about suit them, and that they will like this one. They offer me as good a rate for it as I have received for stories in the *Atlantic*, will begin[3]

TCU (fragment): TNF

[1] On 29 May, Garrison replied to an unlocated letter of the 16th in which Chesnutt made reference to "the revision" of *House*, the final-version manuscript of which he had not yet given to Houghton, Mifflin, despite its acceptance for publication on 24 March (see [April 1900] to Johnson, n. 4). Garrison explained that the firm would no longer be interested in allowing Chesnutt's personal representatives to sell his books through unconventional channels (see 24 November 1899 to Houghton, Mifflin); the experiments in Washington, Buffalo, Pittsburgh, and Worces-

ter "have not proven very encouraging." He closed by announcing, "We shall have to rely on our well-tried methods and channels more than on these showy but unremunerative expedients."

[2] *House* was given periodical publication as follows, with the title of the monthly magazine changing as indicated during the course of the serialization: *Self Culture* 11 (August 1900), 497–510; *Modern Culture* 12 (September 1900), 22–41; (October 1900), 125–37; (November 1900), 251–62; (December 1900), 355–63; (January 1901), 464–71; and (February 1901), 560–68.

[3] On 5 June 1900 Garrison approved the serialization plan; he hoped "that the publication can begin at once so that it will be finished by early fall and we can bring out the book ourselves in October." He then advised Chesnutt to copyright the text and explained how to do so. Finally, he asked if Chesnutt was going to give a copy of the manuscript to the magazine and hold back another for Houghton, Mifflin. Or would he send the firm "revised copy from the sheets or proof slips of the [magazine] when the time comes?" Finally, Garrison noted that the typesetting copy for the book should be in the hands of the printer by 1 August.

Harry D. Robins

◦᠊ᴖ᠊

September 27, 1900.

My dear Mr. Robins:—

I am in receipt of your letter asking my cooperation in presenting my book, *The House Behind the Cedars*, to the public who ought to be eagerly awaiting something from my pen—I only wish I knew they were! I will take up in their order the various points you suggest:[1]

1st. I do not really know of any cities, except Cleveland, where I might hope to sell many books on the strength of my personal acquaintance. I have friends all over the country, and hope to have more, but they are more or less scattered, and many of them have been made through the medium of my writings. You could probably tell from your own order book where most books have been sold, which would be a better index than I could furnish of the number of my readers in such places. As to Cleveland, where the circulating libraries are well supplied with my books, I am told that neither of them stays upon the shelves, but that they remain constantly in circulation. That ought to be a good sign.

The sales at Washington, you will find from books shipped there to have been very good. These sales, however, were not made through the regular trade—I mean the sales I know about—but through a special agent of my own. Washington is a large city, however, with a cultivated and reading people, who are at a point where the race problem is discussed and considered from every point of view. I should not at all wonder if a number of books might be sold there through the regular trade, if proper attention is called to them.[2]

2nd. I do not know that I can specify any particular locality where the subject of the book, bluntly stated as the story of a colored girl who passed for white, would tend to cause any great rush for the book. I rather hope it will sell in spite of its subject, or rather, because of its dramatic value apart from the race problem involved. I was trying to write, primarily, an interesting and artistic story, rather than a contribution to polemical discussion.[3]

I am inclined to think that perhaps a little judicious advertising in Ohio towns, suggesting that the author is an Ohio novelist, might be effective. I am quite sure of the hearty cooperation of the local book trade, and am going to ask their opinion about this Ohio advertising, and let you know about it immediately. How far the local sales will be affected by the serial publication of the story I do not know, but perhaps not materially; and as the book will be out before the story is completed in the magazine, it may on the contrary help its sale. I leave it to you whether any stress should be laid or mention made of the fact that the story had appeared serially in the *Modern Culture Magazine*;[4] if it were a more widely known publication, that would be one thing. If you think it would help it or would not hurt it, it would be a nice thing to do.

3rd. I have enclosed several notices along the line of what would seem to me a good way to advertise this book.[5] These of course you can use in any form you like, changing or combining them or cutting them as you like. If you are going to use any biographical matter about me, I should like to modify it somewhat, as it goes perhaps unnecessarily into detail.

I hope the book may raise some commotion, I hardly care in what quarter, though whether, from the nature of the theme it will, I don't know. I published recently a series of articles in the Boston *Transcript* on the same general subject, which brought me a number of interesting letters from places as widely separated as Boston and Los Angeles.[6] In the Washington, D.C., *Times* of August 18, 1900, was published a long editorial under the head of "The Yellow Peril in the United States," in which the writer said that the white race was becoming insidiously and to a large extent unknowingly corrupted with negro blood, and cited a number of well-known Americans who were well-known, under the rose, to have a remote negro ancestry; of course he did not mention names, but his descriptions were easily recognized by the well-informed. The question of "miscegenation" was brought up at the recent conference of leading white men of the South who met in May at Montgomery, Ala., to discuss the race problem, and one of the solutions put forth involved the future amalgamation with the white race of at least a remnant of the black population.[7] So that the subject I think may be regarded as generally opened up for discussion, and inferentially for literary treatment. I choose it because I understand it, and am deeply interested in it, but I hope to make it interesting to others because of the element of human interest involved.

I shall no doubt be in Boston during the Fall or Winter, I do not yet know just when. I shall probably give some readings in various towns, and if they can be utilized to promote the sale of my books, so much the better. I shall be glad to cooperate with you in any way I can in the matter, and shall write again in a few days, and will answer more promptly any other suggestions you may make.

I am delighted to learn of Mr. Plummer's staunch friendship. I hope to get some more men of the same stamp interested in my work.[8] With the hope that the book may meet our reasonable expectations, I remain,

Cordially yours,

TCU: TNF

[1] On 20 September 1900, Robins announced that publication of *House* was scheduled for 27 October and that marketing plans were being made. He posed three questions to which Chesnutt responds here: in what places and by what book dealers was he so well known that that could be turned to advantage; in what localities would the subject of the book be a stimulant to sales if "show-cards, circulars, advertisement, [and] newspaper paragraphs" publicized it; and should Chesnutt send some paragraphs that are "vital in their character, going to the root of the author's artistic idea and moral purpose in writing the book"? He then explained the last request: "You must be aware that in certain quarters the book will no doubt raise a commotion. This is one of the reasons why we would like to have" the paragraphs which "would guide us in the tone to give our paragraphing, advertising, etc."

[2] At this point in his correspondence with Houghton, Mifflin, Chesnutt becomes more insistent in regard to the need for aggressive advertisement of his books, implying—as he does here—that the firm is in part responsible for smaller-than-hoped-for sales.

[3] Compare Chesnutt's description of the didactic purpose of the short stories in *Wife* in [10 December 1899] to Houghton, Mifflin.

[4] See 2 June 1900 to Houghton, Mifflin, n. 2.

[5] These notices have not been located.

[6] Three articles sharing the same title, "The Future American," appeared in the *Boston Evening Transcript* with the following subtitles: "What the Race Is Likely to Become in the Process of Time," 18 August 1900, 20; "A Stream of Dark Blood in the Veins of the Southern Whites," 25 August 1900, 15; and "A Complete Race-Amalgamation Likely to Occur," 1 September 1900, 24.

[7] See 16 May 1900 to Washington, n. 2. For a jeremiad against the conference speakers who lamented miscegenation—including the Wilmington, N.C., mayor, Alfred M. Waddell, who delivered the opening address on 9 May—see "Race Conference," *Cleveland Gazette*, 19 May 1900, 1.

[8] Robins' 20 September letter closed with a postscript: "Met your friend Clifford Plummer a few evenings ago. Spoke warmly of you. Seems to be *very* acute and forceful." He also asked if Chesnutt would be in the East "this season." Clifford H. Plummer (1861–?) was an African-American lawyer who lived in Boston and was one of Washington's most ardent loyalists. He served as an informer regarding anti-Washington developments among the followers of William M. Trotter (see [January 1902] to Trotter, n. 1) and was instrumental in thwarting the disruptive efforts of Trotter at events attended by Washington in the Boston area.

Houghton, Mifflin & Co.

·☙·

October 29, 1900.

Dear Sirs:—

I am in receipt of the advanced copy sent me of *The House Behind the Cedars*, for which please accept my thanks.[1] You have given it a very handsome and appropriate dress, and an outside cover which would seem to indicate that you meant to push the book as much, at least, as its merits warrant. I am pleased to see also, that you have placed it at the head of your current publications in your advertisements in the literary journals. I have been approached, during the past week, by two of the most prominent publishing houses of the United States, on the subject of a race problem novel of the present day, which makes me think that this novel might well be exploited along that line;[2] for although dated a little in the past, the problem there presented is much the same today as yesterday.[3] I am willing to cooperate in any way in advancing the interests of the book, but of course shall have to rely mainly on your skill and experience.

Kindly send copies, of the eleven[4] still subject to my order, to the following addresses:-

Mr. A. J. Chesnutt, Fayetteville, N.C.

Mr. H. C. Tyson, 2124 K. St., N.W., Washington, D.C.[5]

W. D. Howells, Esq., 40 West 59th St., New York.[6]

TCU (fragment): TNF

[1] On 16 April 1900, Garrison thanked Chesnutt for his "favor of the 13th" (unlocated) and noted the promise of the *House* manuscript "in the course of a week or two." On 24 July, Garrison expressed his desire to have it by 1 August; and on 4 August he acknowledged its receipt as well as announcing that the manuscript was now being sent to the typesetters and that the publication date would be 20 rather than 6 October. He also requested individual titles for the thirty-one chapters (the published text included thirty-three). Chesnutt appears to have sent him the titles for the first twenty, but he also appears not to have kept a copy of the remaining chapters of the novel. Thus on 13 August, "Chapters xxi to the end" were mailed to him. On 21 August, Garrison acknowledged receipt of "the last 12 chapters" (rather than the thirteen that actually appear after chapter twenty). The first sixteen pages of proof were sent to Chesnutt on 27 August according to a letter from Garrison dated 24 August. Unlocated are additional letters concerning the proofs. The sheets for 1,530 copies of *House* were printed on 5 and 17 October (MH:P), and copyright deposit copies were received at the Library of Congress on 26 October.

[2] On 25 October 1900, William Dean Howells invited Chesnutt to submit a manuscript to Harper & Brothers. On 9 November 1900, William C. Bobbs, president of the Bowen-Merrill Company, formally solicited a manuscript in light of a conversation that one of his representatives had recently had with Chesnutt.

[3] This qualification reflects Howells' 25 October description of a manuscript that would be attractive to Harper & Brothers: "We should like it to be, as it probably would be, something about the color-line, and of as actual and immediate interest as possible—that is of American life in the present rather [than] the past, even the recent past."

[4] The recipients of eight of the copies are unknown because the source-text of this letter is incomplete.

[5] H. Clay Tyson was an assistant of Principal Chesnutt at the Fayetteville Colored Normal School in 1882–1883.

[6] On 12 November, Howells thanked Chesnutt for a copy of *House*—"which I hope soon to read." Whether he did read it is moot; he never reviewed it, though Chesnutt appears to have sent him a letter (unlocated) encouraging him to write another appreciation like the one devoted to *Conjure Woman* and *Wife*; see [1 May 1900] to Howells, n. 2. This is suggested in the same 12 November letter from Howells where, without explanation, he replies, "I only did letters a service in praising your stories."

Booker T. Washington

Oct. 29, 1900

My dear Mr. Washington,—

Your favor of recent date, inviting me to visit Tuskegee in February next, was duly received. I think I can safely accept your invitation, with the proviso that if I should come before that time, I would not be unwelcome. I am writing a novel[1] which may require me to visit the South sooner than February, in which event I might visit Tuskegee & kill two birds with one stone. If I decide to come earlier, I will let you know, & try to time my visit so as to catch you there. I am sure I shall enjoy the visit.

I hope you will see my new novel, *The House Behind the Cedars*, which runs along the "color line." My next book on the subject will be square up to date, & will deal with the negro's right to live rather than his right to love.

Mrs. Chesnutt joins me in regards to you, & I remain,

Cordially yours,
Chas. W. Chesnutt.

ALS: DLC

[1] *The Marrow of Tradition.*

Walter Hines Page

November 1, 1900.

My dear Mr. Page:—

Thanks for the sample copy of your new magazine, *The World's Work.*[1] It is impressive both in quality and in quantity, and is most beautifully gotten up, the illustrations being especially fine. It ought to find a place in the homes of thoughtful people everywhere, and a warm welcome at the hands of those who are trying to do the world's work.

Please put me on the subscription list, for which I enclose P.O. order. I shall hope to make the money back out of *The House Behind the Cedars*, which has just appeared.[2] H.M. & Co. have made a beautiful book of it, and I trust the sales will be equally satisfactory.[3] Sincerely yours,

TCU: TNF

[1] Since Chesnutt wrote his last known letter to Page in October 1899, Page had ended his relationship with S. S. McClure and cofounded Doubleday, Page & Co., which published *World's Work*. Page had offered to publish the "Rena" manuscript with "The House Behind the Cedars" as its title on 24 January 1900, proposing royalties of 10 percent for the first 2,000 copies, 12½ percent for the next, and 15 percent on all over 4,000. While waiting for Chesnutt's decision, he

also offered on 17 February a contract for a full-scale biography of Frederick Douglass that Chesnutt planned: on 30 January 1900, Chesnutt had obtained permission from Small, Maynard to write a second book on Douglass. Although Chesnutt, without informing Page, instead submitted the novel to Houghton, Mifflin, where it was accepted for publication at 15 percent per copy on 24 March 1900, their friendly relationship did not change. For example, on 8 May 1900 Page acknowledged receipt of the "Rainbow Chasers" manuscript, which had already been rejected by Houghton, Mifflin and *Century*. It was with sadness that, on 19 July, he had to inform Chesnutt that he and the other readers decided against its acceptance. He explained that in "The Rainbow Chasers" there "is a certain unreality about these people that prevents them from being convincing."

[2] Page's 24 January 1900 letter reveals that Chesnutt had made some important changes in the text of the novel since Page returned it to him. The North Carolinian editor and publisher wrote: "I suppose you are wise in using Old Judge Strange's name and old Mrs. McRae's name and all the familiar old family names and landmarks of Fayetteville, but some of our friends down there will be—well, I will say interested—." Neither name appeared in the published novel.

[3] Houghton, Mifflin reported on 3 November that it had sold "nearly a thousand copies of the book" since its publication *circa* 26 October. On 12 November, Page informed Chesnutt that he would "find a word" about *House* in the December issue of his magazine. "Appraisals of New Books" tersely summarized *House* thus: "A dramatic story of the color-line in Southern life. The heroine, an octoroon who 'passes for white,' almost succeeds, but her failure is one of the most tragic things in recent fiction. A well-constructed and well-written story of great directness and power" (*World's Work* 1 [December 1900], 211–12).

Booker T. Washington

᠙

Nov. 10, 1900.

My dear Mr. Washington:

Your favor of Nov. 3d is at hand. I shall try to regulate my visit to Tuskegee so as to meet you there, as it would otherwise be like seeing the play of *Hamlet* with Hamlet left out. In one sense, at least, you are Tuskegee; as Page says in his new magazine "Every successful industrial or financial combination is built on a strong personality,"—and so is every other great enterprise, Tuskegee included.[1]

I read the first of your *Outlook* serial with great interest and pleasure, and look forward to reading them all with similar profit. I am pleased to know that you read "The Sway-backed House" & hope you may see my new novel, which is already winning golden opinions.[2]

Sincerely yours,
Chas. W. Chesnutt.

ALS: DLC

[1] Chesnutt quotes the unsigned article, "The Outlook for Young Men," *World's Work*, 1 (November 1900), 8–9.

[2] *Up from Slavery* appeared serially in *Outlook*, 3 November 1900–23 February 1901; "The Sway-Backed House" was published in *Outlook* 66 (November 1900), 588–93.

Harry D. Robins

᭡᭡᭡

Nov. 19, 1900.

My dear Mr. Robins:—

I hope you are doing what you can to call attention to The *House Behind the Cedars*.[1] The verdict around here is that it is a novel of the sort that one having begun doesn't want to lay down until it is finished: and the least friendly of the few criticisms I have seen concerning it admits that it is a well constructed novel. I did not see it mentioned at all in any of your advertisements in the New York papers of November 11th. I hope it is one of those novels that will work its way on its merits, which is of course the best sort of success, but in doing so it has to contend against an enormous number of books which are not left to that method. One bookseller here bought 1,000 copies of *Alice of Old Vincennes*[2] and another 250, before publication, relying on the publishers' advertising;—what else they could have relied on in that particular case, in advance of publication, it is difficult to see. Stone & Co., Small, Maynard & Co., and such houses, have a way of stacking up books around here, especially in one bookstore, which the booksellers get, I suppose at special rates, or on consignment; and it is quite evident that it is these books which they try to work off in all sorts of ways. I know that it is not your method, and that it is not a good method, and that it seldom makes a poor book go very far. It does, however, stand in the way, to a certain extent, of even the best books; and I want to feel that I am getting the benefit of your best methods.

I don't know whether you attach much value to the matter I sent you for use in advertising.[3] I rather suspect, from the very handsome little circular which the house has printed, that your people there can write better advertisements than I can.

If you can tell me anything at any time that will be cheerful reading, I shall be obliged to you.[4] I hope to see you sometime during the Winter, and in the meantime remain,   Yours cordially,

TCU: TNF

[1] This is one of two letters written on 19 November to the Houghton, Mifflin staff, and the second in which Chesnutt is markedly more aggressive regarding the need for greater advertising effort in behalf of *House*.

[2] This best-selling historical romance by Maurice Thompson, published in 1900, was set in the American Revolution period. Chesnutt's dislike for Thompson can be seen in his 13 June 1890 letter to Cable. The cause of Chesnutt's query about the absence of advertisements in the New York papers may have been the ad for *Alice of Old Vincennes* placed by the Bowens-Merrill Co. in the *New York Times Saturday Review of Books* on 10 November. It occupied two-thirds of page 10, proclaiming Thompson's work "The Great American Novel." It is noteworthy that, when *House* was advertised in the *Review* on 8 December, 867, it was not given such treatment but merely listed among forty-four other books.

[3] Chesnutt apparently sent advertising copy not used by the firm.

[4] On 8 December, Robins acknowledged this letter and another of 27 November (unlocated). He reported that the "book has gone to press again, and all the jackets in which it shall be sent out will be imprinted 'Third Thousand'"; that double-column advertisements had been inserted in papers in Cleveland, Cincinnati, Toledo, Indianapolis, Kansas City, Omaha, Milwaukee, St. Paul, Minneapolis, St. Louis, New York, Boston, and Philadelphia; that a circular including press commendations was planned for distribution to book dealers; and that the firm would be glad to provide circulars for audiences at readings. A 13 December letter from Robins acknowledges Chesnutt's expression of approval of the firm's efforts (unlocated).

John P. Green

⟡

Dec. 1, 1900

My dear John:—

Your very handsome letter, which reached me on Thanksgiving Day, as it was apparently intended to, gave me much pleasure. One finds appreciation from those who *know*, a very agreeable thing. I think you understand how difficult it is to write race problem books so that white people will read them,—and it is white people they are primarily aimed at. Mine are doing as well as could be expected. I shall write at least one more along the same general line, but of broader scope, attempting to sketch in vivid though simple lines the whole race situation.[1] If I could propose a remedy for existing evils that would cure them over night, I would be a great man. But I am only a small social student who can simply point out the seat of the complaint. I thank you for the comparison with *Uncle Tom's Cabin*; if I could write a book that would stir the waters in any appreciable degree like that famous book, I would feel that I had vindicated my right to live & the right of a whole race.

I'm sure you'll say to others some of the nice things in your letter, & keep the ball moving. Permit one to hope that your official tenure is secure under the next administration.[2] Mrs. C. joins me in regards to you & yours & I remain as ever

Yours sincerely,
C. W. Chesnutt.

ALS: OClWHi

[1] Over the next seven months, Chesnutt continued developing an outline for *The Marrow of Tradition*; see 3 July 1901 to Mifflin.

[2] The reelection of President McKinley made uncertain appointee Green's tenure as U.S. Postal Stamp Agent.

Francis J. Garrison

·◌·

December 27, 1900.

My dear Mr. Garrison:—

Your letter of 24th inst. came duly to hand, and I note what you say respecting orders filled in Cleveland.[1] I saw the adv. in the *New York Times*, and received a letter from the editor stating his willingness to give space to any news items or references to my literary work.

And now with reference to the Cleveland market. Burrows Bros. of this city sell a great many books, and they keep a lot of them stacked up in their store in conspicuous places. They are very nice people, in a way, and have treated me very well, but I have an idea that they sell most of the books on which they can get the best terms, for they have intelligent and pushing salesmen, who tell people what books they want. I spoke to Mr. Cathcart, their buyer, yesterday, about getting in a good lot of my books, stacking them up conspicuously, and selling them. He said to me that if you would consign 250 to them, he would do it.

I have an idea that your house seldom if ever consigns books,[2] but I want these books here, and would like to have you send them. I have no doubt whatever that they will go off in short time. I am so sure of it that if you do not care to consign them, you may secure the account by charging it against me. Of course the transaction will be at the 250 rate. So many good things have been said and written about this book that I want to see everything done that can be done to acquaint the public with its merits. If you can oblige me in this matter, as no doubt you will, please ship the 250 copies to the Burrows Bros. Company. Ship the books anyway, and then notify me what plan you have shipped them on.   Yours very truly,

TCU: TNF

[1] Garrison explained that fifteen copies of *House* were shipped to Cleveland's Helman-Taylor Co., as were 100 to Burrows Brothers, and 110 to the Cleveland News Co. In response to Chesnutt's sense of urgency regarding the advertising effort, he wrote: "We have given special care to pushing & having the book in stock." Robins also informed Chesnutt on 29 December that the "book has sold to the number of about 2,000 copies, and we feel that its sale is by no means over."

[2] On 28 December, Chesnutt was assured that, while the firm never sends out books on consignment, 250 copies were being shipped to Burrows Brothers "on what is practically consignment," though unsold books "must be returned within ninety days."

Booker T. Washington

⌁·

March 13, 1901.

My dear Mr. Washington:—

I arrived safely home, after a roundabout trip with numerous stops, and have brought with me many pleasant impressions of Tuskegee, and of the great work you have under way there.[1] I have put some of my impressions in the shape of letters to the Boston *Transcript*, which will no doubt see the light, unless I have delayed them too long.[2] I hope they may please you.

But, personally, I don't like the South. I couldn't tell the people any better place to go to, and I hope they may work out a happy destiny there; you are certainly doing a great deal to help them to that end. I hope to meet you sometime at the North, and meantime I remain,

Yours cordially,
Chas. W. Chesnutt

ALS: DLC

[1] Chesnutt left Cleveland for a Southern lecture tour on 6 February. On 14 February he read from his stories in Wilmington, N.C.; he did the same on 19 February at Tuskegee, 21 February in Birmingham, 22 February in Atlanta, and 25 February in Charlotte, N.C.

[2] "The White and the Black," *Boston Evening Transcript*, 20 March 1901, 13; "The Negro's Franchise," *Boston Evening Transcript*, 11 May 1901, 18. See also "A Visit to Tuskegee," *Cleveland Leader*, 31 March 1901, 19.

W. Charles Bush

⌁·

April 10, 1901.

My dear Mr. Bush:—

Your kind favor of recent date came duly to hand. I am greatly obliged for your interest and effort to promote the introduction of my books into Great Britain, and I hope my publishers may agree upon something with Messrs. Oliphant, Andrews and Perrier.[1]

I have ordered a copy of *The House Behind the Cedars* sent to you, and you will doubtless receive it within a few days. I hope you may find it as readable as the others; the general verdict is that it is a pronounced advance.

Mrs. Chesnutt joins me in regards to yourself and Mr. Gleed,[2] and we hope to meet you again upon some one of your future visits to Cleveland.[3]

Very cordially yours,

TCU: TNF

[1] W. Charles Bush, who had previously engaged in conversation or correspondence with Chesnutt, wrote from Port Dalhousie, Ontario, Canada, on 2 April 1901 that he had written Oliphant, Andrews & Perrier about the possibility of publishing *Conjure Woman* and *House*; and interest was

expressed in the latter. Cleveland city directories do not list Bush or the Mr. Gleed referred to below.

[2] On 2 April Bush asked Chesnutt to send him a copy of *House*, which he had not been able to purchase; on 6 May Bush thanked him for the copy and extended the best wishes of Mr. Gleed to Chesnutt and his wife.

[3] On 1 April 1901, Houghton, Mifflin acknowledged Chesnutt's letters of 10 and 11 March (unlocated); it reported that Oliphant, Anderson & Perrier of Edinburgh was interested in sheets for 1,000 copies of *House* to be delivered in time for the autumn season. (On 3 September 1901, however, Houghton, Mifflin informed Chesnutt that the Scottish firm had decided against publishing the novel.) Also answered, in the affirmative, was Chesnutt's query about a fourth printing of the novel: "We printed 1500 to begin with, then 500, 1000 and 500 respectively, making 3500 all told, and we hope before long we shall have to print another impression."

George H. Mifflin

·◇·

July 3, 1901

My dear Mr. Mifflin:—

I have n't sent in the manuscript of which I spoke to you, because I am doing a little more work on it.[1] Every day's delay improves it, I feel safe in saying, but I will send it in for consideration in a few days now.[2]

I have just received a check for royalties due July 1st, which comes in very handily, and which I have acknowledged formally under another cover.[3]

Cordially yours,

TCU: TNF

[1] George Harrison Mifflin (1845–1921) was a partner in the firm of Houghton, Mifflin & Co. (1880–1908).

[2] When Chesnutt was in Boston and spoke to Mifflin about his new manuscript, "The Marrow of Tradition," is not known. On 5 and 27 July Mifflin promised Chesnutt a sympathetic reading; the receipt of the manuscript was acknowledged on 29 July, and the contract for the novel—specifying royalties of 15 percent and 7½ percent per copy on regular sales and at the reduced price for export, respectively—was dated 6 August 1901. The sales of *House* resulted in enthusiasm for the new work: according to a 10 August 1901 letter from Garrison, the manuscript had already been sent to the printer. On 16 August, proofs of the first sixteen pages were forwarded to Chesnutt, and a publication date of 12 October was announced in a 4 September letter.

[3] On 3 July, Chesnutt acknowledged a check for $484.15.

Booker T. Washington

·◇·

October 8, 1901.

My dear Mr. Washington:—

I have just requested my publishers to send you an advance copy of my new novel, *The Marrow of Tradition*, which will be out in a week. It is by far the best thing I have done, and is a comprehensive study of racial conditions in the

South, in the shape of what is said to be a very dramatic novel, which my publishers boldly compare with *Uncle Tom's Cabin* for its "great dramatic intensity and its powerful appeal to popular sympathies." It discusses, incidentally, miscegenation, lynching, disfranchisement, separate cars, and the struggle for professional and social progress in an unfriendly environment—and all this without at all interfering with the progress of an interesting plot with which they are all bound up. It is, in a word, our side of the Negro question, in popular form, as you have presented it in the more dignified garb of essay and biography.

If you feel moved, after reading it, to write a word or two, concerning it, I am sure it would be highly appreciated by my publishers and myself; or if you find it too strenuous for you to publicly approve, I feel pretty certain that in private you can do it almost as much good. I should like to feel that I had been able, in the form of a widely popular work of fiction, to do something tangible and worth mentioning to supplement your own work, and to win back or help retain the popular sympathy of the Northern people, which has been so sorely weakened by Southern deviltry in the past decade; for while the tolerance of the South is necessary to the progress of the colored race, and their friendship desirable, you know better than I can how absolutely essential is Northern sympathy to the work of Southern education.

I have read your utterances on the subject of the president's death, and its connection with national lawlessness; and I say amen to it.[1] The country is suffering from blood-poisoning, and the South is the source of the infection. It is refreshing to note the growth of a small party of Southern whites who are beginning to perceive the truth. I see Mr. Page has been telling the North Carolinians some wholesome but unpalatable truths; my novel will tell them some more in the same strain.[2] I hope they may profit by both.

My daughter is very much pleased with Tuskegee.[3] I hope she is making herself useful, and I am glad to be able to contribute through her, a little more work for the good cause.

With regards to Mrs. Washington, I remain,

Cordially yours,
Chas. W. Chesnutt.

TLS: DLC

[1] Washington's statement regarding the assassination of President McKinley has not been located.

[2] A description of the burning of a black male accused of murdering a white woman in Winchester, Tenn., appeared in "Barbarism and Heroism in the South," *World's Work* 2 (October 1901), 1250. On the next page was a commentary on the infeasibility of return-to-Africa emigration and deportation proposals regarding the four million African Americans who had become eight million since the end of the Civil War ("No Artificial Solution to the Race 'Problem'").

[3] Ethel Chesnutt; see 26 October 1901 to Ethel Chesnutt, n. 1.

Houghton, Mifflin & Co.

ᕁ

October 24, 1901.

Dear Sirs:—

Replying to your favor of October 22nd,[1] raising the question whether in line 5, page 58, of *The Marrow of Tradition*, "'Captain,' said Miller," should not be, "'Conductor,' said Miller," I would say that the expression is not an error, but was written advisedly. It is the common custom in the South to address the conductor of a passenger train as "Captain." The proximity of the word to the same word as applied to McBane a few lines later doubtless suggested that it might be an oversight. If you think, however, that the reader unfamiliar with Southern conditions, as perhaps most of the readers of the book will be, would be led to think a mistake had been made either by the Riverside Press or by me, there would be no great harm in changing it to read "'Conductor,' said Miller." Miller, being an educated and traveled man, might very properly use the word, "Conductor."

On page 22, line 6, the last word of the line, "its" should be "their," making it read, "ambition or passion, or their partners, envy and hatred."

Yours very truly,

TCU: TNF

[1] On 20 September, Chesnutt was sent an editorial query about the *Marrow* text: on page 12 of the page proof Charles I was referred to as "the last but two of the Stuart kings," and the appropriateness of that was questioned since there were only four Stuart kings. Chesnutt appears to have provided a replacement description of "King Charles the Martyr, as the ill-fated son of James I. was known to St. Andrew's." This incident may have inspired Chesnutt to give his copy of the proof a much closer reading. On 23 September he wrote to H. R. Gibbs (unlocated), asking for additional changes and promising to send more shortly. Although the printing of the book had already begun, Gibbs agreed on 26 September to delay the printing until the remaining alterations were sent to him. He asked about one of the changes made: on page 59 of the proof Chesnutt had changed "Chinaman" to "chinaman"; Gibbs asked why and apparently did not receive a good reason since the reading in the first printing is "Chinaman." On 8 October all of the proof had been returned, and the publication date was changed from 12 to 23 October: Chesnutt was asked to "advise us by telegraph if you are likely to have any further changes." An advance copy was mailed to Chesnutt on 17 October, the same date on which copyright deposit copies were received at the Library of Congress. That is, *Marrow* had already been published when Chesnutt wrote the present letter.

Houghton, Mifflin & Co.

ᕁ

October 26, 1901.

Dear Sirs:

I beg to acknowledge receipt of your two letters of recent date, also of Boston Theatre programme, poster and of the several remaining complimentary copies of *The Marrow of Tradition* credited to me, for all which please accept my thanks.[1]

The poster is very striking and significant and should prove impressive. The theatre program advertisement is very ingeniously written and ought to help the book materially.

If *The Marrow of Tradition* can become lodged in the popular mind as the legitimate successor of *Uncle Tom's Cabin* and the *Fool's Errand* as depicting an epoch in our national history, it will make the fortune of the book and incidentally of the author, which would be very gratifying.[2]

I had already forwarded you, before receiving yours of the 22nd, copy of large photograph, which you had asked for in a previous letter.

I also note in the Cleveland morning papers an advertisement of the story which is, it seems to me, very strikingly worded.[3] The books are not in the stores yet but I presume they will be to-day or certainly on Monday. There is considerable advance interest in it here and it ought to sell largely.[4]

I also have the list of newspapers forwarded me, to which editorial copies have been sent. It is apparently a very complete list. I wish, however, that you would add to these, a copy to the *Tuskegee Student*, Tuskegee, Ala.; one to Mrs. Ida Wells Barnett, 2939 Princeton Ave., Chicago, Ill.; one to J. E. Bruce, 97 Orange St., Albany, N.Y., one to T. Thomas Fortune, editor of the *New York Age*, 4 Cedar St., New York City, and one to the *Colored American*, Washington, D.C. This is a book of which a considerable sale ought to be had among colored people, if their attention is called to it. Mrs. Barnett is Secretary of the Anti-lynching Bureau—I forget the name of the rest of it, and lectures on the lynching habit and other questions of the race problem. She disseminates literature with reference to lynching and her interest in the book could do much to promote its sale, especially if it could be accepted as an epoch marking novel.[5] Mr. Bruce is a correspondent of many colored newspapers, and a copy sent to him would be a good investment.[6] The other papers mentioned are the leading newspapers which circulate among the colored people, and it would be well in sending out items to the press to include them in your list.

As you suggest, it was my idea concerning which I had a somewhat definite understanding with Mr. Mifflin that special efforts should be made by you in the arranging of this new book. I am very much pleased with the interest that has so far been manifested by the house and the enterprise displayed in the preliminary advertising. It is particularly gratifying to me because it is evident that you really think the book worth the trouble for I do not think for a moment that a conservative house like yours would do so unbusinesslike a thing as to make any considerable investment which you do not reasonably hope would be a good one. Your course in regard to the book is, therefore, doubly pleasing to me since it considers my ideas and at the same time indicates your confidence.[7]

I shall be glad to send you any direct criticisms which I receive from persons whose opinions would be valuable and I hope to receive a number. I stand at all times willing to co-operate with you in furthering the sale and wide reading of the book.

I have not yet seen a copy of the November *Atlantic* but shall look for one to-day and shall examine it with interest for the page devoted to the *Marrow of Tradition.*   Very truly yours,

TCU: TNF

[1] Two letters dated 23 October were received by Chesnutt: the first referred to an enclosed list of "papers" to which copies of *Marrow* had been sent or would be sent shortly (a 4 October letter to Chesnutt indicated the original plan of rushing copies quickly bound in wrappers to magazine editors, newspapers, and "prominent individuals"); the second referred to the copy of a Boston theater program, forwarded under separate cover, advertising the novel. A previous letter, dated 21 October, informed him that that week the theater program for a Boston performance of *Uncle Tom's Cabin* included an advertisement and that the play's star, Wilton Lackaye, was given a copy of *Marrow*.

[2] Chesnutt here sees within reach at last a primary goal of his, first articulated in his journal on 16 March 1880, when he described himself as more qualified by his experience as an African American in the South to write the kind of successful novel that Tourgée had in *A Fool's Errand* (1879). *Marrow*, promising to transcend the success of *House*, appears certain to provide the answer to the question he had posed to himself then: "why could not such a man, if he possessed the same ability, write a far better book about the South than Judge Tourgée or Mrs. Stowe has written?"

[3] The text of the advertisement read "Upon a background of contemporary Southern life Mr. Chesnutt has written a strong, virile, and exciting novel. The scene is laid in a Southern city, and the time is that of the exciting movement for negro disfranchisement. The story narrates great wrongs, terrible injustices, yet is relieved by successful love, Mr. Chesnutt has in *The Marrow of Tradition* far outstripped his earlier successes; he has written a story that will recall at many points *Uncle Tom's Cabin*, so great is its dramatic intensity, and so strong its appeal to popular sympathies" (*Cleveland Leader*, 26 October 1901, 3).

[4] Chesnutt appears to have been active in ensuring that the local press was aware of the forthcoming volume. "C. W. Chesnutt's New Novel" was earlier blurbed thus in the *Leader*: "Charles W. Chesnutt, the well-known Cleveland author, has recently completed another novel which is to be placed on sale October 12. . . . The title of the new book will be 'The Morrow [sic] of Tradition,' in which the author portrays his views of the present condition of society in the old slave States" ("Clevelanders Who Are Talked About," 13 October 1901, 15).

[5] Ida Bell Wells-Barnett (1862–1931) was a Memphis teacher who challenged a Jim Crow law, unsuccessfully taking her suit to the Tennessee Supreme Court in 1887. She was half-owner of the Memphis *Free Speech*; she wrote vigorously against lynching; that paper's offices were destroyed by a mob in 1892. Her first pamphlet on the subject was *Southern Horrors* (1892). Her next, *A Red Record* (1895), included statistics on lynchings and their causes over a three-year period. This was followed by *Mob Rule in New Orleans* (1900). She was the chairperson of the Anti-Lynching League. Her husband was Ferdinand Lee Barnett, attorney and editor of *Chicago Conservator*, one of the periodicals which Chesnutt identified as a potential review medium for his books in a 14 December 1899 letter to Houghton, Mifflin.

[6] John E. Bruce (1856–1924), was a successful journalist whose work appeared in both white and black periodicals. He successively founded three newspapers in Washington, D.C., and then became editor of the *Norfolk Republican*, an editor and business manager of the *Baltimore Commonwealth*, and associate editor of *Howard's American Magazine*. His widely distributed "Bruce Grit" column is his best-known accomplishment.

[7] Although the advertising effort bespoke confidence in *Marrow*, the firm's records indicate a more cautious attitude, with printings occurring in response to actual demand for copies, despite the greater cost of repeated individual printings: 2,542 sets of sheets went to the bindery on 10 October; 992 sets on 24 October; and 1,004 sets on 28 October (MH:P).

Ethel Perry Chesnutt

October 26th, 1901.

My dear Ethel:

I am sending you by mail to-day a copy of *The Marrow of Tradition*.[1] The publishers are displaying considerable enterprise in presenting it to the public, and I hope the results will warrant their seeming confidence in the merits of the book. They have got out a striking poster of which I will procure and send you a copy. It is published here to-day, and is likely to have a large sale here; nine hundred copies were ordered in advance from this city, and it was necessary to print the book twice before publication.

I have asked the publishers to send Mr. Washington and Mr. Scott a copy each and I shall hope for the Tuskegee influence in promoting the publicity of the book—unless the southerners should look into it so severely as to make it prudent for them to remain discreetly silent.[2] Of course you do not want to say anything to any of them about this particular suggestion.

All are well. I have substantially recovered from my slight indisposition. Mr. Boyd was out the other night and suggested that I go to Mt. Clemens.[3] The suggestion was enough to cure me on the spot.

I hope you still continue to like it down there. I presume you have noticed a little flurry in the newspapers about the attention paid Mr. Washington by the President;[4] and the *New York Age* states that Wellesley College denies that it is contaminated by any such thing as race prejudice.[5]

Your affectionate father,
Chas. W. Chesnutt

TLS: TNF

[1] Daughter Ethel Chesnutt (1879–?) was graduated from Smith College in 1901; she was an instructor at Tuskegee Institute when she received this letter. Following the 1901–1902 academic year, she returned to Cleveland, where she married librarian Edward C. Williams in November.

[2] Emmett J. Scott (1873–1957) was Booker T. Washington's private secretary at Tuskegee from 1897 to 1915. Because Washington unhesitatingly delegated responsibility to him for the handling of a wide range of activities, Scott wielded extraordinary influence within the African-American community and among its Caucasian sympathizers. Chesnutt here indicates his sensitivity to the probability that Scott and Washington would be unlikely to publicize a novel that might exacerbate Southern hostility or alienate supporters of Tuskegee. See 5 November 1901 to Washington, in which Chesnutt spells out the compelling reasons why Washington and others associated with Tuskegee had to pursue an expedient course.

[3] William T. Boyd was one of Chesnutt's long-term friends (see 3 September 1895 to Tourgée, n. 1). Mt. Clemens, located in southeastern Michigan, was a fashionable locale at which mineral water cures were sought by the well-to-do.

[4] Although it was not the first time that Theodore Roosevelt had done so with an African American, Washington's dining with him in the White House on 16 October 1901 was treated as a sensation by the press, and editorials in Southern newspapers energetically condemned Roosevelt for his behavior. A more sympathetic, untitled editorial quip in the *Cleveland Leader* read thus: "Senator Tillman says it will be necessary for the white people of the South to kill a thousand

Negroes because President Roosevelt entertained Booker Washington at dinner. Then many of the people of the South are probably happy. They are always glad to find an excuse for killing a Negro" (25 October 1891, 3).

[5] The issue of *New York Age* referred to is not extant. The reference is perhaps to Portia Washington, who alleged having experienced racial discrimination while at Wellesley.

Houghton, Mifflin & Co.

November 4, 1901.

Dear Sirs,—

I seem to have mislaid your letter of several days since, but I remember only one subject which called for an answer. The question asked me was whether or not I would drop a line to the parties to whom complimentary copies of the book were sent at my request, or whether you should do so. I have written to some of them, but have not before me the list of these persons, and if you will kindly drop each of them a little note, in such form as you know how to put it suggesting that books were sent at my request and that both you and I would appreciate any expression of opinion which they might desire to make concerning the book, it will perhaps come with better grace from the publisher than from me, excepting the case of several of my intimate friends to whom I would feel like making a direct personal request.

I observe with much satisfaction that of the reviews which I have so far received of the book all but one are of column length, and that one packs a column of commendation in a much shorter space. I had an idea that the lighter part of the story would make people read the more serious part, but it is interesting to note that the book is accepted seriously from the start and discussed from that point of view.[1] I presume there were a considerable number of reviews in the Sunday papers, of which I shall probably receive cuttings in a day or two. I imagine there will be considerable diversity of opinion in regard to the book, although so far no one has suggested seriously that it is at all overdrawn or that I have drawn from any other fountain than the well of truth.

I notice the book advertised much more extensively, so far as I can see, than any of my former books, and I trust that its reception by the critical public will be such as to make you feel justified in keeping it before the public.[2] I think the book may serve a very useful purpose, beyond the pecuniary returns which it will bring to author or publisher. Fortunately the two things, in the case of a book are very nearly co-terminous, and there is every inducement from either point of view, to push a good thing along.

I have not seen the review in the *Nashville Banner*, but I gather its purport from the brief extract in the advertisement which was published in Saturday's

Leader and Wednesday's *Boston Transcript* and elsewhere.[3] The editor of the *Banner* was very enthusiastic and wrote me personal letters after the appearance of *The Conjure Woman*,[4] but while he has since recognized the literary quality of my work very frankly and fairly, he evidently regards me as a good man gone wrong.[5] I regret that I cannot retain both his literary and his personal appreciation, but I am afraid that upon the subjects concerning which I write our opinions diverge too widely to ever harmonize.

With hopes for the success of the book, I remain

Yours sincerely,

TCU: TNF

[1] What Chesnutt had in mind regarding a "lighter" side of *Marrow* is not clear. Perhaps Jerry's step-ter-fetchit service when waiting upon the Caucasian conspirators, which now appears a self-abasement by the character, was intended by Chesnutt as risible.

[2] Houghton, Mifflin invested a good deal more in the advertisements for *Marrow*; see 29 June 1904 to Page, n. 1.

[3] The review in question actually appeared in the *Nashville American* and was quoted in an advertisement for *Marrow* that appeared not in the *Leader* but in the *Cleveland World*, 2 November 1901, 4. The review was summarized in a 29 October letter from Houghton, Mifflin thus: "This [notice] speaks in a very complimentary way of the ability of the book and its interest, but it groans over the unworthy subject to which it is devoted!"

[4] Chesnutt is recalling Richard W. Yancey of the *Banner* who wrote him in a friendly manner on 22 April 1899, in reply to Chesnutt's letter of thanks (unlocated) for an appreciative review of *Conjure Woman*. Yancey was particularly impressed by Chesnutt's rendering of dialect, despite the fact that in the unsigned "For Literary Folks," *Nashville Banner*, 1 April 1899, 14, fault was found with the reproduction of Southern black dialect. Still, the tone of the review was dominantly positive: "The novelty of these tales and the artistic and entertaining manner in which they are told are sure to win for them a wide popularity and give the author an enviable place among American story-writers."

[5] How the reviewer at the *Nashville American*—not Yancey at the *Banner*—did, indeed, see Chesnutt as "wrong" was indicated in a quotation from the review included in the *Cleveland World* advertisement: "While the book teems with fine writing and a masterly handling of incident, yet it is a wanton attack upon something that the South holds sacred."

Isaiah B. Scott

November 4, 1901.

My dear Dr. Scott,—

I have not forgotten your very strong expressed appreciation of my writings, which gave me much pleasure when I met you last winter at Tuskegee.[1] I have several times meant to write and return the compliment by saying how much I admire the wisdom, the temperance, and yet the courage of your utterances through the columns of the *Southwestern Christian Advocate*. Our southern friends see things through a glass darkly, but we can perhaps by constant iteration gradually help to undeceive them.

I have made an effort in this direction through my latest novel, *The Marrow of Tradition*, of which I have requested the publishers to send you an editorial copy. I assume in advance that you will approve of it and perhaps more. It is both a novel and a political and sociological tract—a tremendous sort of combination if the author can but find the formula for mixing them.

If you feel after reading the book as I think you will, I should very much appreciate anything you may say concerning it editorially, or any brief personal expression of opinion, which might help promote the circulation of the work.

With kindest regards and best wishes,

Cordially yours,

TCU: TNF

¹ Isaiah B. Scott (1854–?) was president of Wiley College (1893–1896) in Marshall, Tex. A Methodist Episcopal minister, he was in May 1896 elected editor of the *Southwestern Christian Advocate*, a position he held until 1904. He met Chesnutt in February 1901.

Booker T. Washington

‹❧›

November 5, 1901.

My dear Mr. Washington,—

Your kind favor of October 28th is before me. Replying first to a question that you ask me, I would say that I started to read *The Crisis* but got switched off before I finished it.¹ It is said to be quite a good novel, although the best critics say it lacks several of the elements of greatness. It is in the popular vein, which is sufficient to account in large measure for its popularity.²

Yes, I have seen something of the storm that has been blowing down your way, and like you I think that everything of the sort will tend in the end toward the result which we seek. I think, however, that the feeling manifested by southern expressions concerning the little incident is very deep-seated. Underneath it all lies the fear of what they consider corruption of blood. But whatever they may call it or consider it, I think that it would be vastly preferable to the sort of thing toward which they are tending under the present condition of things.

I quite agree with you that the medium of fiction offers a golden opportunity to create sympathy throughout the country for our cause. It has been the writings of Harris and Page and others of that ilk which have furnished my chief incentive to write something upon the other side of this very vital question.³ I know I am on the weaker side in point of popular sympathy, but I am on the stronger side in point of justice and morality, and if I can but command the skill and the power to compel attention, I think I will win out in the long run, so far as I am personally concerned, and will help the cause, which is vastly more important. I am really inclined to think from the reception so far accorded to *The Marrow of Tradition* that I may have "arrived" with this book. You and your machinery can do a great deal to further its reading.[4]

For instance, your Mr. Robert W. Taylor called on me the other day while in Cleveland.[5] I gave him a copy of the book. He writes me from Boston that he has read it with great interest and spoken of it widely, that a number have promised to buy it and that, in his opinion, it is bound to make a great hit. He has also dropped the suggestion here and there that I can be secured for lectures—for all which I am under obligations both to him and to Tuskegee.

I see that you received pronounced attentions at Yale College.[6]

Everything that you accomplish, every upward step that you may take redounds to the credit and advances the interests of millions of people. I for one am most sincerely and unselfishly delighted at all of your successes.

Very cordially yours,

Chas. W. Chesnutt.

TLS: DLC

[1] On 28 October, Washington thanked Chesnutt for the copy of *Marrow* that he sent him, promising to read it and relating that he had been slow in finishing Winston Churchill's *The Crisis*, even though it was "worth reading." He observed that Chesnutt had a great opportunity as a novelist to elicit sympathy for "our cause" and to compensate for the "infinite harm" done by Joel Chandler Harris and Thomas Nelson Page. He then alluded to the "storm" caused by his visit to the White House; see 26 October 1901 to Ethel Chesnutt, n. 4. He closed his letter by describing his strategy for dealing with the furor over President Roosevelt's having socialized with an African American: "The only thing that I am going to do is to keep still and saw wood."

[2] Winston Churchill (1871–1947) was a best-selling author who wrote a series of historical romances at the turn of the century. *The Crisis* (1901) presents an "eternal triangle" story set in St. Louis before and during the Civil War. The Southern heroine spurns the hero with Northern sympathies but eventually marries him, thus sounding a long-popular theme regarding the need for the North and South to unite.

[3] Southern authors Harris and Page had, in Chesnutt's view, falsified the condition of the African American. See 13 June 1890 to Cable.

[4] The Tuskegee "machine," as it was known, was the organized center of communications within the national African-American community and the major means of projecting a positive image to the Caucasian world. Chesnutt here has in mind the public-relations capabilities of Washington's organization.

[5] Robert Wesley Taylor was an 1890 graduate of Tuskegee Institute who taught in Pensacola, Fla., and returned to Tuskegee in 1893 as a mathematics instructor. An effective speaker, author of *Harriet Tubman: The Heroine in Ebony* (1901), and very successful fund-raiser, he was one of Washington's principal representatives in the North; by the fall of 1902 he was Tuskegee's financial secretary.

[6] On 21 October 1901, Washington and President Roosevelt received honorary degrees from Yale University.

Booker T. Washington

༼ঌ

November 16, 1901.

My Dear Mr. Washington:—

Your personal letter of November 11th is before me. I am sorry to know that you have been unwell, and hope that ere this you have recovered your usual vigor. I feel complimented at your having read *The Marrow of Tradition* so promptly, and I need not say that I appreciate in the highest degree your commendation of the work. I have a letter from T. Thomas Fortune, for which I quote a line or two:

"I have just finished reading *The Marrow of Tradition*. I thank God that He has given you genius to write such a work. It is the strongest work of fiction on our side since *Uncle Tom's Cabin*, which it equals in dramatic power and excels in plot and literary finish. I would not be surprised if it should work such a revolution in public sentiment as *Uncle Tom's Cabin* wrought, at any venture it will accomplish vast good."

I have taken a leaf from your own experience in regard to this book. I think that although you draw the sinews of war from the white people, your own influence is vastly strengthened by the fact that you have the moral support of the best element of our own people. It is a source of much satisfaction to me to have men of your stamp and that of Mr. Fortune approve this book and recognize its evident purpose. I sincerely hope for several reasons that it may do some little good. I have no doubt that you can find a dozen ways, without any embarrassment to yourself, in which you can induce people to read this book. The southern whites are filling the eastern papers with pleas for sympathy in their hard situation; I have done my best to give the southern blacks a hearing.

I hear from my daughter occasionally; she is pleased with her work and likes to think that she is helping on a good cause.[1] Mrs. Chesnutt joins me in regards to yourself and Mrs. Washington.

Cordially yours,
Chas. W. Chesnutt

TLS: DLC
[1] See 26 October 1901 to Ethel Chesnutt, n. 1.

Booker T. Washington

༼ঌ

November 25, 1901.

My dear Mr. Washington:—

I have just sent a copy of my book, *The Marrow of Tradition*, to President Roosevelt, sending under another cover a note calling his attention to it, in which I say: "It deals with the race problem in the South, and is written from a point of view which may be interesting to one who must also face that problem, and who has shown a disposition to meet it with fairness to all parties concerned. I should like to hope that you may read the book, and that you may accept it as the tribute of a co-worker in the field of letters to one who in addition to the literary gift has both impulse and opportunity for effective action in national affairs."

I am very anxious that the President should read this book. He has shown himself very friendly, so far, to our people, and I should like to help brace him up in this particular. I know that things of this kind sent to the President are likely to escape his attention, unless it is particularly directed to them, and it has occurred to me that you might possibly be willing to drop Mr. Roosevelt a note suggesting that he read the book.[1] If you should feel any embarrassment in doing this, pray do not consider my suggestion for a moment, but if you think a line from you might prove effective in this regard, I should be pleased to have you write it.[2]

Cordially yours,

Chas. W. Chesnutt.

TLS: DLC

[1] Washington's influence on Roosevelt was extraordinary, to the degree that political appointments of African Americans were not possible without his approval.

[2] On 5 December 1901, Washington replied from Boston, assuring Chesnutt that he would call attention to his book when he next saw the President. Whether Roosevelt read it is moot; no reply to Chesnutt has been located.

Houghton, Mifflin & Co.

December 30, 1901.

Dear Sirs:—

How is the *Marrow of Tradition* doing?[1] Is it moving along with any degree of satisfaction; and if not, how seriously are you disappointed in it? It has been selling fairly well here I am told, though not quite up to the expectations of the dealers. It has evoked a great deal more comment than anything else I have written, so far as I can gather from the reviews and letters and personal statements that have been made to me, and I should like to know whether the sales have been anything in proportion.

A question which I have for a long time been wanting to ask you is whether there is any quarrel or misunderstanding between your house and the New York *Independent* which would prevent them from reviewing my books. The *Independent* is a staunch and uncompromising advocate of the equal rights of all citizens, and comes nearer to my personal views with regard to what ought to be the status of the colored people than any other periodical in the country;

and yet for some reason it has never, so far as I remember, seen fit to notice my books at all.[2] I do not know that this has made any difference in any respect but it has made me wonder whether there was some other reason for this neglect besides the possible lack of sufficient merit in the books to justify any attention.

I would also like your opinion, as the publishers who have handled my books, as to what the chances are, so far as you might be able to guess from your long experience, as to my being able to write a book dealing with the color line from my point of view which would be likely to make a popular success? By popular success I mean a sale of 20,000 or 30,000 copies, enough to produce a modest return for the amount expended in writing it. It is true that I have not been writing primarily for money, but with an ethical purpose entirely apart from that; yet I have always hoped that I might perchance strike a popular vein, for, unless my books are read I shall not be able to accomplish even the ethical purpose which I have in view.[3]

I am beginning to suspect that the public as a rule does not care for books in which the principal characters are colored people, or with a striking sympathy with that race as contrasted with the white race. I find a number of my friends advise me to break away from this theme for a while and write something which is entirely disassociated from it. They suggest that the line between zeal and fanaticism is a very narrow one and I gather that they suspect me of being perilously near it in my latest book; they suggest further that considering the extent to which I have been advertised as a member of that race I might do it just as much good by a worthy achievement in some other field, as by writing books about them which the public does not care for. I am beginning to think somewhat the same way. If a novel which is generally acknowledged to be interesting, dramatic, well constructed, well written—all of which qualities have been pretty generally ascribed to *The Marrow of Tradition*, of which in addition, both the author and the publishers have good hopes—cannot sell 5,000 copies within three months after its publication, there is something radically wrong somewhere, and I do not know where it is unless it be in the subject.[4] My friend Mr. Howells, who has said many nice things about my writings—although his review of *The Marrow of Tradition* in the *North American Review* for December was not a favorable one,[5] as I look at it—has remarked several times that there is no color line in literature.[6] On that point I take issue with him. I am pretty fairly convinced that the color line runs everywhere so far as the United States is concerned, and I am even now wondering whether the reputation I have made would help or hinder a novel that I might publish along an entirely different line.

If you can answer my inquiries or give me any suggestions along the line of what I have been discussing, I shall be very much obliged. In the meantime I remain   Very truly yours,

TCU: TNF

[1] Since his last letter to the firm, two important developments had occurred. Garrison, who was typically curt with Chesnutt but an enthusiastic supporter of Booker T. Washington, was won over by his reading of *Marrow*, delayed because of an illness that began in August. On 9 November, his tone was that of the equal-rights enthusiast, fellow editor Harry D. Robins. Now it was Garrison, son of William Lloyd Garrison, who was stirred to champion Chesnutt as an artist and advocate of civilization. He praised him especially for his fairness toward both blacks and whites, which struck him "as remarkable as was that of Mrs. Stowe in *Uncle Tom's Cabin*." Garrison closed by lamenting the furor in the South over Booker T. Washington's visit to the White House, which "shows how barbarous the whites of that section still are." Chesnutt had finally made him an ally. The second, less sanguine development was first indicated in an unsigned letter from Houghton Mifflin, dated 27 November: "we have been somewhat disappointed recently in the movement of the book. . . . For example, we took the leading bookstore in Boston, and displayed a thousand copies, with portraits, press notices, newspaper advertisements, and display posters, and the result was the sale of 43 copies during the whole week." On 29 November, Chesnutt was informed that the book "has not quite responded" to the energetic advertising campaign: "we have sold something over 3000 and have on hand about 1100." Another letter, dated 9 December, equivocated with the announcement that the "book is moving, slowly to be sure but on our daily reports we are pleased to note its progress." Note below that Chesnutt himself views a successful book as one having sales of 20,000 to 30,000 copies. (By the end of its first year in print, 105,000 copies of the truly popular novel by Thomas Dixon, *The Leopard's Spots* [1902], had been sold; and the 1903 sales of Frank Norris's *The Pit* totaled 94,194 copies.)

[2] A survey of *Independent* from the 1880s through 1901 confirms Chesnutt's description of this weekly magazine showcasing not only Caucasian but African-American sensitivity to the effects of slavery and to contemporary problems resulting from racial discrimination. Chesnutt, however, did receive notice from it. *The Conjure Woman* was succinctly characterized thus: "Several short stories, somewhat after the style of Joel Chandler Harris's Uncle Remus sketches, but yet quite different, make this a very enjoyable little book. The oddities and drolleries of negro life are happily depicted amid scenes peculiar to North Carolina, and there is considerable freshness shown in both incident and dialogue. The author has a fine sense of humor" ("Literature," *Independent* 51 [21 September 1899], 2569–70).

[3] Chesnutt is downplaying the critical nature of his situation as a would-be professional author. Principle aside, he had to write for profit: as early as 1895 he had accumulated a considerable cash reserve to fund his experiment with a writing career (see 11 April 1895 to Cable), and it must have been quite large by the time that he "retired" from his stenography business (see [11 October 1899] to Page). By late 1901, however, he probably felt anxious as his liquid assets diminished.

[4] The sales records indicate that 3,276 copies were sold in 1901; 111 in 1902; and 0 in 1903–1905 (MH:P).

[5] On 9 December 1901 (DLC), Chesnutt saw the matter differently when writing to Washington, announcing that Howells had "paid his respects" to *Marrow*.

[6] In "Mr. Charles Chesnutt's Stories" Howells focused on the genre of the short story, "where Americans hold the foremost place. In this there is, happily no color line" (see [1 May 1900] to Howells, n. 2). Perhaps significantly, Howells was silent regarding *House*, and when he reviewed *Marrow*, he was ambivalent: sympathetic to African Americans in his own fiction, he acknowledged the power with which Chesnutt presented the case for social equality; on the other hand, he observed that Chesnutt "stands up for his own people with a courage that has more justice than mercy in it"; "The book is, in fact, bitter, bitter" ("A Psychological Counter-Current in Fiction," *North American Review* 173 [December 1901], 872–88).

William M. Trotter

᷾

[January 1902]

My dear Mr. Trotter:—

I enclose you herewith P.O. Order for $1.50 annual subscription to *The Guardian*, beginning with the week of January 1st.[1] I have found it interesting and instructive and I admire its uncompromising stand on all questions pertaining to the rights of the Negro. You have the opportunity to conduct a high-class, dignified and helpful newspaper, which will be of much service to the colored race.

I note your various suggestions to myself, mostly with reference to Mr. Washington. I feel quite as deeply interested as any one can in maintaining the rights of the Negro, North, South and everywhere; but I prefer, personally, to do it directly, rather than by attacking someone else. As a public man, Mr. Washington's views are of course a fair subject of criticism, and it is the privilege of a newspaper to express its views on his utterances. I think, however, that you overrate his influence on the course of public affairs; he has merely swum with the current, rather than directed it. I could not have followed his course; neither do I see my way to adopt the extreme position you have taken.[2] His school has accomplished a great deal of good; I have been there and seen it.

I am willing to approve the good, and where I disagree with him, to preach the opposite doctrine strenuously. But I aim to be a literary artist, and acrimonious personalities are the death of art.[3] (They sometimes kill even a newspaper.) With best wishes for the *Guardian* and that we may all work together, each in his own way for truth and justice, I remain,

Cordially yours,

TDU: TNF

[1] William Monroe Trotter (1872–1934) left a career as a mortgage broker to found with George Forbes in 1901 a weekly Boston newspaper, the *Guardian*. In his quest to end racial discrimination he opposed what he saw as Booker T. Washington's too-conciliatory approach; indeed, he served a one-month jail term for disrupting a Boston speech made by Washington in July 1903 (see 11 August 1903 to Washington in which Chesnutt criticizes Trotter for this). In 1905 Trotter collaborated with W. E. B. Du Bois in organizing the Niagara Movement but later refrained from involvement with its successor, the National Association for the Advancement of Colored People, in large part because of white funding and participation. His own organization begun in 1908, the National Equal Rights League, was more exclusively black in character. That Chesnutt was writing to Trotter as he carried on a friendly correspondence with Washington was, however, a portent of a change in his tone that would occur: see the markedly candid 27 June 1903 letter to Washington, written well after Chesnutt was soliciting his promotion of *Marrow*.

[2] The revised draft of the present letter was originally dated 28 December 1901. The unlocated final version was apparently sent to Trotter after the beginning of the new year. On 1 January, Trotter did not mince words about his attitude toward Washington: "I hope . . . you have noticed what . . . Washington has been saying about the Negro and the Jim-Crow car and I hope that it can

no longer be truly thrown at us here that you are a warm personal friend to him. I hope that this contemptible campaign he is now waging against the Negro's civil rights, will cause you to come out stronger than ever for our rights and to refuse Washington any further endorsement. Any man who argues that the Negro should give in just where the white man most wants him to step down and aside is an enemy to every honest Negro, no matter how many schools he is running."

[3] Ironically it was the "bitter" tone of *The Marrow of Tradition*, noted by William Dean Howells in his essay on Chesnutt, that has been traditionally viewed as one of the reasons for that novel's commercial failure. See 30 December 1901 to Houghton, Mifflin, n. 6.

George H. Mifflin

◈

March 20, 1902.

My dear Mr. Mifflin:—

I was duly in receipt of your favor of March 14th, in which you enclosed a letter from Dr. Du Bois,[1] and some correspondence between yourself and Mr. Bowen of the *Independent*, with reference to the review of *The Marrow of Tradition* which appeared in that magazine.[2] Permit me to thank you for taking the matter up. The notice was not only unjust, I felt, to the book, and to my motives, but was personal to the point of offensiveness.[3] I had expected what Mr. Bowen's explanation reveals, that some Southerner had reviewed the book. I think your last letter to Mr. Bowen in which you express the hope that in some way justice may be done to us in the columns of the *Independent*, was precisely the way to go back at him. An apology in private for an injury in public is poor compensation. The *Independent*, however, is so cock sure about all its views and opinions,[4] that I shall be curious to see what form anything they may say will take, if they say anything at all upon the subject.[5]

I thank you also for the letter of Dr. Du Bois; it does not say a great deal, but what it does say is intended I presume by way of

TCU (fragment): TNF

[1] On 8 March 1902, Du Bois thanked Houghton, Mifflin for a copy of *Marrow*. He declared it one of the best sociological studies of the 1898 riot in Wilmington, N.C., that he had seen.

[2] Since December 1901, sales of *Marrow* had not improved. On 18 January 1902, Garrison described a development that must have been particularly embarrassing for Chesnutt: Burrows Brothers bookstore in Cleveland "had a large number" of copies of *Marrow* on sale, and it "wrote us a few days ago asking whether they should return to us the very considerable balance which they have of them." On top of that, Chesnutt's inquiry on 30 December regarding the absence of a review of *Marrow* in *Independent* prompted Houghton, Mifflin to put pressure on that magazine, and the resulting review was withering. Chesnutt sent the review to Garrison (unlocated) who replied on 10 March 1902, informing him that George H. Mifflin had fired off an indignant note to the publisher, Clarence W. Bowen. Bowen explained to Mifflin on 13 March that the review had been assigned to a Southerner, and he apologized for the mistake.

[3] The unsigned review, "Literature," appeared in *Independent* 54 (March 1902), 582: "A novel written apparently by a man with a racial grievance, and for the purpose of exposing conditions rather than to gratify any literary instinct in the author. All the traditional virtues of the negroes are

contrasted with all the reputed vices of Southern whites with the lively distinctions of a mulatto imagination. And the result is vigorous and vindictive to a remarkable degree. Mr. Chestnut [*sic*] will do well to remember that in order to make his enemy appear thoroughly despicable, he should be treated with a show of fairness instead of a malignant hatred, which always excites sympathy. He tips the scales of justice too far in favor of his own indignant emotions. But these, however justified by the fact of his own experience, are never safe foundations to build a romance upon. They are too rash, too personal. And art at least is no respecter of persons. There is no color line in its eternal fairness." Although Chesnutt did not comment on it, as "offensive" a review appeared in the magazine edited by Walter Hines Page: "It is a contemporary *Uncle Tom's Cabin*, a story of racial hatred in the South. . . . The book is palpably a tract. If the Negroes were not so blameless and the Whites not so unrelievedly bad, it would be more convincing" ("A Short Guide to New Books," *World's Work* 3 [February 1902], 1,788).

⁴ For very different opinions of *Independent* and its editor, William Hayes Ward, see 30 December 1901 to Houghton, Mifflin and 31 October 1903 to Washington. It should be noted as well that the magazine had not, in fact, changed in its sympathetic attitude toward things African-American. In the same issue, Washington was the subject of an article by Charles S. Morris who praised him as "the natural leader of the colored race by the divine right of a coronet of brains" ("Booker T. Washington," 565–68). In the same volume, an editorial entitled "The Top and the Bottom" positively focused on the need for endowments made to black colleges (13 March 1902, 646–47); and African-American author L. J. Coppin's article "The African Negro's Religion for the African Negro's Soul" appeared in the 27 March issue (748–50).

⁵ *Independent* did not publicly acknowledge that the review was problematic. Publisher Bowen wrote Mifflin on 26 March 1902 that its literary editor, scholar Paul Elmer More (later associated with Irving Babbitt as a leader of the New Humanism movement), had read *Marrow* and judged the review correct: "This is a novel written with a 'purpose' and the purpose stands out more predominant than the story itself. The intention is to show the injustice which the blacks have suffered at the hands of the whites since the War. This, of course, is a justifiable theme, but in working out this theme Mr. Chesnutt has done what he could to humiliate the whites. . . . The last chapter . . . was utterly revolting to me, although I have no Southern sympathies."

William H. Moody

༺ঙ༻

March 28, 1902.

Dear Sir:—

At the suggestion of Hon. T. E. Burton, Member of Congress from this district, that you have taken special interest in the question of disfranchisement and conditions in the South—a fact which of course was public property—I take pleasure in sending you under separate cover a copy of my novel, *The Marrow of Tradition*, which discusses Southern conditions, political and otherwise, from a standpoint friendly to the colored race.¹ The following extract from the New York *Nation* of March 20th, which also appeared in *The Evening Post* of March 22nd, will afford some suggestion as to the scope of the book and perhaps as to whether or not it is worth your reading:

"The medium of fiction is used by the author of *The Marrow of Tradition* to make a statement of existing relations between negroes and whites in several of the Southern States. Plot, characters and situations are all conceived with this object in view. The combination of fiction and fact is not perfect, but it is closer and smoother than in most of the current purpose novels. The characterization of both races is excellent, and to many of the scenes the author has given a genuine dramatic touch, the touch that thrills and convinces. In statement of conditions and in criticism Mr. Chesnutt is calm, acute, and just—surprisingly so when he discusses lynch law and disfranchisement by the 'grandfather clause' and other ingenious methods.[2] The tone of his argument throughout is admirable, and the expression often eloquent."[3]

If you find time to read the book and are at all impressed by its point of view, I shall feel myself amply repaid in having lodged a new point of view in the mind of a gentleman of influence, whose position gives him opportunity to act where the rest of us can often do nothing more than talk.

Sincerely yours,

TCU: TNF

[1] William Henry Moody (1853–1917) was a Massachusetts attorney who experienced a meteoric rise to public prominence and power, serving as congressman, secretary of the navy, and attorney general between 1895 and 1906—whereupon he began his term as a U.S. Supreme Court justice. Having failed to create a popular success with *Marrow* via the conventional marketing route, Chesnutt now resorts to a moral appeal to the leaders of the country who might influence public policy. This letter represents several with the same text that Chesnutt sent to influential public figures in Washington.

Theodore Elijah Burton (1851–1929), an Ohioan, was a member of the U.S. House of Representatives (1889–1891, 1895–1909, 1921–1929) and the U.S. Senate (1909–1915). The author of *Life of John Sherman* (1906) and *Corporations and the State* (1911), he was famous for his independence of thought and hostility to pork-barrel legislation. On 10 February 1902 he aided Chesnutt in his plan to distribute *Marrow* among political figures, sending him a copy of the *Congressional Directory* and identifying Moody, C. E. Littlefield, Edgar Crumpacker, and Marlin E. Olmsted as influential figures interested in disfranchisement and "the conditions in the South." Crumpacker's 5 May reply was noteworthy: he praised both *Marrow* and Thomas Dixon's *The Leopard's Spots*, "a very readable story upon the other side of the question."

[2] The "grandfather clause" disqualified those potential voters whose grandfathers had not enjoyed the franchise in a state, thus excluding African Americans who did not have the right to vote until the Reconstruction Era (see [22 March 1899] to Page, n. 5).

[3] Chesnutt quoted all but the final sentence of the review: "While his novel is inferior to his short stories in form and method, it shows more vigorously than they do the capacity for cool observation and reflection" ("More Fiction," *Nation* 74 [20 March 1902], 232).

PART V

DISCONTENT IN 1903–1904

◦

A Turn to Argumentative Prose

◦

*We are directly concerned with the interests
of some millions of American citizens of
more or less mixed descent, whose rights are
fixed by the Constitution and laws of the
United States; nor am I ready yet to accept
the doctrine that those constitutional
rights are mere waste paper.*

James Pott & Co.

෴

January 31, 1903.

Dear Sirs:—

I am in receipt of your favor of January 12th, to which absence from the city has prevented an earlier reply, in reference to your proposed volume presenting the negro question from the negro's point of view.[1] If you finally determine upon the plan, I see no reason why I should not undertake to write such an article as you suggest, upon the question of disfranchisement.

I should of course like to know of the other writers with whose contributions mine would be bound up—the names mentioned in your letter are all right. And if the book is intended as a business enterprise, I should be pleased to know what you would consider a proper compensation for such an article.[2] Any other letter you may write will be more promptly answered.[3]

Very truly yours,

TCU: TNF

[1] The sang froid of this delayed reply to what once would have been enthusiastically received by Chesnutt as an acknowledgment of his accomplishments may be a consequence of the déjà vu nature of the situation: an essay on "the negro question from the negro point of view" was the ill-fated project he undertook at the suggestion of George Washington Cable in 1889 (see 12 February 1889 to Cable). Chesnutt did not, however, have the opportunity to recycle the essay he produced then: on 12 January 1903, he was asked to write 2,500 to 3,000 words on "the general subject of disfranchisement of the negro in the south." Chesnutt's gruffness and pecuniary focus, too, may reflect his disillusionment with commercial authorship per se, given the poor sales of both *House* and *Marrow* and the depletion of his savings during his 1899–1902 "retirement" from business.

[2] In the 12 January letter to Chesnutt, Washington, Du Bois, and Paul Laurence Dunbar were named. In the 5 February reply to Chesnutt offering $50.00 for 2,500 words and advising him about "the advisability of making as conservative a statement of the facts as is possible," Bishop Benjamin T. Tanner was also cited, though his planned essay, "Characteristics of the Negro Race" did not appear in the volume.

[3] "The Disfranchisement of the Negro," Chesnutt's only essay to be published in a book during his life, appeared in *The Negro Problem* (New York: James Pott & Company, 1903), 79–124. The relationship between publisher and author became strained. Mid-June was initially the submission date given him; but, on 28 April, Chesnutt was asked to submit the piece as soon as possible. He did not and was reminded of the need for copy on 15 June. On 16 June he finally forwarded it, with an excuse rather than an apology, noting that his article had become "at least twice as long as what you asked me for." Hoping for a greater return on his investment of time and energy, he then posed the possibility of giving the essay periodical publication first and sharing the payment for it. Pott declined on 30 June and asked Chesnutt what remuneration he expected for the longer-than-requested article.

W. E. Burghardt Du Bois

᭡

June 27, 1903.

My dear Doctor Du Bois:—

I beg to acknowledge receipt of the clipping which you return to me; it was not important but I thank you just the same.[1]

Potts have accepted my article on the disfranchisement of the Negro. I take a firm stand for manhood suffrage and the enforcement of the constitutional amendments. I take no stock whatever in these disfranchisement constitutions. The South is suffering a great deal more from the malignity of the whites than the ignorance of the Negro. I have wondered whether your book on the *Souls of Black Folk* had any direct effect in stirring up the peonage investigation in Alabama; it might well have done so.

I have not forgotten what you say about a national Negro journal. It is a matter concerning which one would like to think and consult before committing himself. There are already many "colored" papers; how they support themselves may be guessed at from the contents—most of them are mediums for hair straightening advertisements and the personal laudation of "self-made men," most of whom are not so well made that they really ought to brag much about it. The question of support would be the vital one for such a journal. What the Negro needs more than anything else is a medium through which he can present his case to thinking white people, who after all are the arbiters of our destiny. How helpless the Negro is in the South your own writings give ample proof; while in the North he is so vastly in the minority in numbers, to say nothing of his average humble condition, that his influence alone would be inconsiderable. I fear few white people except the occasional exchange editors, read the present newspapers published by colored people. Whether you could reach that class of readers and at the same time get a sufficient subscription list from all sources to support the paper is the thing which I would advise you to consider carefully before you risk much money. The editing of a newspaper is the next vital consideration. To do it properly would require all the time of a good man—he ought to be as good a man as yourself.[2] I wish I could talk with you. Where will you spend the summer? Let me know your movements and it is possible that I might find it convenient to be at the same place some time before the fall.

I presume what you have written concerning me has not yet appeared, but have no doubt it will be just and complimentary, and I thank you for it in advance.[3]

Sincerely yours,

Chas. W. Chesnutt

TLS: MU-Ar

[1] With a previous, undated letter (MU-Ar), Chesnutt enclosed clippings of comments on his work by Horace Traubel, editor of *Conservator*, along with an autobiographical sketch that Du Bois had requested.

2 Du Bois did not succeed in establishing a magazine until 1906, when publication of the *Moon* commenced.

3 In "Possibilities of the Negro," *Booklovers Magazine: The Advance Guard of the Race* 2 (July 1903), 2–15, Du Bois observed: "Chesnutt wrote powerfully, but with great reserve and suggestiveness, touching a new realm in the borderland between the races and making the world listen with one short story." After including Chesnutt as one of three African-American artists who have risen "to places of recognized importance," Du Bois observed that Chesnutt faces a "peculiar temptation": "of money making—why leave some thousands of dollars a year for scribbling about black folk?"

Booker T. Washington

࿐

June 27, 1903.

My dear Mr. Washington:—

I have meant for some time to write you again on the subject mentioned in your last letter to me, to-wit, the restricted franchise in the South.[1] Before doing so let me express with you my regret at your loss of Mr. Thrasher.[2] He was a fine man and did a good work. I liked him very much.

I am squarely opposed to any restriction of the franchise in the South on any basis now proposed. It is wholly and solely an effort in my opinion to deprive the negro of every vestige of power and every particle of representation. How completely this leaves him in the power of the whites and exposes him to their cruelty and contempt, is indicated by the disclosures of the peonage investigation now in progress in your State.[3] I have no faith in the Southern people's sense of justice so far as the Negro's rights are concerned. Their own public opinion on the subject is hopelessly corrupt and they have poisoned the North until we scarcely feel that our rights are secure in this part of the country. The time is coming when every man who speaks upon these subjects will have to take sides one way or the other, and if you are going to stand with the Lyman Abbotts and men of that stamp I fear you will be on the side which other colored men who have the interests of the race at heart will feel to be the wrong side.[4] On this proposition I stand squarely with the *New York Evening Post*.[5] I realize some of the difficulty and delicacy of your position, and yet at the same time I do not see how the recognized leader and spokesman of a people whose rights are in jeopardy can afford to take a stand less high, or demand less for his people than white men do.

In your letter you say that at the time of Mr. Douglass's death there were but few Negroes in the state legislatures and only one or two in Congress; I think there were more in the state legislatures than you have in mind. You speak of our condition when Mr. Bruce was swept out of the senate;[6] from present indications, long before Mr. Washington, who has followed these distinguished gentlemen as the leader of his people, shall have disappeared from public view, they will not have a rag of any right whatever left in the Southern States; they may be allowed to live and to do certain kinds of manual labor through the favor of the Southern whites,[7] but their guaranteed rights will be a thing of the past.

I am very much in earnest in this thing, and I hope to write and say a great deal upon the subject, which it seems is destined to be widely discussed in the near future.

I appreciate all you say and have written about education and property; but they are not everything. There is no good reason why we should not acquire them all the more readily because of our equality of rights.[8] I have no confidence in that friendship of the whites which is to take the place of rights, and no expectation of justice at their hands unless it is founded on law.

Pardon my frankness; your letter invited it. I feel deeply on this subject. I want my rights and all of them, and I ask no more for myself than I would demand for every Negro in the South. If the white South will continue to ignore the Constitution and violate the laws, it must be with no consent of mine, and with no word that can be twisted into the approval or condonation of their unjust and unlawful course.   Sincerely yours,

TCU: TNF

[1] On 6 May 1903 (DLC), Emmett J. Scott acknowledged a 2 May letter to Washington (unlocated) in which Chesnutt made a "frank statement" regarding Washington's "position with regard to southern affairs." Washington replied on 16 May to Chesnutt's assertion that "the policy of conciliation" has effected a diminution of "the Negro's rights," suggesting that conciliation had nothing to do with the loss of political power since 1873. Citing the defeat of U.S. Senator Blanche K. Bruce and the decrease in the number of less prominent African-American legislators, Washington identified the problem as the lack of African-American influence in local communities and the need to rectify the situation by creating the sine qua non for legislative representation, an "intelligent property holding taxpaying constituency" capable of electing black representatives—ones for whom the white voters would also be willing to cast their ballots. An "increase of knowledge and wealth and character" among African Americans will eventually insure their political rights, argued Washington.

[2] Max Bennett Thrasher (1860–1903)—author of *Tuskegee: Its Story and Its Work* (1900) and "Mr. Chesnutt at Work," *Boston Evening Transcript*, 4 September 1901, 13—was an administrator at Tuskegee. On 29 May 1903 he died of peritonitis in the Tuskegee Institute Hospital after an appendectomy.

[3] In "The Disfranchisement of the Negro" Chesnutt argues that the "country stands face to face with the revival of slavery; at the moment of this writing a federal grand jury in Alabama is uncovering a system of peonage established under cover of law" (*The Negro Problem*, 89). There was a proliferation of peonage investigations in Alabama in 1903, especially in Coosa, Lowndes, and Tallapoosa counties. They received much attention from the Northern press, especially the *New York Evening Post*. Although landowners were reprimanded by the courts, and four of them served four months in jail and paid $500 in fines for their unlawful activities, peonage did not end in Alabama. See Pete Daniel, *The Shadow of Slavery: Peonage in the South, 1901–1969* (Urbana: University of Illinois Press, 1972), 43–64.

[4] Lyman Abbott (1835–1922) was a "Social Gospel" minister whose reform concerns ultimately led to a close relationship with Theodore Roosevelt. He was the editor of *Outlook* (1881–1923), a religious and literary weekly that had serialized Washington's *Up From Slavery* immediately prior

to its book publication in 1901. Abbott here symbolizes to Chesnutt those who, like Washington, demonstrate their credulity by assuming that the South will deal fairly with African Americans, particularly in regard to preserving their right to vote. The optimism that Chesnutt found so alarming and which his next published novel, *The Colonel's Dream* (1905), grimly attempts to rebut, will be seen in an editorial (presumably by Abbott) entitled "The Race Problem," *Outlook* 73 (14 March 1903), 607–10. For example, it declares that, at "no time since the Civil War has the eventual solution of the race problem seemed to us so hopeful as it seems to-day"; this is "due to the increasing manifestation of Southern interest in the education and elevation of the negro." Particularly galling to Chesnutt, given his anger over clear evidence of systematic disfranchisement, must have been the assertion that Southerners "are trying to solve this problem on principles consonant with justice and freedom." Only slightly less offensive, perhaps, was the editorial's echoing of the Washingtonian article of faith regarding the wisdom of educating African Americans in manual-labor skills and the reassurance it offered that, however elevated in the future, there is no serious likelihood of African Americans ever intermarrying with Caucasians in significant numbers. See 28 July 1903 to *Outlook*.

[5] In 27 May 1904 to Robert C. Ogden, Chesnutt characterizes the *Evening Post* as a newspaper that takes a radical stand in regard to protecting the civil rights of African Americans. Oswald Garrison Villard (1872–1949) owned the *Evening Post*, in which his sympathetic attitude toward African Americans was manifested from 1897 to 1918. Rollo Ogden (1856–1937) joined the editorial staff in 1891 and became editor-in-chief in 1903. A former minister at the Case Avenue Presbyterian Church in Cleveland (1883–1887), his editorials argued in behalf of full civil rights for all, including the extension of the franchise to women.

[6] Douglass died in 1895. Bruce lost his seat in the U.S. Senate when Democrats returned to power in Mississippi in 1881. See 7 December 1897 to Green, n. 2.

[7] Chesnutt makes a pointed allusion to Washington's well-known emphasis on manual-labor education as appropriate for most African Americans, which would be reinforced in 1904 with the publication of his *Working with the Hands*. The tension between Washington and individuals like Chesnutt over this issue had, in part, to do with the demeaning way in which Washington had characterized African Americans—like Chesnutt—who had not followed the Tuskegee model for economic advancement. In 1901 Washington explained in *Up From Slavery*, a volume that Chesnutt owned, the problem for which he saw the teaching of practical vocational skills as the solution: during the Reconstruction Era "two ideas were constantly agitating the minds of coloured people," a "craze for Greek and Latin learning" (see Chesnutt's journals, where such an enthusiasm is pellucidly clear) and "a desire to hold [political] office"—both of which Washington interprets as manifestations of a desire to avoid manual labor, or hard work of any kind. The ministry and the teaching profession Chesnutt entered, he explains, thus became popular because they did not involve hard work. In his opinion, the consequences were often lamentable when not comically ludicrous: "Many became teachers who could do little more than write their names. I remember . . . one of this class, who was in search of a school to teach, and the question arose . . . as to the shape of the earth and how he would teach . . . this subject. He explained his position in the matter by saying that he was prepared to teach that the earth was either flat or round, according to the preference of a majority of his patrons" (*Up From Slavery*, 80–81).

[8] See *Up from Slavery*, where Washington laments the granting of the franchise to Reconstruction era African Americans not prepared to exercise it wisely: "I cannot help feeling that it would have been wiser if some plan could have been put in operation which would have made the possession of a certain amount of education or property, or both, a test for the exercise of the franchise, and a way provided by which this test should be made to apply honestly and squarely to both the white and black races" (84).

James Pott & Co.

∽

July 2, 1903

Dear Sirs:—

Replying to your favor of June 30th, which reached me this morning, and to your previous letter, I appreciate the force of what you say about magazine publication of my article on the Disfranchisement of the Negro and we will let that matter drop.[1]

As to the length of the article, your letters made it clear that you wanted an article of from 2500 to 3500 words long, although in your letter of February 5th you said: "We would be glad to give you $50 for an essay of 2500 words upon The Disfranchisement of the Negro. . . . If the paper should run beyond 2500 words we should be glad to pay you at the rate of 2 cents per word for anything over that number."

I surely had no desire to stretch out the article for the sake of the money that was in it, but the subject was hardly capable of any sort of adequate treatment in much less space. I realize that the article is somewhere near three times as long as you had in mind, and I shall not attempt to hold you to anything more than you regard as fair compensation. You would have been willing to pay me $70 for an article of 3500 words. If you will send me a check for $100 I shall not complain, though if you make it larger I shall appreciate your liberality.[2] This is scarcely more than a cent a word which is by no means extravagant.[3]

*TCU (possibly a fragment):*TNF

[1] Chesnutt had proposed both magazine and book publication of his essay; see 31 January 1903 to James Pott & Co., n. 3.

[2] On 1 August, the firm accepted Chesnutt's terms with the promise of a "further remittance" if *The Negro Problem* sold well.

[3] James Pott & Co. mailed proof to Chesnutt on 1 August; it sent him duplicate proof on 11 August, with the complaint that he had held up production; and it mailed to him a copy of the book on 16 September.

Outlook Publishing Co.

∽

July 28, 1903

Dear Sirs:

I enclose herewith my check for renewal of my annual subscription of the *Outlook.* I do not like its attitude in regard to suffrage restriction in the South, and do not share its rose-colored confidence in the intention of the white South to treat the black South fairly, do not indeed believe that the white South is yet able to put itself in proper mental attitude to even see what is fair treatment of the Negro.[1] The *Outlook*, however, has many valuable features, and I am pretty well satisfied that its editors mean well in this matter, and I shall follow in its columns the process of its conversion to the correct point of view. There is no safety for the rights of the citizen until the equality of all men before the law is fully and everywhere recognized, and when this is done, the present discriminating laws and constitutions of Southern States will have gone to the legislative scrap-pile. They may be all right on paper, as the *Outlook* laboriously explains—the voice is the voice of Jacob, but the hand is the hand of Esau.[2]   Yours very truly,

TDU: TNF

[1] See 27 June 1903 to Washington, n. 4, concerning the editorial viewpoint of *Outlook*.

[2] This is a paraphrase of Genesis 27:22. The allusion is to the way in which Jacob, pretending to be his brother Esau, deceived his father Isaac: the South may give the appearance of being just, but it intends to continue violating the civil rights of African Americans.

Booker T. Washington

◦◦◦

Personal.

August 11, 1903.

My dear Dr. Washington:—

I should have replied sooner to your private and confidential letter of July 7th, but have been very busy, and could not find time to express myself as I would like to—will probably not do that even here.[1]

Permit me to express my strong disapproval of the conduct of Mr. Trotter and his adherents at your Boston meeting. A man who has a cause, or thinks he has a cause, which cannot be presented, at the proper time and place, in calm and dignified argument, has mistaken his calling as an advocate.[2]

Replying to that portion of your letter in which you invite the expression of my opinion on matters pertaining to the race, I wish to say that I differ from you most decidedly on the matter of a restricted franchise.[3] It is an issue gotten up solely to disfranchise the Negroes, and with no serious intention of ever applying it to any one else. I see nothing at all to justify what you term "the protection of the ballot, for a while at least, either by an educational test, property test, or by both combined." It is a complete acquiescence in the withdrawal of the ballot from the Negro, and his entire deprivation of any representation; it means that you are willing, in your own State and county, to throw yourself upon the mercy of the whites, rather than to claim your share in your own government under a free franchise. You may reply that you would have to do it anyway.[4] But you need not approve of it, thereby tying the hands of the friends of the race who would be willing and able to cry out against the injustice. The little handful of colored voters registered in Alabama, for instance, cut no figure in the general result of an election.[5] The State of Mississippi, where the ballot is "protected" in the manner you approve of, has just nominated a governor and a U.S. Senator on an anti-negro platform.[6] The world is not having long to wait nor much need to watch, to see how the white South, under the policy of non-interference, is carrying out its "sacred trust"— I doubt whether "sacred" is quite the word for a trust which was acquired by highway robbery of another class. Your qualification that "whatever tests are required, they should be made to apply with equal and exact justice to both races," would be all right if we could see or hope for any disposition on the part of even a decent minority of Southern white men to apply these tests fairly. I for one prefer to wait until I see this disposition before I will agree that the ballot should be "protected" by restrictions which have but one purpose and can have but one result—to deny the colored race all representation. Such a restriction could never be fair so long as there remained any disparity in the condition of the races, so long as there was any race question in Southern politics; and therefore it could never be fair in your lifetime or mine.

Nor do I think it the part of policy to dwell too much upon the weakness of the Negro race. That their condition should be lowly, in view of their antecedents, is entirely natural, and scarcely calls for any lengthy disquisitions.[7] It is altogether contrary to the spirit of our institutions and to the Constitution to pick out any one class of people, differentiated from the rest by color or origin or anything else, make some average deduction concerning their capacity, and then proceed to measure their rights by this standard. Every individual Negro, weak or strong, is entitled to the same rights before the law as every individual white man, whether weak or strong; nor is there any good reason in law, in morals or anywhere else, why the strong Negro should have his rights and opportunities measured by those of the weak.[8] I think that by recognizing and dwelling upon these distinctions, and suggesting different kinds of education and different degrees of political power and all that sort of thing for the colored people, we are merely intensifying the class spirit which is fast robbing them of every shadow of right. Let the white man dwell upon the weakness of the Negro, if he will; it is not a matter which you or I need to emphasize. The question with which, in principle, we have to deal, is not the question of the Negro race; what the black race has or has not been able to do in Africa should no more enter into the discussion of the Negro's rights as a citizen, than what the Irish have not done in Ireland should be the basis of their citizenship here. We are directly concerned with the interests of some millions of American citizens of more or less mixed descent, whose rights are fixed by the Constitution and laws of the United States; nor am I ready yet to accept the doctrine that those constitutional rights are mere waste paper. The

Supreme Court may assent to their nullification, but we ought not to accept its finding as conclusive: there is still the court of public opinion to which we may appeal.[9]

You speak of Jim Crow work for Negroes at the North; I am unable to think of any colored man in this city, possessed of any art or trade, who cannot find employment and earn a living at it.[10] There are plenty of them in shops and factories, sometimes as foremen, and they are not badly represented in offices and stores. *All* the Negroes down South must ride in the Jim Crow cars. Northern prejudice at least discriminates. Southern prejudice doesn't. I would by no means confound the good Southerners with the bad. Judge Jones is a noble man and worthy of all praise; I only wish he represented a larger constituency.[11] But the white South insists upon judging the Negroes as a class. They themselves must be measured by the same rule—must be judged by the laws they make, the customs they follow and the crimes they commit, under color of law, against the colored people. They seem to me, as a class, barring a few honorable exceptions, an ignorant, narrow and childish people—as inferior to the white people of the North—barring a few of the lower class—as the Southern Negroes are said to be to the whites of that section. I make no pretense of any special love for them. I was brought up among them; I have a large share of their blood in my veins; I wish them well, and first of all I wish that they may learn to do justice. My love I keep for my friends, and my friends are those who treat me fairly. I admire your Christ-like spirit in loving the Southern whites, but I confess I am not up to it.

I have taken occasion in the article which I have written for James Pott & Company, to express my disagreement with you upon the matter of the suffrage.[12] I have done so without heat, and with what I meant to make ample recognition of your invaluable services to the country. If I have not said more along that line, it was because I could not believe that anything I might say would add in any degree to your well won fame. But I believe in manhood suffrage, especially now, and especially for the Negro. And I do not believe in a silent submission to any form of injustice.

I think the feeling with reference to yourself on the part of some colored men, which has resulted in occasional and sometimes very unjust and rancorous criticism—a feeling which seems to puzzle you, and which is not very easily explainable,—may grow out of a somewhat obscure consciousness of this fact:—No man living in the heart of the South, and conducting there a great institution in the midst of a hostile race, can possibly be in a position to speak always frankly and fearlessly concerning the rights of his people. He is not at liberty to express that manly indignation which is always the natural and often the most effective way to meet injustice. He must choose his words; he must trim his sails; he must apply the salve so soon after the blow, that it takes away all the sting of the lash. I do not believe there is in the United States another colored man, situated as you are, who could have said even as much by way of criticism of the Southern whites as you have said. But I still recognize the limitation.[13] But you Southern educators are all bound up with some one special cause or other, devotion to which sometimes unconsciously warps your judgment as to what is best for the general welfare of the race. Your institution, your system of education, whatever it may be, is too apt to dwarf everything else and become the sole remedy for social and political evils which have a much wider basis. The civil and political rights of the Negro would be just as vital and fundamental if there were no question at all of the education of the Southern Negro.[14] It is not at all essential to the comparative happiness of the race that they should be highly educated in any particular way; they might be happy in comparative ignorance if they had the same education and the same chances as the other people among whom they live. It is the *differences* which make the trouble. Educate them all to a high degree and leave the same inequalities, and as old Ben Tillman[15] is so fond of saying—he occasionally tells the truth by accident—you merely shift the ground of the problem, you do not alter its essential features.

Permit me to compliment you upon the pamphlet on lynching; I do not see that the President's is any more forceful.[16] His letter, in spite of all its noble sentiment, I think unduly magnifies the importance of the crime of rape. It is no worse a crime now than it has always been, and cannot, that I can perceive, deserve any different or greater punishment than it has always had. I do not believe it is any more common than it has always been; and it has only seemed so since the fashion grew up of burning Negroes for it and making display headings in the newspapers upon the subject. In the eye of the law it is no greater crime when committed by a Negro upon a white woman than when committed by a white man upon a Negro woman; and yet from the hysterical utterances on the subject one would be almost inclined to believe that rape committed by a white man upon a white woman was scarcely any offense at all in comparison. It is the rape that is the crime, and not the person who commits it; and it is scarcely less unjust to railroad a man to the gallows without opportunity to prepare a defense and give the public time for calm and cool deliberation, than it is to put him out of the way upon the spot with the rope or the torch.

I wish you godspeed in the conversion of the Southern white people; encourage the good ones all you may, but I think the rest of us, when we can get a hearing, should score the bad ones; it will do them good. Your ability and your influence are so great that I should like to see them exerted always in favor of the highest and the best things, which are also, in the long run, the wisest and the most successful, though perhaps at times not seemingly the most immediately practical. On this franchise proposition I think you are training with the wrong crowd. I wish that you were in a position to undertake the political leadership of the colored race, or that there were one or two men as able and as honest as yourself to do so. I think we might then reasonably hope that the Fourteenth and Fifteenth Amendments would become vitally operative.[17]

Cordially yours,
Chas. W. Chesnutt.

TLS: DLC.

[1] In a 7 July letter, Washington focused upon the "weak" condition of African Americans, observing that it can only be overcome by "education and experience" and that no "law passed by congress or any state" can prevent oppression: "I fear, in one form or another, the Negro will have to continue to take his medicine until he gains material, mental, moral and political strength enough to enable him to change his present condition." Washington then self-defensively pointed out that he had always spoken in behalf of the African American: "whenever I feel that the proper time has come for an utterance upon any subject concerning my race I have never hesitated to give that utterance." Inviting further correspondence on the subject, he protested, "I cannot understand what you or others want me to do that I have left undone."

[2] William M. Trotter was the aggressively militant editor of the Boston Guardian; see [January 1902] to Trotter, n. 1. Here Chesnutt is sympathetically reacting to what Washington suffered on 30 July 1903 at the Columbus Avenue A.M.E.Z. Church in Boston when he attempted to address the National Negro Business League. After T. Thomas Fortune succeeded in introducing Washington amidst heckling and the red pepper which had been scattered on the platform, Washington was prevented from speaking by Trotter and his associates. Only after Trotter and others were arrested was Washington able to deliver his address.

[3] See 27 June 1903 to Washington, n. 8, regarding Washington's seeing the wisdom in a restricted franchise equitably applied to Caucasians and African Americans by the states.

[4] In "The Disfranchisement of the Negro," Chesnutt categorizes individuals who do not see the franchise issue as truly meaningful thus: "The argument of peace-loving Northern white men and Negro opportunists that the political power of the Negro having long ago been suppressed by unlawful means, his right to vote is a mere paper right, of no real value, and therefore to be lightly yielded for the sake of a hypothetical harmony, is fatally short-sighted" (96).

[5] Chesnutt provided the figures in question in "The Disfranchisement of the Negro": "Out of a total, by the census of 1900, of 181,471 Negro 'males of voting age,' less than 3,000 are registered; in Montgomery county alone, the seat of the State capital, where there are 7,000 Negro males of voting age, only 47 have been allowed to register, while in several counties not one single Negro is permitted to exercise the franchise" (86).

[6] Chesnutt explains in "The Disfranchisement of the Negro" the nature of the limitation in Mississippi and other Southern states: "These restrictions fall into three groups. The first comprises a property qualification—the ownership of $300 worth or more of real or personal property (Alabama, Louisiana, Virginia and South Carolina); the payment of a poll tax (Mississippi, North Carolina, Virginia); an educational qualification—the ability to read and write (Alabama, Louisiana, North Carolina)" (83). He then examines in more detail the ways in which these restrictions are rendered even more exclusive than they at first appear. The Mississippi gubernatorial candidate in question is James K. Vardaman (1861–1930), a newspaper editor who served in the state legislature; he was elected governor in 1904 by developing a power base among agriculturists and poor whites who feared "Negro dominance." The senatorial candidate is Hernando D. Money (1839–1912), an ally of Vardaman who was also successful at the polls.

[7] Typical of Washington's pragmatic approach to winning the confidence of Caucasian readers was his repeated concession in regard to the argument that African Americans as a whole were not yet as sophisticated as the white community: for example, "Of course the coloured people, so largely without education, and wholly without experience in government, made tremendous mis-

takes [when serving in public office during the Reconstruction era], just as any people similarly situated would have done." Washington further qualified his point in a more positive way, though: "the Negro is a much stronger and wiser man than he was thirty-five years ago" and many are now truly qualified to vote with probity and intelligence, and even to serve in office as well as Senator Blanche K. Bruce did (*Up from Slavery*, 86; concerning Bruce, see 27 June 1903 to Washington, n. 6).

[8] How absolutist Chesnutt is in his attitude toward male franchise may be measured in light of distinctions between superior and inferior kinds of blacks and whites that he draws in his own fictional writings. But the right to vote was not, for Chesnutt, qualified by these or any other classifications of individuals.

[9] In "The Disfranchisement" Chesnutt describes two Supreme Court rulings: the first having to do with "a case based upon the 'understanding' clause [see n. 5] of the Mississippi Constitution, in which the Supreme Court held, in effect, that since there was no ambiguity in the language employed and the Negro was not directly named, the court would not go behind the wording of the Constitution to find a meaning which discriminated against the colored voter"; and the second, "the recent case of Jackson vs. Giles [i.e., Jackson W. Giles], brought by a colored citizen of Montgomery, Alabama, in which the Supreme Court confesses itself impotent to provide a remedy for what, by inference, it acknowledges *may* be a 'great political wrong.'" Referring later to the Alabama case, Chesnutt was outraged that the Court has "declared the legislative and political department of the government to be the only power which can right a political wrong" (*The Negro Problem*, 86–87, 93).

[10] On 7 July, Washington wrote, "Our race has disadvantages in every part of the country. In the North you have Jim Crow work, in the South we have Jim Crow cars. In most sections of the North as much of a sensation would be created by a Negro going into a shoe factory or a printing office as if he went into a railroad car set aside for white people in the South."

[11] Thomas Goode Jones (1844–1914) served in an Alabama regiment of the Confederate army, rising from private to major. After achieving prominence in the state legislature, he was elected governor of Alabama; and during that state's 1901 constitutional convention, he did much to effect the adoption of a provision regarding the removal of sheriffs who cooperated with mobs. That year Roosevelt, who soon publicly opposed lynchings (see n. 16), appointed him to a federal judgeship in the northern and middle district of Alabama. In his 7 July letter, Washington alluded to Jones thus: "You say you have no faith in the southern people's sense of justice so far as the Negro's rights are concerned. I have yet the most faith in the sense of justice of a large proportion of them, but just now in proportion to those who would do us wrong the number is small, but we should not condemn the good with the bad. Judge Thomas G. Jones of this state, a white Southern Democrat, is as pure, brave and honest a man and as good a friend to the Negro as any white man in this country."

[12] "The Disfranchisement of the Negro" in *The Negro Problem* would be published in mid-September.

[13] Chesnutt gives here a fair assessment of Washington's situation as the internationally visible representative of those with his racial background and as the primary figure in the black-white rapprochement that had been achieved. Admitted is the fact that Washington could not use Chesnutt's incendiary language in "The Disfranchisement," for example: "I shall say nothing about the moral effect of disfranchisement upon the white people, or upon the State itself. What slavery made of the Southern Whites is a matter of history. The abolition of slavery gave the South an opportunity to emerge from barbarism" (102). Whatever Washington said might immediately affect the condition of millions in the North and South, and it behooved him to be judiciously circumspect when necessary for his own sake and theirs.

[14] In "The Disfranchisement" Chesnutt describes Washington as a "promoter" of education whose "career is bound up in the success of an industrial school"; he insinuates that Washington has surrendered the ballot for the sake of seeing his own approach to obtaining equality prosper (109–110).

[15] Benjamin R. ("Pitchfork Ben") Tillman (1847–1918) rose to power in South Carolina as an agrarian champion opposing the monied class represented by attorneys and merchants. He was elected governor (1890–1894) and exercised extraordinary control of the political situation, hand-picking his successor when he became a U.S. Senator (1894–1918). He pushed for a convention to rewrite the state's constitution: in 1895 he thus directed both the gerrymandering that diminished the effective representation of African Americans and the origination of educational and property qualifications legally disfranchising them. He even advocated the repeal of the Fifteenth Amendment and justified lynching in cases of rape.

[16] *"Lynchings in the South," An Open Letter by Booker T. Washington* (Tuskegee, Ala.: Tuskegee Institute Print, 1901) is a pamphlet in which Washington decries the exercise of "lynch law" against African Americans. On 9 August President Roosevelt released to the press a letter commending Governor Winfield T. Durbin of Indiana for his strong stand against lynching. Roosevelt's position was that it is incompatible with the continued existence of the republic: such forms of anarchy inevitably give rise to tyranny. As Chesnutt goes on to note, Roosevelt focused on rape committed by African Americans, arguing that even for such an heinous crime mob violence, and particularly torture, cannot be tolerated ("President Denounces Mob Lawlessness," *New York Times*, 10 August 1903, 1–2.)

[17] The Fourteenth Amendment provides that no state shall make or enforce any law abridging the privileges or immunities of U.S. citizens, or depriving any of life, liberty, or property without due process of law, or deny any the equal protection of the law. The Fifteenth provides that the right of U.S. citizens to vote shall not be denied or abridged by any state on the grounds of race, color, or previous condition of servitude.

William H. Richards

◦⌒◦

September 4, 1903.

My dear Professor Richards:—

Replying to your letter of August 31st, in which you kindly suggest that it is about time for me to appear again before a Washington audience, I have just written a letter to Mr. Jackson, president of the association, in reply to one of his dated August 19th, inviting me to address the association and offering to turn over to me the receipts of the evening.[1] As I am a business man as well as an occasional writer, my time is worth something to me, and while I would expect no large remuneration, you will see from my letter to Mr. Jackson, that I would like to be assured that at least my expenses would be met; anything over would of course count as compensation. I do not know that I could do any particular good by a lecture which I might deliver; anything which I might say upon current topics affecting the race would probably not be novel, and I imagine that most of my audience would agree with me upon them. The other subject which I suggest, "The Value of Ideals," would offer a wider field of discussion and at the same time afford me an opportunity to say anything I like that might have a special or particular interest to my audience.[2]

I thank you for this very kindly invitation, which no doubt I owe to your suggestion. I was sorry I could not see more of you at Washington,[3] but hope to make good the loss at some future time.

Cordially yours,

TCU: TNF

[1] William H. Richards, former president of the Bethel Literary and Historical Association in Washington, D.C., and presently a lecturer for the organization, wrote Chesnutt on 21 August, noting that it had been approximately four years since he had spoken "before a Washington audience." He hoped that Chesnutt would accept the invitation soon to be sent him by the president, George W. Jackson.

[2] Chesnutt did not again address the Bethel audience until 10 May 1904 (see 27 May 1904 to Ogden, n. 9).

[3] The date of a recent visit to the District of Columbia to which Chesnutt refers is not known.

J. A. Hopkins

٭❀٭

September 4, 1903.

Dear Sir:—

I am in receipt of your favor of August 22nd, which came during my absence from the city, with reference to my contributing to your magazine to be entitled "The Voice of the South."[1] I regret to say that at present my engagements for the fall are such that I do not see how I can promise you anything for several months at least, and certainly not in time for your first number. As soon as I can find time, I will take up with you the question of becoming a regular contributor, if you are still in the notion. I have no doubt that such a magazine you describe will serve a useful purpose, and I wish you all success with it.

Sincerely yours,

TCU: TNF

[1] On 22 August 1903, J. A. Hopkins, general agent and assistant manager of the Negro Department, J. L. Nichols & Co., Naperville, Illinois, described the new magazine that was planned as a means of providing "the learned negro a chance to discuss vital questions concerning the progress of the race." He invited Chesnutt to "accept the position of one of our regular contributors," asking what terms he would expect and when he could furnish the first article. The name of the monthly magazine actually published was *The Voice of the Negro*.

Charles F. Thwing

٭❀٭

September 29, 1903

My dear Doctor Thwing:—

I have looked over the paper you handed me.[1] The propositions which you lay down are so fair, so just, so entirely consistent with my own view of what should be the position of civilization and enlightened Christianity in regard to this question, that I find nothing to criticise or to add. Any argument which you should base upon these propositions could scarcely fail to be all that the Negro's best friend could ask.

If I might make any suggestion at all it would be with reference to the first and fourth propositions, and then only as seeking to understand a little more closely what you mean when you say the "negro." If you mean the race in its ancient seats in Africa, that is one thing, but if you mean the variety which now lives in the United States, the point of view should be a little different. A very casual glance at any gathering of colored people, and a moment's reflection upon the personality of most men known as Negroes who have at all lifted themselves above the mass, will show that there is in the American Negro so called, a very large infusion of white blood. It is by the blood that the characteristics of a race are transmitted; hence in referring for instance to the one million colored people in the country who were classified by the census of 1900 as "mulattoes, quadroons and octoroons," that is to say, half or more than half white, and the several other millions who must possess this heritage in less degree, it is scarcely technically correct to say that they have had only a hundred years of civilization. For instance, if you were to figure it mathematically, the civilization of the mulatto would be equal to half that of a white man, plus half that of a Negro, or a total of 1050 years; that of a quadroon on the basis of your figures would be 1525 years, and so on in proportion to the blood. This of course leaves out any question of environment which may obscure or dwarf inherited characteristics, and leaves out any consideration of the claimed deterioration which results from a mixture of races.

Of course this is purely a fanciful speculation but there is a principle underlying it, and where our Southern friends insist upon reading the Negro out of the human family because of claimed inferiority of race, the Negro is entitled to every advantage which nature has given him. After all, however, the key of the whole problem is stated in your proposition that it is to be treated as a problem of the individual and not one of races. The saddest spectacle in history is that of warring races upon the same territory, and if the American people can fuse out of the diverse races which now inhabit this continent a really free people, among whom every individual, regardless of anything but his talents and his citizenship, shall find open to him every worthy career for which he may demonstrate his fitness, it will in my opinion have achieved very nearly the ultimate problem of civilization. This I am convinced was foreshadowed at the founding of this republic, and was intended to be proclaimed as a principle in our organic law by the enactment of the constitutional Amendments.

Respectfully yours,

TCU: TNF

[1] Charles F. Thwing (1853–1937) was president of Western Reserve University in Cleveland (1890–1921) and a prolific essayist on educational topics. Thwing's paper does not appear to have been published, and its title is not known.

Jesse Lawson

·❧·

October 8, 1903.

My Dear Mr. Lawson:

I beg to acknowledge receipt of your favor of October 22d, enclosing invitation to attend the conference of the National Sociological Society in November.[1] I thank you very much for the compliment and for the invitation to speak. I am not able just at this writing to state positively whether I shall be able to attend. I expect, however, to see Mr. Miller[2] here during the American Missionary Association meeting, by which time I shall know definitely whether I can come or not.[3]

Cordially yours,
CHAS. W. CHESNUTT.

Source: *How to Solve the Race Problem: The Proceedings of the Washington Conference on the Race Problem in the United States Under the Auspices of the National Sociological Society, 9–12 November 1903* [edited by Jesse Lawson], (Washington, D.C.: Beresford, Printer, 1904), 104.

[1] Jesse Lawson (1856–1927) was a teacher who became an attorney and, in 1882, began a forty-four-year career as legal examiner at the Bureau of Pensions in Washington, D.C. In 1890 he formally began his involvement in sociology as a lecturer at the lyceum of the Second Baptist Church. A former editor of *The Colored American* (1893–1897), he became a professor of sociology and ethics at Washington's Bible College and Institute for Civic and Social Betterment; he was also the founder and president of the National Sociological Society.

[2] Kelly Miller (1863–1939) was, beginning in 1890, a professor of mathematics at Howard University; he effected the addition of sociology to the curriculum in 1895, teaching in both subject areas until 1907 when he turned exclusively to sociology. At this time, he was corresponding secretary of the National Sociological Society. In 1896 Miller stood as a critic of Booker T. Washington, principally because of Washington's Cotton States Exposition speech in Atlanta (1895); by 1903 he was thoughtfully steering a middle course between Washington and radical critics of Washington such as William M. Trotter. He was also acknowledging the positive aspects of Washington's emphasis on practical education while insisting that "higher education" was necessary as well.

[3] The assurance is a peculiar one, since the three-day meeting did not begin until 20 October, two days before the Sociological Society conference commenced. Further, Miller delivered an address on the importance of education on the evening of 22 October and was thus not able to inform Lawson of Chesnutt's plans. The focus of the A.M.A. meeting was on what should be done about improving the status of African Americans; and Thomas Dixon's novel *The Leopard's Spots* was the subject of criticism. Chesnutt did not play a role in the proceedings.

Booker T. Washington

·❧·

Oct. 31, 1903.

My dear Dr. Washington:—

Replying to your favor of Oct. 26th, in which you make inquiry concerning the letter addressed to you by Rabbi Moses J. Gries of this city, (which I return,) I would say Mr. Gries is pastor of the leading Jewish congregation of Cleveland, (and a very fine man,) and that the lecture work concerning which he writes you is that of the Temple Course, which is a lecture course carried on under the auspices of the Temple congregation.[1] They present talent of various sorts; among their oratorical attractions are Thomas Dixon, Russell Conwell and others. Elbert Hubbard has lectured to them, and Mayor Sam Jones of Toledo, and other distinguished men.[2] I have appeared before them myself, but local talent cuts no great figure in such affairs.[3]

The congregation is made up of Jews, and while a great many people of other creeds patronize the lecture course, I do not imagine there are among them many persons of considerable wealth and social influence, though of course a few such people might be attracted by the presence of a distinguished speaker who could not be heard elsewhere. And Jews, you know, have many charities and philanthropic enterprises of their own, which I imagine require the bulk of their resources available for such purposes.

I read your article in the October *Atlantic*, and I agree with it perfectly so far as it preaches the doctrine of labor, patience, and industrial training.[4] I disagree with it most pointedly where, even by inference, the registration of the twenty-five teachers of Tuskegee or even the twenty-five hundred colored voters in Alabama is accepted in lieu of the 180,000 votes to which, under manhood suffrage, the negroes of Alabama would be entitled. I commend to your consideration the editorial in the *Independent* of this week, which expresses my views upon your work exactly.[5] I had the pleasure of meeting Dr. Ward,[6] the editor of the *Independent*, here a week ago, while he was in attendance upon the American Missionary Association Convention; I was invited to lunch with him at the residence of an acquaintance, but was unable to be present, and though I met him afterwards our interview was very brief, and did not touch upon your work. However, he evidently thinks upon the subject just as I do. To my mind it is nothing less than an outrage that the very off-scourings of Europe, and even of Western Asia may pour into this Union almost by the millions annually, and be endued with full citizenship after a year or two of residence, while native-born Americans, who have no interest elsewhere and probably never will have, must be led around by the nose as members of a "child race," and be told that they must meekly and patiently await the result of an evolution which may last through several thousand years, before they can stand upon the same level of citizenship which any Sicilian, or Syrian or Turk or Greek or any other sort of European proletarian may enjoy in the State of Alabama.

The article in Pott & Co.'s book[7] is the only thing I have published for a year or two, my time having been mainly absorbed in the somewhat prosaic task of earning a living along other lines; but I hope to do better in the future. I hope that you enjoyed your trip to Europe, indeed I do not see how a man of breadth and culture could do otherwise.[8] My daughter, Ethel, whom you know, has become within a month the mother of a fine boy.[9] She and the child are doing well. Please give my regards to Mrs. Washington and believe me,

Cordially yours,
Chas. W. Chesnutt.

TLS: DLC

[1] Moses J. Gries (1868–1918) was the rabbi of Tifereth Israel Temple from 1892 to 1917.

[2] Thomas Dixon (1864–1946) was a North Carolina Baptist minister and popular lecturer whose novel *The Leopard's Spots* had been recently published, to be followed by *The Clansman* (1905), *The Traitor* (1907), and much later, *The Flaming Sword* (1939)—all of which embody an anti-African American perspective having to do with the threat of "Negro dominance." Russell H. Conwell (1843–1925) was a Baptist minister, the founder and first president of Temple University, and the author of *Acres of Diamonds* (1888). A popular lecturer, he typically spoke on the relationship between Christianity and capitalism, and the need for both self-reliance and a sense of social responsibility. Elbert G. Hubbard (1856–1915) was a bohemian promoter of the Arts and Crafts Movement in America, a book publisher, the editor of *The Philistine* magazine, and a prolific essayist. Samuel M. Jones (1846–1904), an industrialist, served as the reformist mayor of Toledo, O., from 1897 to 1904.

[3] Chesnutt read "The Goophered Grapevine" at the temple on 15 November 1900.

[4] "The Fruits of Industrial Training," *Atlantic Monthly* 92 (October 1903), 453–62.

[5] The editorial observed that both African Americans and Southern whites have recently turned against Washington—the former because of his light emphasis on voting rights and heavy emphasis on industrial rather than "higher" education, and the latter because of his dining with President Roosevelt. It defends him, observing that industrial education is indeed appropriate for most and that Washington does not disparage liberal studies at Fisk University and Atlanta University; it argues that Washington is not responsible for increasingly widespread disfranchisement. "If Dr. Washington has been in fault at all it has been chiefly for his prudent reticence. He has encouraged the negroes to lie low till the storm be [passed]. . . . We should give the opposite advice. We should urge every negro to vote that can get his name on the registry" ("Booker T. Washington," *Independent* 55 [29 October 1903], 2,590–91).

[6] William Hayes Ward (1835–1916) was a linguist, specialist in Near East cultural history, teacher, and minister who joined the *Independent* in 1868, becoming its editor in 1896 and serving as honorary editor after 1913. Liberal in theology, he was well known for his passionate dedication to social amelioration.

[7] "The Disfranchisement of the Negro"; see 31 January 1903 to James Pott & Co., n. 3, and 11 August 1903 to Washington where Chesnutt expatiated upon the explicit and implicit criticisms of Washington made in this essay.

[8] Washington's tour occurred in late September through mid-October. While in Europe Washington spent most of his time in Normandy and Paris.

[9] Charles Waddell Chesnutt Williams.

Booker T. Washington

✺

March 5, 1904

Dear Dr. Washington:

Some one has sent me from Tuskegee a copy of part of the Montgomery *Advertiser* containing your letter to the *Age-Herald* concerning the shocking outrages against negroes in the South.[1] It is a timely word and I hope may make some impression. I fear however that the race has not yet touched the depths to which the present movement seems tending. The refusal of the Kentucky Legislature to adopt the disfranchising amendment scarcely offsets the destruction of Berea College.[2] The bill to disfranchise the negroes in Maryland went through with no more commotion, no more show of interest, than would have gone with a bill to repair a bridge across a creek.[3]

I have always admired your cheerful optimism, and I sincerely hope it many stand the strain upon it. But the present state of public opinion upon the race question is profoundly discouraging. I had imagined that we had reached the depths of contemptuous disregard in the case of Senator Tillman,[4] but Governor Vardaman has gone far beyond him, and Bishop Brown of Arkansas—a product of this city, by the way, or at least a former resident, and a bishop of my own church here—has out-Heroded Herod.[5] Even these things could be endured, but when Pres't Eliot of Harvard comes out with his curious speech in New York, justifying by inference the rigid caste system of the South which is the real thing that is holding the colored people down, I feel the foundations falling.[6] I am profoundly convinced that a race without political power or influence is and will continue to become even more so a race without rights. From its present attitude there seems no immediate remedy through the Supreme Court of the United States.

I hope that you do not underestimate the power of education, but these ferocious outbreaks such as that which disgraced the State of Mississippi and called forth your letter, make me wonder if we do not underestimate the power of race prejudice to obscure the finer feelings of humanity. With best wishes for your continued success, I remain,

Cordially yours,
Chas. W. Chesnutt.

TLS: DLC

[1] Washington's letter to the editor of the *Birmingham Age-Herald*, 29 February 1904, 2, was reprinted in many newspapers. It deplored the burning at the stake of three Mississippians, none of whom had been formally charged with a crime.

[2] The disfranchisement bill lost by a "close vote" according an untitled paragraph in *Cleveland Gazette*, 13 February 1904, 2. The "destruction" of Berea College as a racially integrated school became unavoidable on 4 March when the Kentucky legislature made segregated schools mandatory. Although Berea unsuccessfully appealed to the state courts (1906) and even the national Supreme Court (1908), it had to dismiss its African-American students as soon as possible because of the fines for infractions of the law.

[3] On 10 March, Washington replied that Chesnutt was "mistaken about the disfranchising bill having passed the Maryland Legislature. It may go through, but so far it has only passed one house.'" The bill did, however, pass in both houses and was then ready for presentation to Maryland's voters as an amendment of the state's constitution (see the untitled paragraph on this development, *Cleveland Gazette*, 12 March 1904, 2).

[4] See 11 August 1903 to Washington, n. 15.

[5] On 19 January, the newly elected governor of Mississippi, James K. Vardaman, delivered an inaugural address in which he declared that blacks should not participate in the government of whites; that education suitable for white children should not be afforded black children; that criminality among blacks is rampant; and that God created blacks to serve the needs of the superior race. The Right Reverend William Montgomery Brown (1855–1937) was the Episcopalian

bishop of Arkansas; Chesnutt is here alluding to statements by Brown such as those quoted in "The Week," *Nation* 78 (25 February 1904), 140–41: "I extenuate the offense of lynching, for it is the only remedy for attacks on women"; "the South is obliged to lynch because women would not appear in court"; and "lynchers are justified in the sight of God, because lynching is a form of self-protection."

[6] Charles William Eliot (1834–1926) was president of Harvard University from 1869 to 1909; in 1903 he held the influential office of president of the National Education Association. He had recently shared the podium with Washington in New York City at a meeting on industrial education sponsored by the Armstrong Association. Washington provided statistics demonstrating that most Southerners favored public education for African Americans. Eliot supported the concept of universal education but opined that both blacks and whites were in agreement regarding the undesirability of both social integration and interracial marriages ("President Eliot and Dr. Washington on the Race Question," *Outlook* 76 [20 February 1904], 439–40).

Robert C. Ogden

∽

May 27, 1904.

Dear Sir:—

Dr. Booker T. Washington has forwarded me a copy of a letter from you[1] in which you ask for information concerning one William Hannibal Thomas, the author of a libelous book called *The American Negro*, published by The Macmillan Company a few years ago.[2] Shortly after the appearance of the volume in question, I devoted some time to the investigation of Mr. Thomas's career, and had some subsequent correspondence with The Macmillan Company in reference thereto.

Having learned that Thomas had been in his youth a student of Western Theological Seminary, at Allegheny, Pa., I addressed a letter to that institution and received the following reply:

Western Theological Seminary,
Allegheny, Pennsylvania.

Mr. Chas. W. Chesnutt,
Dear Sir:—

Mr. W. H. Thomas was a student in this seminary between the years 1865–1868, and in the latter year was dismissed because of criminal intercourse with the woman whom he subsequently married. He first denied the charges, but later confessed their truth and was sent out. I have just written out a transcript from the Faculty Minutes for a lawyer in New Bedford, Mass., and mailed it to him.

Yours sincerely,
T. H. Robinson,
Pres. of Faculty.

Being informed that Thomas had been a teacher at Clark University, Atlanta, Ga., subsequent to his leaving school, and that he had got into some sort of trouble there, in connection with school funds, I traced the matter down to the criminal court in Atlanta, from which I procured a certified copy of the following record, showing that Thomas had been indicted twice in that court for crime:

The State	)	*Larceny after trust*
vs.	)	True Bill.
Will H. Thomas	)	A. M. Parker, Foreman.

Oct. 24th, 1873.

The State	)	*Forgery.*
vs.	)	True Bill.
Will H. Thomas	)	Alvin K. Seago, Foreman.

Nov. 17th, 1873.

	)
State of Georgia,	)
County of Fulton,	)

I, Arnold Broyles, Clerk of Superior Court said County, do hereby certify that the above is a true transcript of the record in the case of the "State vs. Will H. Thomas", of findings of the Grand Jury as appears on Minute Book J, pages 577 and 633, respectively, minutes of said Superior Court.

Witness my official signature and seal of said Court this April 4th, 1901.   (Signed) Arnold Broyles,
Clerk Superior Court,
Fulton Co., Ga.

These cases, I have been reliably informed, were dismissed or nolled[3] at the instance of Bishop Gilbert Haven, to avoid scandal, Bishop Haven at that time presiding over the Methodist Church there, or at least having by virtue of his office, supervision of the school.

Having been informed that some time after leaving Atlanta Thomas had moved to Newberry, S.C., where he had further trouble, I addressed a letter to one E. H. Phillips, Sr., of that town, asking information concerning Thomas, and received the following reply,

Newberry, S.C.,
April 6th, 1901.

Chas. W. Chesnutt, Esq.,
Cleveland, Ohio.
Sir:—

This is to inform you that I knew the Wm. Hannibal Thomas you refer to in your letter of recent date, that I was one of his bondsmen with Burr Raines, Henry Kennedy and Wm. Snead, and he did jump his bond leaving it for us to pay, which we had to pay. He was a justice of the peace at that time and he seized and sold a bale of cotton unlawfully, for which he was afterward arrested and convicted, though he was not present at his trial and there remains a sealed sentence in the Clerk's office in the County Court. While here he had or lived with two women. I cannot say that he was or was not married to either. He is known by such colored men as R. E. Williams, C. C. Brown, S. P. Cannon, Wm. Dawkins, Gifford Snowden.

Respectfully yours,
E. H. Phillips, Sr.

Upon receipt of the above letter I wrote to John C. Goggans, Clerk of Court at Newberry, S.C., asking information with regard to the facts, as above stated, and received the following reply:

Newberry, S.C.,
April 1st, 1901.

Chas. W. Chesnutt, Esq.,
Cleveland, Ohio.
Dear Sir:

Your favor of the 29th ult. received. Will send you certified copy of records in case State vs. Wm. Hannibal Thomas for five dollars ($5.00). Your information as to the case is correct.

Respectfully,
Jno. C. Goggans,
C.C.C.P.

Some subsequent step in Mr. Thomas's checkered career landed him in Wilberforce University, an institution for colored students at Wilberforce, Ohio. Having every reason to believe that his record at Wilberforce would be consistent with what had preceded it, I addressed a letter to the president of that university, and from him received the following reply:

Wilberforce University,
Wilberforce, Ohio,
April 4, 1901.

Mr. Charles W. Chesnutt,
Cleveland, Ohio.
My dear Sir:—

Yours of March 25th to hand and contents noted.

In reply to the same, I beg to say that about 26 or 27 years ago Mr. W. H. Thomas was connected with Wilberforce University in a financial capacity. There were some actions on his part in relation to the institution that were very questionable, much of which was not recorded. The Secretary of the College at that time is now living in Wilberforce and will give you a detailed statement of the transactions, if you choose to write to him. His address is, John A. Clark, Wilberforce, O.

Respectfully yours,
J. H. Jones,
Pres., Wilberforce University.

A letter to Dr. Clark above referred to developed the fact that the books of the university were not at that moment available for examination.

Desiring information in regard to the later life of Mr. Thomas I addressed a letter to Butler R. Wilson, a colored attorney and counsellor at law, 32 School Street, Boston, Mass., Mr. Wilson being a lawyer of character and standing and numbering among his clients Mr. Francis J. Garrison of the firm of Houghton, Mifflin and Company. Mr. Thomas was at that time and for aught I know is now a resident of Everett, a suburb of Boston.

Mr. Wilson's reply was as follows:

2/11/1901

My dear Mr. Chesnutt:–

The author of *The American Negro* published his own biography and misnamed it. It is news to me that he claims to be a lawyer. Living in Everett, just out of Boston, financially irresponsible, having posed as editor of magazine in interest of colored race, erstwhile preacher, lecturer and jack-at-all-trades except one productive of an honest living, he was years ago repudiated in this community. For years he has been struggling to get his name before the public, and here's hoping that it may be gibbetted.

Sincerely,
Butler R. Wilson.

I have heard many other damaging facts relative to the private life and character of Mr. Thomas, but I was not, for lack of time, able to trace them with any degree of definiteness.

Having collated the foregoing information, I enclosed a summary of it to the Macmillan Company with the following letter:

Cleveland O.,
April 20, 1901.

The Macmillan Company,
New York.
Dear Sirs:

Several months ago your house published a volume entitled *The American Negro*, by one William Hannibal Thomas. I do not know how fully the responsible heads of your firm were informed of the contents of this volume, but I quote a few choice morsels:—

"Soberly speaking, Negro nature is so craven and sensuous in every fiber of its being that a Negro manhood with decent respect for chaste womanhood does not exist."

"It is almost impossible to find a person of either sex, over fifteen years of age, who has not had actual carnal knowledge."

"Marriage is no barrier to illicit sexual indulgence, and both men and women maintain such relations in utter disregard of all their plighted troth. In fact, so deeply rooted in immorality are our Negro people, that they turn in aversion from any sexual relation which does not invite sensuous embraces, and seize with feverish avidity upon every opportunity that promises sexual gratification."

"Most Negro women marry young; when they do not, their spinsterhood is due either to physical disease, or sexual morbidity, or a desire for unrestrained sexual freedom."

"Marital immoralities are not confined to the poor, the ignorant and degraded among the freed people, but are equally common among those who presume to be educated and refined."

"In view of all the known facts at our command, we shall be justified in assuming that not only are ninety per cent. of the Negro women of America lascivious by instinct and in bondage to physical pleasure, but that the social degradation of freedwomen is without a parallel in modern civilization."

Another passage charges the entire youth of the race with masturbation. Still another gravely suggests castration as a punishment for criminal assault committed by Negroes.

When it is borne in mind that the term "freedman," or the word "Negro," as used in this book, is taken as meaning the whole colored race in the United States, who number some eight or nine millions, largely mixed with white blood in varying proportions, the publication in cold blood of a book, the general tenor of which is indicated by the above extracts, becomes, unless the book be truthful, nothing less than a crime, from which immunity is secured only by the fact that to libel a whole race is not an offense indictable in any court except that of public opinion. The only excuse for a libel is that it states the truth. There is no possible way of disproving such statements as the above, except by mere denial, in which event it is the word of one man against as many others as may choose to contradict him. This book has stirred up among the colored people of the country, and among some of the whites, a storm of indignant protest and denial. The issue therefore as to the truthfulness of this book, lies between William Hannibal Thomas on the one side, and practically his whole race and their friends upon the other.

I have taken it for granted that if The Macmillan Company knew in advance of its publication, that any book the value of which rests upon the character of the writer, was written by a man notoriously untruthful, without character or standing anywhere, and with a long record in the criminal courts and on the threshold of them, they would not put the sanction of their imprint upon such a publication. I can scarcely believe that your house would be a party, and the principal party—for only your name gave the book any title to consideration—to so grave an attack upon a class, merely because they are supposed to be poor and ignorant and defenseless.

I take the liberty of enclosing a statement of some facts I have collected at some trouble and expense, bearing upon the character of William Hannibal Thomas.[4] His record is so bad that no one need hesitate, for prudential reasons, to make it known.

I do not know whether the ethics of publishing ever require the withdrawal of a book from circulation or from sale, but if there was ever a case where decency and fair play demanded it, this seems to me to be one of them.

As to my own right to speak on this subject, and as to my own character and probable motives in thus addressing you, I refer you to my own books, and to the following persons:

Messrs. Houghton, Mifflin and Company,
Walter H. Page, of Doubleday, Page & Co.,
James MacArthur, with Dodd, Mead & Co.,
William Dean Howells,
Booker T. Washington,
Samuel E. Williamson, Esq., Gen. Counsel,
   N.Y.C. & H.R.R.R.

Yours very truly,
Charles W. Chesnutt.

To this letter The Macmillan Company replied as follows:

THE MACMILLAN COMPANY,
Publishers,

66 Fifth Avenue,
New York,
April 22, 1901.

Charles W. Chesnutt, Esq,
Cleveland, Ohio.
Dear Sir:—

Before replying to your letter of the 20th, may we ask you if you will be kind enough to do so and if you happen to have the memoranda by you, to give us the numbers of the pages of the book from which the extracts on pages 1 and 2 of your letter are taken?

Speaking generally, we may say that we rely upon our "readers" to inform us as to the character of books of this kind that we publish, and the book in question passed our "readers" with very considerable praise, these readers being men whose acquaintance with sociology and the study of works of this character entitles their opinions to serious consideration.

In the last resort our contracts with our authors make them responsible for the statements in books that we publish, but before taking up this aspect of the matter we should like to get the information asked for above and we should also be glad to have your permission to send a copy of your letter with its enclosure to the author of the volume in question.

Awaiting the favor of your reply, we are

Yours very truly,

THE MACMILLAN COMPANY,

George P. Brett,

President.

I replied to this letter giving the following extracts from Thomas's book, which are evidently the passages upon which Mr. Thomas Nelson Page based his article in the May *McClure's*, in which he deflowered the virginity and defamed the womanhood of an entire race:[5]

Cleveland, O.,

April 26, 1901.

The Macmillan Company,

New York.

Dear Sirs:—

Replying to your very prompt acknowledgment of my letter of the 20th, I here repeat the passages quoted in my former letter, with some additional ones, citing the pages of *The American Negro* where they may be found:—

"Soberly speaking, Negro nature is so craven and sensuous in every fiber of its being, that a Negro manhood with decent respect for chaste womanhood does not exist." (Middle of page 180.)

"Marriage is no barrier to illicit sexual indulgence, and both men and women maintain such relations in utter disregard of all their plighted troth. In fact so deeply rooted in immorality are our Negro people, that they turn in aversion from any sexual relation which does not invite sensuous embraces, and seize with feverish avidity upon every opportunity that promises sexual gratification." (Page 183, last paragraph.)

"So great is their moral putridity that it is no uncommon thing for stepfathers to have children by their step-daughters with the consent of the wife and mother of the girl. Nor do other ties of relationship interpose moral barriers, for fathers and daughters, brothers and sisters, oblivious of decent sexual restrictions, abandon themselves without attempt at self-restraint, to sexual gratification whenever the desire and opportunity arises." (Page 179, last 9 lines.)

"Most Negro women marry young: when they do not, their spinster-hood is due either to physical disease, or sexual morbidity, or a desire for unrestrained sexual freedom." (Page 184, lines 8 to 11.)

"Marital immoralities are not confined to the poor, the ignorant and degraded among the freed people, but are equally common among those who presume to be educated and refined. (Page 184, last 4 lines but 2.)

"But while the negro is thoroughly imbruted with lascivious instincts, there are many contributory causes which accelerate libidinous acts. For instance, the practice of masturbation is common among the children of both sexes, and the physical desire awakened and stimulated by organic manipulation inevitably leads to sexual intercourse. It is, therefore, al-most impossible to find a person of either sex, over fifteen years of age, who has not had actual carnal knowledge." (Page 182, last par., 183 first 3 lines.)

"For like reasons rum drinking is also universal among both sexes; and all grades of negro society, preachers and laity, seem to vie with each other in the use of intoxicating liquors." (Page 190.)

The next paragraph imputes syphilis to the whole race.

On page 191 there are some "facts" given to "substantiate" the preced-ing statements:

"For example, a noted teacher in a Southern negro school, who has charge of several hundred children, ranging in age from six to fifteen, has informed us that it was well nigh impossible to keep the boys and girls from indulging in immoral practices even while together in the school-yard, and that several instances of carnal contact had taken place despite the presence of numerous onlooking companions. This is not an excep-tional experience. Co-sexual assemblages of negroes, whether of children of adults, in the schoolroom or sanctuary, would, if the light were turned on, disclose an equal degree of moral turpitude. We have also been in-formed by a trustworthy physician, who has had an exceptionally large female practice, that he had professionally examined over 900 negro girls, ranging in age from ten to 25 years, and that out of that number only two furnished proofs of virginity, while most of the others exhib-ited."[6] (Page 192, beginning with line 11.)

Who are this "trustworthy physician" and this "noted teacher," from whom this person has received this "information"?

"We shall, however, in view of all the known facts at our command, be justified in assuming that not only are fully 90 per cent. of the negro women of America lascivious by instinct and in bondage to physical plea-sure, but that the social degradation of our freedwomen is without a par-allel in modern civilization." (P. 195, 6th to 12th lines.)

In the paragraph beginning in the middle of page 234, castration or emasculation is gravely proposed as a punishment for criminal assault.

The whole of the chapters on "Moral Lapses," "Criminal Instincts," and in almost equal measure that on "Characteristic Traits" are open to the same condemnation as the passages I have quoted. The fact that the author contradicts himself broadly here and there, and that with a certain ingenuity he has woven some incontestable facts with his mass of falsehood, which might deceive one who approached the book in ignorance of the subject or without prejudice against the negro—an almost inconceivable thing among white Americans, so thoroughly is the atmosphere impregnated with it—I say that even these contradictions and facts cannot be held to qualify the sweeping statements above quoted. As I said before, the only possible excuse for making such statements—even if that would be a sufficient excuse—would be their truthfulness. In putting your imprint upon such a book, your house makes itself sponsor for their truthfulness, or at least for the man who wrote them, upon whose candor and means of knowledge their truthfulness must finally rest.

If such a book dealt with the manners and customs of the Fiji Islanders, and were equally false and ill founded, it might do no great harm. But gravely put forward, under the imprint of a great publishing house (which has given the world some of its best literature), concerning neighbors and fellow citizens, who have already a heavy handicap of race prejudice to carry, it might easily have a far-reaching and disastrous effect. The Negro in the United States stands at present in a critical position: his status as a slave is ended; his position as a freeman has not yet been made secure. The least that could be asked, in view of these facts, is absolute fairness in any discussion which involves their position in society. I may say in this connection that this book has been excluded from the Cleveland Public Library, on the ground that it would tend to increase race prejudice, and was therefore not fit for general circulation—and as well because of the language employed and the subjects discussed. If a book is not fit for library circulation, the only other place which one can conceive it as fit for is in a scientific library, where it might properly belong if written by some reputable scientist who had made candid study of a problem in sociology. How near the person who indited this gross libel on a race meets this description may I think be gathered from the enclosure in my former letter. My point is emphasized by the fact that I have heard it claimed here that the book was written by an educated colored man, who would undoubtedly be fair toward his own race, and that therefore his statements could be taken as the truth. This was probably the argument which influenced The Macmillan Company in bringing out this book; but its fallibility as a conclusive test, or as proof that culture implies character, is illustrated by the fact that a Harvard College instructor is today on trial for murder, and that a distinguished English author recently died in obscurity and disgrace after having served a penal sentence for an unnameable crime.[7] A Negro may become a degenerate as well as a man of any other race—his author would have you believe that all the colored people belong in that category.

Referring to your question of responsibility, mentioned in your letter, of course the only kind of responsibility involved here is a moral one. I should imagine, from reading Mr. Thomas's book, together with what I have learned about his life, that he might fairly be classed as morally irresponsible. On no other hypothesis can one account for the putting forward of a great part of this volume. But in any event the chief onus would rest upon your house, for Mr. Thomas was a man absolutely obscure, who had never done anything toward the world's work which would entitle him to hearing as spokesman representing a people; so obscure, indeed, that he must have imagined that his past could be concealed, or he never would have risked the inevitable exposure. He may indeed be so far gone as not to be affected by these disclosures—which, by the way, are now being widely disseminated in the "colored" press at other hands than mine—but with the possibility remaining that he may, I have no objection to your sending him a copy of my letter and of the enclosure therein. I think perhaps I ought to leave off the last letter, as I have not asked permission of the writer to use it—I could get fifty to replace it from residents of Boston—and I would therefore prefer that you send him the copy I enclose herewith, which merely leaves off the last letter.

The fact of the matter is that the Macmillan Company have been grossly imposed upon, and have permitted themselves to be made the tool of a corrupt and conscienceless seeker after notoriety. If I can convince The Macmillan Company of this fact, I shall have accomplished the purpose of this correspondence. What steps they will take, or can take, I do not know. I am quite aware that if I were addressing a publisher of a different class, I might run the risk of still further increasing the circulation of this infamous book; in the case of your house I will take the chance. Whatever the outcome may be, I am only one of many who are determined that Mr. William Hannibal Thomas shall have nothing more out of this book than his royalties, and that its dangerous influence shall be counteracted as far as may be.

Very sincerely yours,
Chas. W. Chesnutt.

Shortly afterwards I learned that The Macmillan Company had withdrawn the book from sale and had endeavored as far as possible to withdraw it from circulation. Certainly they tried to get the copies which they could trace to the city of Cleveland.

I have given this correspondence in full, because the argument contained in it applies with equal force in many respects to what Mr. Page has said.[8] I spent several days in Washington recently,[9] and I was unable to ascertain that Mr. Page had visited any colored church or school or home, in a city of 90,000 colored people, for the purpose of ascertaining the facts concerning the condition of the race, but he had preferred to keep on his own side of the Chinese Wall of prejudice which separates the races in Washington, and to take the statements of this man Thomas at second hand. I had thought myself of replying in some quarter to what Mr. Page has said, but I am very glad if the enclosed matter will be of service to Mr. Schurz or any other widely known and influential man who will take a tilt with Mr. Page in the cause of fairness and decency.[10] The article to which I refer is contained in the May number of *McClure's Magazine*, under the title "The Negro of Today."

Permit me, though unknown to you, to take this opportunity of expressing my appreciation for your well known interest in the cause of an oppressed people. As you are aware, there are two schools of friendly thought with reference to the rights of the Negro in the South. Personally I belong to the more radical school, in which I should class such organs of thought as the *New York Evening Post* and the *Independent*; as I do not think the matter of race or racial development under our constitution and theory of government should be considered by the law at all, and I believe the political and social structure of the South to be destructive of liberty. I imagine from what I read that you belong to the more conservative school. But we are both working, you in your large influential way and I in a smaller and less conspicuous field, toward the same great end.

I had the honor of an introduction to you one day at the Lawyers' Club in New York, at which time I was the guest of Mr. W. H. Baldwin;[11] doubtless you have forgotten the circumstance.   Cordially yours,

TCU: TNF

[1] Robert Curtis Ogden (1836–1913) was manager of the Wanamaker retailing enterprise in Philadelphia and then New York City. He was a friend of Samuel C. Armstrong, the founder of the Hampton Institute in Virginia at which Booker T. Washington was educated. Inspired by Armstrong to engage in similar kinds of public service, Ogden was a trustee of Hampton (and later of Tuskegee) and devoted considerable attention to education—especially industrial education for blacks and whites—in the South. With a 24 May 1904 letter, Washington forwarded to Chesnutt Ogden's request for information on William Hannibal Thomas.

[2] William Hannibal Thomas (1843–?), *The American Negro: What He Was, What He Is, and What He May Become, A Critical and Practical Discussion* (New York: Macmillan; London: Macmillan, 1901).

[3] *Nolle prosequi* is a declaration that prosecution has been stopped; to have "nolled" is to have stopped prosecution proceedings.

[4] Chesnutt's undated, typed "statement" was entitled "In Re William Hannibal Thomas, Author of *The American Negro*." It began, "In the month of February, 1901, while traveling through the Southern States, I made inquiry from time to time with reference to the career of one William Hannibal Thomas, author of a defamatory book against the Negro race, published by the Macmillan Company." Following the letter from Butler R. Wilson, it concluded, "I have heard many other damaging facts relative to the private character of William Hannibal Thomas, and with reference

to his alleged services while a member of the South Carolina legislature. While what I have heard is entirely consistent with what is above set forth, not having the means of proof at hand I refrain from mentioning the facts in detail." Chesnutt sent a copy to Walter H. Page, who complimented him on a thorough piece of research on 6 May 1901. Washington was also a recipient; he thanked Chesnutt on 3 May 1901 for the "transcript of the evidence" concerning the character of the "execrable" Thomas.

[5] Thomas Nelson Page's reliance on *The American Negro* was not a matter for inference but explicit in the text and footnotes. Page's "The Negro: The Southerner's Problem" appeared in three parts in *McClure's Magazine*: 22 (March 1904), 548–54; 22 (April 1904), 619–26; and 23 (May 1904), 96–102. In the second part Page attributed black-white tensions to the vindictiveness, uninformed idealism, incompetence, and self-aggrandizing behavior of those associated with the Freedmen's Bureau and similar Reconstruction era expedients for altering conditions in the South from without. The third part, to which Chesnutt refers, focuses on a large number of African Americans who have regressed rather than progressed because of education; it also emphasizes the propensity for immoral and illegal behavior demonstrated by a sizeable proportion of the African-American population.

[6] Chesnutt's transcription reads thus.

[7] Oscar Wilde (1856–1900); the "unnameable crime" was consensual sexual activity with a male, illegal in England in 1895 when he was convicted and sentenced to a two-year prison term.

[8] That is, Thomas Nelson Page; see n. 5.

[9] Chesnutt lectured on "Elements of Citizenship" on 10 May for the Bethel Literary and Historical Association in the District of Columbia.

[10] Carl Schurz (1829–1906) was a politically active foe of slavery before the Civil War. During Andrew Johnson's administration he toured the South at the President's request, reporting on conditions there and unsuccessfully recommending strict supervision of the states' political and economic restructuring. After serving as secretary of the interior in Hayes' administration he began a long-term association with the *New York Evening Post*—whose editorials on race problems reflected Chesnutt's views, as he explains below—and wrote for other periodicals as well. Schurz, in short, was sympathetic to the African American and had immediate access to the print medium; Chesnutt is here threatening to expose Macmillan in his references to Schurz and, below, the *New York Evening Post*. Another reason for Chesnutt's allusion to Schurz is that Page and he were already engaged in debate. Two months before Page's series of articles on "The Negro" in *McClure's* began, Schurz's "Can the South Solve the Negro Problem?" appeared (*McClure's* 22 [January 1904], 259–75). Page's articles were seen as a response to Schurz's by *Current Literature*: "Carl Schurz on the Negro Crisis" 36 (March 1904), 302–4, was followed by "Mr. Page's Reply to Mr. Schurz" 36 (May 1904), 526–28. What Chesnutt does not allude to is the fact that Schurz differed radically from Chesnutt in his point of view on the franchise: Schurz was, in his *McClure's* article, of the opinion that voting rights should not have been extended to all African Americans but only those who were educationally qualified.

[11] William Henry Baldwin (1863–1905) was an executive associated with several railroad companies. When developing the Southern Railway in the 1890s he became interested in improving the condition of African Americans, was an enthusiastic supporter of Booker T. Washington, and served as a Tuskegee trustee beginning in 1897.

Booker T. Washington

◆

June 8, 1904.

Dear Dr. Washington:—

Replying to your favor of recent date, enclosing Mr. Ogden's letter, which I return herewith, I am glad to see that he is following up the clues concerning Mr. Thomas. He has the means, and if he has the inclination he can doubtless find out all about that interesting if not admirable person.

I note and appreciate what you say concerning my Washington address.[1] I also note, on looking over Mr. Ogden's letter, that you are bringing your influence and that of your friends to bear directly upon problems of the kind which to most Northern men are merely abstract matters.

I really do not know what can be done in the matter of Thomas's book. Publishers seem to be out for the money and to have very little concern about how they get it. As long as the public eagerly welcome matter defamatory of the Negro and are not at all eager for matter to his credit, I presume the publishers will supply them with what they wish. I hope to see the time when there will be a sufficient number of colored men of influence and standing to make it unprofitable to slight or abuse the race. When that time comes colored people will receive not only their rights, but the courtesies due to them as well as to other citizens.

Sincerely yours,

Chas. W. Chesnutt

TLS: DLC

[1] Chesnutt had written on 28 May (DLC), expressing concern about what Washington may have heard regarding the lecture he delivered in the District of Columbia (see 27 May 1904 to Ogden, n. 9): "I have seen in some newspaper since, the statement that I had attacked you in my utterances. The only reference which I made to you was I think entirely complimentary, and if our points of view would conflict at all, that is of course a matter for legitimate argument." Washington replied on 31 May, informing him that he was not upset when someone disagreed with him in the "high-toned, gentlemanly way" that Chesnutt did. Chesnutt had apparently assumed that Washington read "Chesnutt Vs. Washington," *Cleveland Gazette*, 21 May 1904, 1. The *Gazette's* editor, Harry C. Smith, had seized the opportunity to continue his relentless attacks on Washington: the subtitle of the report on Chesnutt's lecture read "the Well-Known Author Assails Some of Booker's Positions." The description of the lecture that followed, however, did not indicate that Chesnutt had, in fact, done so; rather, Chesnutt's animus was directed against Thomas Nelson Page.

PART VI
THE QUEST RENEWED,
1904–1905

✧

Argumentative Art for an
Indifferent Readership

✧

*I have almost decided to foreswear the
race problem stories, but I should like to write
a good one which would be widely read,
before I quit.*

Walter Hines Page

᠂◦᠂

June 29, 1904.

My Dear Mr. Page:—

I received your letter, which gave me much pleasure, concerning my story "The Colonel's Dream."[1] I have always considered you the best judge I knew of a Southern story of that sort, because in addition to the other necessary qualities, you combine a sympathetic knowledge of the South and a freedom from prejudice which are rarely found together. So much by way of appreciation of your kind words.

As to the story, it was hardly meant for more than an elongated short story. But it is not unlikely that I can enlarge the structure, giving it more plot and more characters, as well as more words—more bones as well as more flesh.[2] The general theme is encyclopedic, and I ought to be able to get together a full sized novel out of it. I am only apprehensive of the didactic side, to which the theme gives constant temptation; for I realize that preaching is not art,[3] and as a matter of personal taste I shrink from the sordid and brutal, often unconsciously brutal side of Southern life—as I should from the shady side of any other life.[4] If I can handle some of these things in a broad and suggestive way, without disgusting detail—if I could follow even afar off the Russian novelists of the past generation, who made so clear the condition of a debased peasantry in their own land, I might write a great book. As it is, even with my limited powers, there are several threads of the story which might be developed along this line. Then, too, I could give the colonel a woman friend at the North, a woman of wealth, social standing and fine character, who was interested in his little boy and him, far more than the colonel appreciated, but whom the colonel had lost sight of during his Southern interlude. It would add an element of heartbreaking pathos to have him go back to her and leave Miss Clara; but if I could give him this and other motives for returning to his former life, it would avoid undue emphasis upon the episode of old Peter's digging up. The sand hills tragedy in the background might be elaborated with delicacy, and I might give lazy, long legged Ben Dudley a rival.[5]

Send me the MS. back, and I will see what I can do with it. When I have thought it all out I will let you know my plan of development, or come down and talk it over with you.

I know you are a publisher and in business to make money, but I like to think that you are fundamentally in sympathy with my views on most Southern subjects, and for that reason I shall set a high value on your suggestions. I have not forgotten that the most popular of my novels up to date—at least the one which people speak oftenest to me about, The House Behind the Cedars, was rewritten by me in pursuance of a suggestion of yours similar to that which you make concerning this story.[6] I have almost decided to foreswear the race problem stories, but I should like to write a good one which would be widely read, before I quit.

Cordially yours,

TCU: TNF

[1] Since 20 March 1902 when he wrote to George H. Mifflin, Chesnutt's correspondence with Houghton, Mifflin appears to have consisted mainly of royalty checks sent to him and the firm's comments on the disappointing sale of *Marrow*. Chesnutt, however, was working on a new manuscript, "The Colonel's Dream," and Houghton, Mifflin acknowledged receipt of it on 26 April 1904. Garrison's letter to Chesnutt, dated 12 May, reveals that "Dream" was preceded by another, unnamed manuscript as well. Like this other manuscript, "Dream" was declined by Garrison: "If we could follow our wish and impulse, we should like to publish the book, but we cannot shut our eyes to the fact that the public has failed to respond adequately to your other admirable work in this line, and that we have netted a large aggregate loss on the several volumes of which we had such hopes, and on which we expended far more for advertising than the results justified." The manuscript was then sent to Page, who apologized on 24 June 1904 for the delay in reporting on it. He had been away on two trips made over the previous two months.

[2] On 24 June, Page rejected the manuscript of "Dream" after praising Chesnutt's use of "old Fayetteville" as the setting and presentation of "the race problem in a most vivid and pathetic way": "It is not long enough nor full enough; in fact, it contains hardly more than the one telling and touching incident of the digging up of Old Peter's body" (see n. 4). He termed it an elongated short story. Chesnutt is here responding to Page's encouragement, for his mentor also suggested that he expand it into a full-scale novel: "Can you give it more body? Make it of larger structure; introduce, if necessary, more characters, and round it out to something like a good hundred thousand words able bodied novel? I hope you can. If the subject admit of this treatment and you are in a mood to do it, I should be very proud indeed to publish it for you." On 1 July, he made another suggestion as he returned the manuscript to Chesnutt: "Don't work the machinery of the alleged hidden treasure too hard."

[3] Chesnutt had been patently didactic in *The Wife of His Youth* and *The House Behind the Cedars*; only *The Conjure Woman* could have been described as either lightly didactic in its implications or free from an aggressively moralistic tone. Chesnutt here displays his sensitivity to negative reactions to his most recent novel, *The Marrow of Tradition*, and to Page's possible awareness of its modest sales—in effect assuring Page that the new work would not be a tract.

[4] Chesnutt is apparently referring to the sensational episode involving the corpse of his hero's saintly one-time slave, "old Peter." When Colonel French inters him in a white cemetery, his coffin is exhumed and carried to the piazza of the Colonel's house, where he finds it in the morning with a note indicating that some local Caucasians will not permit such a violation of sacred ground.

[5] The manuscript Page read appears to have dealt only with Colonel French, accompanied by his motherless son, returning from New York City to North Carolina; attempting to revive his economically depressed hometown and to thwart race prejudice; experiencing the sensational exhumation of "old Peter," and turning his back on the incorrigible South to return to the better world in the North. As indicated here, he soon added the Northern lady who cares for the Colonel, Mrs. Jerviss; and he gave Ben Dudley a rival for the hand of Graciella, for she becomes infatuated with the Colonel. He did not, however, have the Colonel leave Clara (who became Laura Treadwell) for Mrs. Jerviss: Laura, who cannot accompany him to the North because she must take care of her elderly mother, instead appears to convince the Colonel that he never really did love her. Thus, the treatment of "old Peter" by local racists remained the dramatic event precipitating the hero's rejection of the hopelessly evil, unredeemable South.

[6] By the end of 1904, only 3,244 copies of *House* had been sold; *Marrow* was only slightly more successful in that 3,387 were sold.

Judson W. Lyons

✑

July 22, 1904

My dear Mr. Lyons:—

One of our prominent Republicans in this city, who wishes to use the information during the approaching campaign, asked me to find out for him why John Sharp Williams was elected to the 55th Congress from the fifth district of Mississippi, comprising twelve counties, by a vote of 9,385 votes to 17 for his opponent, J. P. Hill.[1] Was it merely the ordinary operation of the disfranchising laws of Mississippi, or were there special circumstances which account for the farcical Republican vote?[2] Perhaps I ought to address myself to Mr. Hill, but as I do not know his address, if you can give it to me or refer me to some one who can furnish the information, I shall be obliged to you.[3] I gather from the census that there were about 36,000 colored males of voting age in that district at the time of Mr. Williams's return to Congress.

I trust that you are enduring life comfortably and with your usual cheerful philosophy during the hot weather.　　　　　　　　Cordially yours,

TCU: TNF

[1] Judson Whitlocke Lyons (1858–1924) studied law at Howard University and was admitted to the bar in 1884, practicing in Augusta, Ga. He was active in Georgia Republican politics, was appointed Register of the Treasury by President McKinley in 1899, and served in that office until 1906. The chairman of the Committee on Politics of the National Sociological Society, he spoke at its Washington Conference on "The Race Problem in the United States," 9–12 November 1903, which Chesnutt did not attend (see 8 October 1903 to Lawson).

John Sharp Williams (1854–1932) was a Democrat who served in the U.S. House of Representatives from 1893 to 1909 and in the U.S. Senate from 1911 to 1923.

[2] On 26 July 1904, Lyons opined that "voters there have, by reason of juggling with the State election laws, become a vanishing quantity. . . . I do not know anything about Mr. Hill and indeed do not know that I ever heard his name before. I am satisfied, however, that the explanation of the reduction of his constituency is the harsh un-American election laws . . . in Mississippi."

[3] Lyons directed Chesnutt to Rev. E. W. Lampton of the District of Columbia, who gave him Hill's address in Meridian, Miss. On 20 August, Chesnutt asked Hill if there were "any special circumstances attending the election" for the 57th Congress: "Were only 17 men registered, or did only 17 vote, or were the votes merely thrown aside"? A reply from Hill has not been located.

T. Thomas Fortune

✑

September 5, 1904.

My dear Mr. Fortune:—

I have just been reading with interest and profit your article on "The Voteless Citizen" in the Voice of the Negro for September.[1] Not the least interesting part is where you quote at length from my article on "Disfranchisement" in *The Negro Problem* and credit the same, with a very fine compliment, to Mr. Wilford H. Smith.[2] I appreciate the compliment, so far as it applies to the article;—however much it may be deserved, so far as Mr. Smith is concerned, he is not entitled to it for that particular bit of writing, over which I worked too long to see, with perfect equanimity, a compliment from so competent a critic as yourself go to some other gentleman.[3]

With regards,

Sincerely yours,

Chas. W. Chesnutt.

TLS (file copy): TNF

[1] "The Voteless Citizen," *The Voice of the Negro* 1 (September 1904), 397–402. (This article was immediately preceded by Chesnutt's "Peonage, or the New Slavery," 394–97.)

[2] Fortune's misattribution of two of Chesnutt's paragraphs appeared on p. 401 of his article. The first paragraph began "These restrictions fall into three groups . . ." and ended "which must precede voting" (*The Negro Problem*, 83–84). The second paragraph began "But the first group, by its own force . . ." and ended "not subject to any of the other restrictions" (84–85). Wilford H. Smith (1863–?), a New York real estate agent and Booker T. Washington's lawyer, was the author of "The Negro and the Law" in *The Negro Problem*, 127–59; Chesnutt was the author of the essay Fortune quoted, "The Disfranchisement of the Negro," 79–124 (see 31 January 1903 to James Pott & Company, n. 3).

[3] Fortune apologized for the misattribution on 12 September, also asking Chesnutt to write for $5.00 per article for *New York Age* "on any phase of the campaign that will be helpful to the Republican ticket." By 21 September, Fortune received an unlocated letter of 19 September with the article by Chesnutt; it appeared in a no longer extant issue of *Age* and was reprinted under the title "For Roosevelt" in the *Cleveland Gazette*, 22 October 1904, 1. Therein, Chesnutt declared it inconceivable that "any Negro voter in the United States" would not vote for Theodore Roosevelt; only an "ingrate and a fool" would vote for Democrats. On 29 September Fortune also wrote, "I hope to see soon in a book the 100000 words you wrote in the summer time." Chesnutt had apparently told him about *The Colonel's Dream*; and Fortune offered him $20.00 for "a *political love story*" of 3,000 words to appear in three parts, "based on the Wilmington damnation . . . giving Editor Josephus Daniels, Chairman Simmons & Ex Congressman Waddell their place of infamy." Daniels was the editor of the Raleigh, N.C., *News & Observer*; Furnifold M. Simmons was the chairman of the executive committee of the North Carolina Democrat party in 1898; and Alfred M. Waddell became the mayor of Wilmington in 1898. All were key figures in the election that precipitated the 1898 race riot in Wilmington.

Robert Anderson

⋅◇⋅

September 18, 1904.

Dear Sir:—

Replying to your letter of recent date, asking me for a definition of what the Negro problem is, I should say that it is a continuing problem which assumes some new stage every now and then, and will probably continue to vex us as long as the Negro in this country exists in the public consciousness as something distinct from the ordinary citizen, and whose rights, privileges and opportunities are to be measured by some different standard from that applied to the rest of the community.[1]

Its first political phase was the abolition of the slave trade; then the question of the morality of slavery was raised by the abolitionists; then came the economic question of the competition of slave and free labor; then, in the turmoil of the Civil War came the question of the abolition of slavery; then Andrew Johnson's policy of reorganizing the Southern States, which threatened to prove so disastrous to the free people that it was replaced by the reconstruction as we know it, of which there are varying opinions, the South claiming it to have been disastrous to them and in view of subsequent events, to the Negro as well; while others who are quite as well informed, for instance, Mr. Carl Schurz (in McClure's Magazine for January, 1904), maintains that it was the best thing that could be done under the circumstances, and that its failure was not entirely due to the Negroes.[2] Then came the movement for disfranchisement and the relegation of the Negro, by statute in the Southern States, to a position of civil and political inferiority, emphasized by various proscriptive laws.

The Negro question which it seems should concern good citizens today is, how shall American public opinion be brought around to the point where it will grant to people of Negro descent, the rights and immunities which are secured to them by the Constitution of the United States? It is difficult to conceive of a free democracy in which there is any recognition by law of caste, whether founded on race, religion or, as in the older aristocracies, blood or descent. And this problem involves the education of the Negro to a point where he can assert by all fair and proper means his claim to equal rights, and the education of the whole people to the point where they will see that the prosperity, peace and progress of the nation are bound up in the ideal of the rights of man as laid down in the social compact.

The Negro question in the South as it is at present in its most acute form, is how can the white people be induced to do justly by the Negro; how can lynching be suppressed? By a strict and impartial enforcement of law. How can crime be suppressed? Certainly not by cruel and unusual punishments inflicted by mobs, but by the fostering of education and the general spread of enlightenment. The subject is too long for a letter; it would take a volume to even define it. The Negro question will not be even placed in the way of peaceful solution until the Southern States, as those of the North have done already, freely concede the equality of the citizen before the law, and leave questions of social intercourse and race integrity to the domain of private life and personal opinion, where they properly belong. There can be but one citizenship in a free country; if the laws make or recognize any distinctions, then that country is not free.   Yours very truly,

TCU: TNF

[1] Robert Anderson, of Landsdowne, Pa., wrote Chesnutt on 3 September 1904 that he would be presenting a paper on "The Negro Problem" to a club to which he belonged, and he asked Chesnutt to give him "a definition of what the Negro Problem is." He also replied to Chesnutt's invitation to speak at a meeting of the Grand Army of the Republic veterans in Cleveland. Chesnutt was chairperson of the "Colored Troops" committee.

[2] See 27 May 1904 to Ogden, n. 10.

Walter Hines Page

‹◯›

September 26, 1904.

My dear Mr. Page:—

I send you by express today, under another cover, the revised and enlarged manuscript of "The Colonel's Dream," and hope it will meet with your approval in its present shape. It is not quite 100,000 words but is very close up in that neighborhood.[1]

I have no pride of opinion in regard to these Southern stories which I persist in trying to write. I am quite aware that they can accomplish no good purpose unless they are read, and I am entirely willing to accept any suggestions from you that may improve the story from the standpoint of the publisher, and from your own standpoint as one who knows the subject even better than I do. I have not put in any chapter headings or any foreword,[2] but if it is thought advisable, in case you find the story available in its present shape, I shall be glad to supply them.[3]

Very sincerely yours,

TCU: TNF

[1] In three months, Chesnutt had changed his "elongated short story" into a novel; see 29 June 1904 to Page.

[2] Although Chesnutt did not add a foreword, he did much later add a dedication accepted for inclusion by Page on 26 January 1905. Despite his concern in his previous letter to Page about the need to minimize the didactic in his writing, the dedication made it clear that this too was a "novel with a purpose": "To the great number of those who are seeking, in whatever manner or degree, from near at hand or far away, to bring the forces of enlightenment to bear upon the vexed problems which harass the South, this volume is inscribed, with the hope that it may continue to the same good end."

[3] On the stationery of a New York City hotel, the Everett House, Page wrote to Chesnutt (then in New York), "I came by to tell you—that we'll be glad to publish 'The Colonel's Dream.'" This note dated "Thursday" was accompanied by a printed invitation to an "informal house warming" at the Doubleday, Page offices on 17 November 1904 (a Thursday). With a 19 November 1904 cover letter, the undated contract for *The Colonel's Dream* sent to Chesnutt in Cleveland for his signature specified a lower royalty rate than Houghton, Mifflin had typically given him: 10 percent of the retail price of the first 2,500 copies; 12½ percent of the next 1,500; and 15 percent of all copies above 4,000. The manuscript was returned to Chesnutt, who most likely revised it further since, on 12 January 1905, he received a reminder: "We are waiting for your MS." On 18 January, Chesnutt was asked to provide a list of the principal characters and, if there was to be one, a dedication.

Booker T. Washington

ɔ·

October 27, 1904.

My dear Mr. Washington:—

As I learn that you are to be in this city on January 11th, to lecture in the Temple Course, I should consider it an honor if you could make my house your stopping place as long as you are in the city.[1]

One of my friends, Mr. Virgil P. Kline, at the head of one of the largest law firms of the city, and counsel for the Standard Oil Company and Mr. Rockefeller, is very desirous of meeting you, and knowing of our acquaintance has asked me to extend to you an invitation to dine with him during your stay in the city.[2] He has a beautiful home and influential acquaintance, and although a Democrat (of the Gold variety),[3] is profoundly interested in the race problem. If your engagements will permit, I am sure you would enjoy meeting him.

Mrs. Washington passed through the city recently on her way to Oberlin and called at the house where we were living when you were last here; but as we had moved several months before, to a point some distance from that place her stay was not long enough to enable her to reach us. Mrs. Chesnutt and I regret very much that she missed us and hope that we may have the pleasure of seeing her on some other occasion.

Cordially yours,
Chas. W. Chesnutt.

TLS: DLC

[1] On 31 October, Washington thanked Chesnutt for the asking him to stay in his home but declined the pleasure. "I am compelled to have my stenographer with me and have to do so much official work that I find it nearly impossible to avoid staying at a hotel as it is the best place for this kind of work."

[2] Washington arrived on 11 January; attended the next day a banquet given by the Cleveland Council on Sociology and then lectured at the Rabbi Gries' temple. On the 13th he addressed the pupils of Central High School where Helen Chesnutt taught, visited the home of Kline for tea, and was the honored guest at a banquet given by two women's organizations, The Minerva Reading and Friday Study clubs. Among the speeches made was one by Chesnutt entitled "The Literary World." See the heated criticism of Washington's speech at the Council of Sociology banquet, during which he told "four 'nigger' stories," in "'Nigger' Stories!" *Cleveland Gazette*, 21 January 1905, 1.

[3] That is, Kline is a conservative Democrat, not to be confused with radicals who had in recent years campaigned for a monetary standard based upon silver rather than gold.

Horace Traubel

ɔ·

December 22, 1904.

My dear Mr. Traubel:—

Replying to your recent letter with reference to Negro music in the South,[1] I shall be very glad to cooperate with Mr. von Sternberg,[2] if the matter is gone into. A great deal of work has been done along this line by the people at

Hampton Institute, at Hampton, Va., and many hundreds of "Spirituals" have been printed in the pages of the *Southern Workman*, which is the Institute magazine.

The late Anton Dvořák[3] also had a theory that Southern Negro melodies were the only indigenous American music and destined to furnish motives for future compositions of a high order; indeed, I think he included some of them in an opera and others of his works. Mr. Harry Burleigh, a colored baritone choir and concert singer in New York, and an artist of no mean ability,[4] was a pupil of Dvořák and would know a great deal about his investigations and records in that field. Mr. Samuel Coleridge Taylor, of London, England, who was in this country a few weeks ago, and whom it was my pleasure to hear conduct a choral society in Washington in the performance of his musical the *Hiawatha* trilogy, has also set a number of Negro melodies to music and is working on others now for Ditson and Company of Boston.[5] Doubtless there are others, who know more about music than I do, who have made investigations in this field.

As I have said, I should be very glad to aid Mr. von Sternberg in any way that I can in the way of information, or if it came to the point, the actual collection of such melodies. I should be pleased to hear of any further development in the matter.   Sincerely yours,

TCU: TNF

[1] Horace Traubel (1858–1919) was founder and editor of *The Conservator* (1890–1919), a Philadelphia monthly magazine, and a close friend of the late Walt Whitman.

[2] Constantin Ivanovich von Sternberg (1852–1924) was a Russian-born pianist, composer, and teacher.

[3] Antonin Dvořák (1841–1904), a Bohemian-born composer, was best known for his Symphony No. 5, which he subtitled *From the New World* (1893). In 1892 Dvořák accepted the position of director of the National Conservatory of Music in New York. It was during this time that he became inspired by American folk idioms, especially the songs of African Americans and the music of Native Americans.

[4] Harry T. Burleigh (1866–1949) was an African-American baritone and composer of folk songs and spirituals. At this time, Burleigh was a soloist in St. George's Protestant Episcopal Church and a member of the choir at Temple Emmanu-el, both in New York. While Burleigh was a student of Dvořák's at the National Conservatory of Music in New York, he introduced his teacher to the African-American songs that in part inspired the *New World* symphony.

[5] Samuel Coleridge-Taylor (1875–1912) was a London-born composer and violinist already famous for his *Hiawatha* oratorio. In the District of Columbia's Convention Hall, he conducted performances on 16 November (*Hiawatha*) and 17 November ("Choral Ballads and Other Selections"). On 20 November he attended a "song service" in his honor at the Metropolitan A.M.E. Church; and on 21 November the 15th Street Presbyterian Church presented a concert and reception for him.

Houghton, Mifflin & Co.

⌒

March 6, 1905

Dear Sirs:—

I beg to acknowledge receipt of statement of royalties on my books for the six months from August 31, 1904, to February 28, 1905, showing $13.70 royalties, of which $8.37 was credited on my account with you and check for the balance $5.33, enclosed to me, for which I thank you. I trust the publication of my book in the fall will start up the sale of these a little more actively.

Yours sincerely,
Chas. W. Chesnutt.

TLS: MH

Virgil P. Kline

⌒

March 19, 1905.

My dear Mr. Kline:—

Recurring to our recent conversation about my son, Edwin J. Chesnutt, and my request that you use your friendly interests in his behalf, I ought to say that he was 21 years of age last September; that he has been a student at Harvard for the past three years, having entered the Sophomore class from a preparatory school in 1902, and will graduate next June. In his course he has given considerable attention to French and Spanish with a view to their use in a practical way; and while he probably has no great conversational facility in them, he has laid the necessary foundation. I would like to have him secure employment, if he can, in some civilized country where the color line does not run; this for reasons which we have talked over; for instance, some healthful part of Latin America, like say the Argentine Republic or Southern Brazil, though he would doubtless go wherever he might be assigned. If we could command your friendly offices with the Standard Oil Company with its world-wide ramifications, they would be more likely than any other company I can think of to be able to find a place for him where he might make himself useful in a foreign country and at the same time remain in touch, through an American institution—I guess the Standard ranks in that category—with his own country and his own people. I need not say how much my family and I would appreciate any interest you might feel disposed to bring to bear in his behalf.

Sincerely yours,
Chas. W. Chesnutt

TLS (file copy): TNF

Edwin J. Chesnutt

 ✑

March 20, 1905.

My dear Edwin,

I am keeping you in mind at this end of the line and doing what I can to promote your interests. I enclose you a copy of a letter which I have written to Mr. Kline as a means of getting this matter in proper shape before the proper people. Mr. Kline will endorse it for himself and the other gentlemen with whom he has spoken, and it will then go to the officer who has charge of the employment of men. I will let you know as further developments occur. Meantime, pursue the even tenor of your way. Attend strictly to business, learn all you can, and you will come out all right, in this matter or elsewhere.

The family are all well, and I hope this will find you in good shape. I shall be down that way in May, at which time I shall give you a thorough investigation; I have no doubts you will be able to stand it, though, if you don't, I could only lock the stable door after the horse has been stolen. You will observe I have had a great deal of confidence in your good sense and ability to take care of yourself.[1]

Your affectionate father,

TCU: TNF

[1] After he was graduated from Harvard in 1905, Edwin lived in Europe, learned shorthand, and was employed by his father, had a position at Tuskegee, and became a dentist in 1915.

Doubleday, Page & Co.

 ✑

March 29, 1905.

Dear Sirs:—

I am in receipt of your letter of March 27th, with reference to the corrections in proofs of *The Colonel's Dream*. Your complaint seems entirely reasonable, and I do not consider it at all small. I quite realize that the publishing end of a book is of vital consequence, though I confess this was borne in upon me more forcibly since I received your letter. I had really gone on making the corrections without any thought of expense.[1]

I have struck out a great many of the changes, leaving only those which I think materially improve the story. I had corrected the second batch of proof-sheets before receiving your letter, and I have also gone over these as well as those returned by you, with the same end in view. I think the changes that are left are justified from the literary point of view, and I hope you will not find them too extreme. From the middle of the book on they will be slight. I notice that I am limited by our contract to ten per cent. of the original cost of composition, and while I have no desire whatever to use that, but would much rather keep within it, if the corrections exceed the margin I will cheerfully make them good either in my account or by a direct remittance. I always try to be reasonable and quite agree with your thoughtful suggestion that checks should go to authors (and I would include publishers), instead of to the robber printers who are sucking our life blood.[2]

I trust that the changes I have made, with the restraint which I shall exercise on the balance of the proofs, will make up for my past recklessness.

Permit me to compliment your editorial reader "L. L." on the quality of his or her suggestions.[3] I accepted them because they were always an improvement, except in one or two instances where my meaning had not quite been grasped.

I am returning the first 65 galleys by this mail. While we are on the subject, do you think that the chances of this novel, and the element of expense, would justify an illustration or two?[4] If you think it would and that such an addition would pay for itself in enhancing the volume's attractiveness, I should like to have it, although of course I will be governed by your views in the matter.

I have had a very good photograph made, a copy of which I will forward to Mr. Marcosson in a few days, and will get up some stories which can be used for advertising purposes.[5] I suppose he will be taking this up before long.

Yours very truly,

TCU: TNF

[1] Chesnutt was effectively rewriting the novel in proof. Postcards from Doubleday, Page indicate that galley proof for *The Colonel's Dream* was sent to Chesnutt thus: galleys 1–27 on 13 March; and galleys 83 to 108 on 20 March. The others were apparently forwarded at some time between these dates. Chesnutt altered the text in the first set of galleys to such an extent that Henry W. Lanier wrote on 27 March that the firm was "somewhat distressed" that the cost of Chesnutt's revisions and corrections would probably be "as much as the complete original typesetting." He was conciliatory in tone, hoping that he did not seem "small minded"; but he closed by indicating that the galleys were being returned to Chesnutt under separate cover for his further consideration in light of the fact that he would be responsible for additional charges.

[2] Lanier had written that "we think the American printer, under the terms of the International Copyright Act, is doing pretty well anyhow without these bonuses," that is, the fee charged for resetting type.

[3] The editor appears to have been Lanier, who initialed his letters to Chesnutt. The "H" of "H L" is malformed and interpretable as an "L."

[4] Lanier reported on 31 March that "our final decision was against them."

[5] Isaac F. Marcosson (1877–1961) was the author of a literary column for the Louisville *Times* before he joined the Doubleday firm in 1903 to work on its magazine *World's Work*. Appreciative of novelists with a penchant for social criticism such as Frank Norris, David Graham Phillips, James Lane Allen, and Ellen Glasgow, he soon enjoyed his greatest promotional triumph when handling for Doubleday, Page the marketing of Upton Sinclair's classic muckraking novel, *The Jungle* (1906).

W. Walter Sampson

◡

April 10, 1905.

My dear Mr. Sampson:—

I was duly in receipt of your letter of March 30th, and wish to thank you and Mrs. Sampson very much for your cordial tender of hospitality.[1] I have not made any arrangements yet with reference to my stay in Boston, nor have I yet determined how long I shall be in the city; and my family are already under so many obligations to you for hospitality that it seems almost like an imposition for me to stop at your house.

With reference to giving you a certain evening, my engagement in Boston is on Monday, May 22nd.[2] If I gave you Thursday, the 18th, I should have to remain in Boston in order to meet my engagement, five days, which with coming and going would keep me away from home for a week; and the same would be true if I accepted your invitation for the 25th. This may be a pleasant little scheme on your part to keep me in Boston that long and I may be able to make my plans fall in with it, and will cheerfully do so if I can. It is, however, about six weeks yet before the time, and I trust you will not consider me unappreciative if I ask you to hold the invitation open for a week or two, with the understanding that I shall give you one evening while I am there, if my time there will meet your convenience, and that I will let you know about accepting your more prolonged hospitality.

Mrs. Chesnutt and the family are well, and join me in cordial regards to yourself and Mrs. Sampson. Trusting that this may find you in good health and spirits, I remain, with cordial appreciation,

Sincerely yours,

TCU: TNF

[1] W. Walter Sampson appears to have been a relative; see 21 October 1899 to Love, n. 2.

[2] As early as 3 April 1901, shortly after the Boston Historical and Literary Society was formed, William M. Trotter invited Chesnutt to help "improve and quicken the intellectual life of the Colored people of Boston" by appearing before its membership. Although Chesnutt stayed with the Sampsons when in the Boston area, he postponed his speaking date until 25 June so that he might attend his son Edwin's graduation from Harvard University. The lecture that he gave was subsequently revised and published as "Race Prejudice: Its Causes and Its Cure," *Alexander's Magazine* 1 (July 1905), 21–26. He may have also given a lecture or a reading in Providence, R.I.; an undated letter, written in late January or early February to W. P. N. Freeman of Providence, when Chesnutt was still planning to speak before the Society on 22 May, proposed possible dates for an appearance.

Hugh M. Browne

⟨◦⟩

June 2, 1905.

My Dear Mr. Browne:—

I am in receipt of your letter in reply to my letter of inquiry with regard to the Committee of Twelve.[1] Of my interest in the subject and my approval of the objects of the Committee, there is no manner of doubt, and with a personnel including men whose views vary so widely as do the views of some of those on the committee, there is probably room for every phase of thought and opinion in regard to the race question. I think, however, that we are all united, in the wish to overcome as far as may be the prejudice against the colored people and to promote good feeling so far as that is possible without the sacrifice of vital principles. I shall be glad to co-operate with the Committee and to do what I can to further its ends.   Cordially yours,

TCU: TNF

[1] Hugh M. Browne was secretary of The Committee of Twelve. He first contacted Chesnutt in a letter of 28 July 1904 in which he outlined the goals, rules, and resolutions of the committee. Browne wrote to Chesnutt on 12 April 1905 that the committee, which, according to its letterhead, was organized "For the Advancement of the Interests of the Negro Race," had unanimously elected him to fill a vacancy on the committee. He did not state that this vacancy resulted from the resignation of Du Bois. Other members of the committee included Booker T. Washington, Hugh M. Browne, Charles E. Bentley, E. C. Morris, Charles W. Anderson, Archibald H. Grimké, George M. Clinton, Kelly Miller, J. W. E. Bowen, T. Thomas Fortune, and H. T. Keating.

J. Edward Nash

⟨◦⟩

August 14, 1905.

My dear Sir:—

I am in receipt of your favor of August 3rd, and absence from the city has prevented my answering it sooner.

I shall be glad to address your Christian Culture Congress, upon certain conditions. As you must be aware, the preparation and delivery of an address which is worth hearing involves time and the expenditure of mental and physical energy. If I were engaged in the promotion of some special work or institution, from which I gained my livelihood, as do most of our public men, I would come up there and talk to you for my traveling expenses. But I am engaged in pursuits where my time and energy are required to earn a livelihood, and what I devote to other pursuits is simply that much taken out of my capital. I therefore feel that in justice to myself I should make a charge for my services. I do not imagine, however, that a Christian Culture Congress is an institution from which one could demand a very large fee, and I would therefore suggest that for $25.00 and my steamboat fare, I would come up Saturday night, and speak to you on Sunday. I could then return to Cleveland, if my affairs required it, by the Sunday night boat.

I am going away to-morrow to be gone for ten days or two weeks. I shall be back, however, before September 3rd, and in time to come to Buffalo and address you on that date. In case you should decide to have me come, upon what subject would you prefer that I speak? Would you like to have me speak on some phase of the race question, or give you a reading from some of my books?

Kindly advise me what you decide in the matter. Any letter that you write me will be forwarded to me, and I will answer it as promptly as I receive it.[1]

With thanks for the kind words contained in your letter, and a high appreciation of the wish on the part of yourself and the Christian Culture Congress to hear me speak, I remain,

Cordially yours,

TCU: TNF

[1] A reply from Nash has not been located; whether Chesnutt spoke before the C.C.C. is not known.

Doubleday, Page & Co.

◦⌣◦

August 16, 1905

Dear Sirs:—

Mr. H. French Tyson, a young relative of mine, and a student of Harvard, wishes to take some orders among the colored people (mainly) of Washington, D.C., where he lives, for my forthcoming book, *The Colonel's Dream,* for delivery upon publication. I have heretofore had an arrangement with Houghton, Mifflin & Co. to furnish him the books on my account, at the author's rate, or as good a rate as they would allow.[1] He has been successful in selling several hundred of my former books, and reaches some people whom ordinary advertising would not reach. If this idea appeals to you, kindly send him a copy of the book, so that he may have a sample, and charge same to me.[2] His address is

H. French Tyson,
2124 K. St., N.W.,
Washington, D.C.

Yours very truly,

TCU: TNF

[1] See 24 November 1899 to Houghton, Mifflin and 2 June 1900 to Garrison, n. 1.
[2] Doubleday, Page accepted Chesnutt's proposal.

Houghton, Mifflin & Co.

⟨⟩

September 5, 1905.

Dear Sirs:—

I beg to acknowledge receipt of your statement of August 31st, of our account for royalties, and of the accompanying check for $6.22 to cover balance due me. I trust the appearance of my forthcoming book may stimulate somewhat the sale of those upon your list.

Very truly yours,
Chas. W. Chesnutt.

TLS: MH

John S. Durham

⟨⟩

September 5, 1905.

My dear Mr. Durham:—

Your letter in reply to mine came to hand while I was away upon my vacation, and I hasten to acknowledge it.[1]

I thank you very much for the suggestions contained in it.[2] They are valuable, and my son wishes me to say that he will bear them carefully in mind in considering the question of a possible future in the Latin countries. If he decides to come down that way, both he and I will write to you more fully later on. I thank you very much for your friendly interest, and shall not hesitate to take advantage of it if events take that turn.

I am bringing out a new book this fall, *The Colonel's Dream*, a study of Southern conditions in the form of a novel, which will appear from the press of Doubleday, Page and Company. They think well of it and I trust the reading public may be similarly disposed. I haven't seen anything of late from your pen;[3] doubtless many of your best thoughts are embalmed in department reports. I should like to know when you do anything in the literary way. Thanking you again for your kindly interest in my son's future, I remain

Sincerely yours,

TCU: TNF

[1] Durham was a Philadelphia attorney whose surviving correspondence with Chesnutt dates back to 1898. His letters repeatedly express admiration for Chesnutt's fiction; he, too, had literary ambitions and often reported on his progress as an aspiring novelist.

[2] On 12 August 1905, Durham was in Cuba, employed by the Francisco Sugar Company. He then responded to Chesnutt's request for advice regarding the placement of his son Edwin in a suitable occupation in South America. Durham suggested that it was essential that Edwin obtain special training in some specific field of endeavor.

[3] Chesnutt is referring to Durham's "Diane: Priestess of Haiti," *Lippincott's* 69 (April 1902), 387–466, the manuscript of which he read and commented upon in 1902; he may also have had in mind "The Labor Unions and the Negro," *Atlantic Monthly* 81 (February 1898), 222–31.

Doubleday, Page & Co.

∽

September 6, 1905.

Dear Sirs:—

When last in New York I called Mr. Marcosson's attention to several typographical errors which escaped both your office proof-reader and myself, in *The Colonel's Dream.*[1] And they pile up so in the first few pages that you will pardon my calling attention to them.

The misspelling of my name on the cover I have already written you about and you have already answered that the dies would be changed and the name spelled correctly upon the cover of all copies except the first small number bound up before the error was noticed.[2]

In the list of "Other books by Charles W. Chesnutt," facing the title page, the name "Douglas" should be "Douglass," doubling the final "s."

In the list of characters, following the table of contents, the name "Miss Clara Treadwell" should be "Miss Laura Treadwell."

On page 254, first two lines, the name "Treadway," which occurs in each line, should be "Treadwell."

There are several minor points like quotations, commas, etc., to which I might call attention, but they do not seem important. Those to which I have called attention are, especially the first three, bunched in such a way as to attract attention, and I trust they will be corrected as early in the publication of the book as the conditions of publication will permit.[3]

Yours very truly,

TCU: TNF

[1] Chesnutt very likely visited New York City in the early summer, circa 25 June, when he was in the Boston area (see 10 April 1905 to Sampson, n. 2). *Dream* was first printed in mid to late June.

[2] A sample of the stamped casing or bound volume was sent to Chesnutt, who discovered that his name had been misspelled on the stamped case. On 5 July, S. A. Everett replied to Chesnutt's letter of 2 July: "Not a great number of the books have been bound. We have already put in hand the correction of the cover dies."

[3] Corrections were made in the plates before the second 1905 printing of *The Colonel's Dream,* a copy of which is in the Charles L. Blockson Collection, Temple University. No copy with Chesnutt's name misspelled on the front cover has been located.

Mr. Isaac F. Marcosson

و‌ه

September 16, 1905.

My dear Mr. Marcosson:—

Your letter enclosing cartoon of "The Colonel's Dream" to hand.[1] It is a clever conceit. I trust the colonel's dream of peace between the czar and mikado may be permanently realized, although it looked a little dubious for a time there.

I am not able to tell you much about the book yet, but as soon as I get hold of anything that will be useful I shall let you know.[2] It is in bookstores here now.

Sincerely yours,

TCU: TNF

[1] The pen-and-ink drawing pictures a man in bed, dreaming. The caption, "The Colonel's Dream," refers to the dream image rendered above the sleeping man's head: figures identified as the Czar and the Mikado are greeted by a man standing before a "Presidential Chair." The allusion is to Theodore Roosevelt, who facilitated the Treaty of Portsmouth and the conclusion of the Russo-Japanese War (1904–1905).

[2] On 12 September, Marcosson requested "anything publishable about the book" that might be used in the advertising campaign. Although *Dream* was printed in June and deposited for copyright at the Library of Congress on 22 July 1905, Lanier's letter of 8 September indicates that it was not published until 9 September.

Shelby J. Davidson

و‌ه

September 18, 1905.

Dear Sir:—

Replying to your letter of September 3rd, I was under the impression that I had answered your letter of August 5th in reference to my appearance in the Bethel Literary and Historical lecture course during the season, to the effect that I was not at present certain whether or not I should be in Washington during the winter.[1] I have business engagements which make it difficult for me to fix dates a long time in advance, without the chance of incurring some considerable loss thereby, and as I do not understand that the society pays anything more than traveling expenses, I would hardly be justified in making any great sacrifice. If I find that I am coming in that direction at any time and can let you know in advance, I will advise you and if you still wish to hear me, will be at your service. But at this writing I cannot conveniently set any definite date when I could appear, on the terms above suggested.

With reference to Judge Tourgée, I knew him personally, have visited at his home and have held him in high esteem for the zeal and perseverance with which he labored in the interests of our race.[2] It would be a pleasure to speak in his praise if I could conveniently do so.

Yours very truly,

TCU: TNF

[1] Shelby J. Davidson was the president of the Bethel Literary and Historical Association in 1905. On 5 August he invited Chesnutt to give an address during the 1905–1906 season which would begin in October. On 3 September he asked Chesnutt if he would like to eulogize Albion W. Tourgée.

[2] When Chesnutt visited Tourgée's home in Mayville, N.Y., is moot. Mayville, located immediately to the east of the Ohio border, was not distant from Cleveland; and Chesnutt may have first visited him when he took a vacation, alone, in nearby Chautauqua during the summer of 1891. On 14 November 1905, a memorial service for Tourgée, who had died in France, was held in Mayville, and Chesnutt was present to deliver a testimonial.

Jerome B. Howard

◦◡◦

September 18, 1905.

My dear Howard:—

I want to thank you for your cordial and appreciative letter in reference to my new book.[1] That which for the colonel was a dream will in the hands of others or a succession of others more patient, become a reality, I trust. I have faith in humanity, and if that faith is justifiable, the problems involved in the Southern situation will in time be worked out in a manner for the best happiness of all concerned.

Faithfully yours,

TCU: TNF

[1] Howard was associated with the Phonographic Institute in Cincinnati, O. Benn Pitman and he were the authors of *The Phonographic Dictionary and Phrase Book* (Cincinnati: The Phonographic Institute Company, 1901), an inscribed copy of which is among the books owned by Chesnutt.

William Hayes Ward

◦◡◦

September 18, 1905.

My dear Mr. Ward:—

I am glad that my novel was sufficiently interesting to hold your attention until you had finished it, and that you found something to commend.[1] I shall consider it a feather in my cap to have broken your non-novel reading habit.

I appreciate your good opinion all the more highly from the fact that I know you approach these subjects with which my novel deals as nearly without prejudice as it is possible for any of us to do in the environment in which we live.
Sincerely and cordially yours,

TCU: TNF

[1] See 31 October 1903 to Washington, n. 6. In that letter Chesnutt praises *Independent* editor William Hayes Ward as a progressive thinker on the subject of voting rights for African Americans, noting that Ward too disagrees with Washington's emphasis on economic improvement at the expense of political equality. Ward's letter, which apparently offered a positive comment on *Dream,* has not been located. Given the denunciation of *Marrow* that appeared in *Independent* (see 20 March 1902 to Mifflin, n. 3), Chesnutt probably expected that Ward would make amends in a forthcoming review of *Dream;* but the review was not only brief but tepid: "This is a Southern story, but not of the Before-the-War type. It is frankly up to the times, with the clash of races and the convict camp, and the decayed old gentry. The Colonel of the Confederate army, hardly yet a man, goes to New York, gets wealth, returns to live in his native village, and tries to put in practice some of his acquired Northern ideas of thrift and fair treatment of all. He finds helpers; there is a love romance; but he fails, and, amid comedy and tragedy, turns his back on his disappointment and his parental home. The style is easy, apparently practiced, and the story does not lack for abundant incident, in which the relations of the races have full expression" ("Literature" 59 [5 October 1905], 816).

Alice E. Hanscom

September 22, 1905.

My dear Miss Hanscom:—

Thanks for your kind letter of September 20th, and especially for the appreciative insight into my motives.[1] I have already heard many good words concerning *The Colonel's Dream,* and I hope it may commend itself to a wide circle of readers—for the sake of the cause as well as for my own sake. I shall be glad to see a copy of your review.[2]

I have been well since I saw you last, and my pen would have been heard from sooner had I not been profitably employed with other matters. I hope with *The Colonel's Dream* to enter upon a period of somewhat fuller literary productiveness.
Cordially yours,

TCU: TNF

[1] Alice E. Hanscom was editor of "The Reading Circle" column in the *Union Gospel News,* published in Cleveland; an admirer of Chesnutt, she was also a book reviewer for *Self Culture* in 1900 and was undoubtedly instrumental in facilitating its serialization of *The House Behind the Cedars;* see 2 June 1900 to Garrison, n. 2. In her letter of 20 September 1905 she wrote that she had received a review copy of *The Colonel's Dream* and had just "finished a notice of it." "I am glad that you are keeping at it,—keeping alive the light by which men may discern the conditions they have inherited and the responsibility resting upon themselves to better those conditions. I don't quite see

how you can so successfully keep the impartial, unimpassioned tone, though I realize the wisdom and the finer literary art in doing so."

[2] Hanscom's review appeared in "The Reading Circle," *Union Gospel News*, in October or November 1905. While the issue in question is not extant, a clipping of Hanscom's positive evaluation of *Dream* is in one of the Chesnutt scrapbooks. It concludes: "With [a] characteristic sense of justice, the author shows the humorous frailties, the more serious mistakes, and the positive wrongdoing of the white and colored townsmen alike. Faith hope, and love weave their brightness among the saddening influences of failure, disappointment, and heartache. Mr. Chestnutt [sic] has the courage of the conviction that, 'slowly, like all great social changes, but visibly, to the eye of faith, is growing up a new body of thought, favourable to just laws and their orderly administration.' Like the leading character of his own story he, too, has a dream, a vision of the time when 'Justice, the seed, and Peace, the flower, of liberty' shall everywhere be found throughout our borders."

Isaac F. Marcosson

September 27, 1905.

My dear Mr. Marcosson:—

Agreeably to your request of recent date, I send you some flashlight pictures of myself at my home. They are not as good as might be, but perhaps out of them you may find one which the *Saturday Evening Post* can use. I think a good picture can be cut out of almost any of them.

In the standing pose the outline of my face came right up against a bust standing on top of the bookcase, and the line of the bust followed my nose, exaggerating it somewhat grotesquely. It has been retouched to about its normal shape, as may be perceived by comparing it with the seated figure. If you cannot use one of these I will make another drive at a better one.

I have had several good reviews of the new book, which I presume you have also seen. They tell me it is selling in the bookstores. Mr. Kauffman of the *Saturday Evening Post* has requested me to send him any gossip or anecdotal matter that I like about myself, for use in the new department of literary gossip. I shall be glad to comply with his request.[1]

Yours very truly,

TCU: TNF

[1] Neither a photograph of Chesnutt nor the information Chesnutt sent Kauffman appeared in the *Post*.

Isaac F. Marcosson

᳐

October 14, 1905

My dear Mr. Marcosson:—

Is *The Colonel's Dream* catching on at all? I presume I have seen most of the reviews, or at least a number of them which have come under your notice, but of course I do not know as well as you what value attaches to those things. I have not seen the book advertised anywhere, except about half an inch in the last number of the *World's Work*, and I fear that a number of my friends around Cleveland have not yet been advised of the fact that I have published a new book.[1] I am willing to co-operate in any way in bringing the book to the attention of the public. All personal expressions of opinion I have had concerning it have been complimentary. A curious but interesting fact is that perhaps the most appreciative reviews have come from the South. They disagree with my conclusions, they deprecate the publication of the book, but they treat it with respect and do not deny its correctness as a picture of widespread conditions. That the conditions are widespread is indicated by the fact that the story has been variously located in the Carolinas, Georgia and in Alabama.

Yours very truly,

TCU: TNF

[1] As he did with Houghton, Mifflin, Chesnutt once again becomes assertive in regard to the need for aggressive advertising. Marcosson replied on 16 October that the "book has been advertised more than you happen to have seen. Be assured that we are leaving nothing undone to give it publicity." He also noted that *Dream* "is moving slowly, but it is showing more life in Boston than any other place. A re-order from there came in today."

Mrs. W. B. Henderson

᳐

Nov. 11, 1905.

My dear Mrs. Henderson:

I am in receipt of your letter of Nov. 6th, and am pleased to hear from a member of your family.[1] Your daughter pays me quite a compliment in selecting *The Marrow of Tradition* as a theme for her essay.

The book was suggested by the Wilmington riot, with the date and details of which you are more familiar than I am, since it was the occasion of your husband's leaving the South.

I am unable to retrace the process by which the book grew. It was suggested by a vivid description given me by Dr. Mask, during a visit of his to Cleveland, of the events of the riot, and a ride which he took across the city during its progress.[2] The personal element of the story is what the most of any novel must be—the fruit of my own imagination.

The book was written, as all my books have been, with a purpose—the hope that it might create sympathy for the colored people of the South in the very difficult position which they occupy. With the events of my life and their presumable relation to the book, your husband is undoubtedly familiar. I share the blood of the race; I lived in North Carolina from the age of 9 to that of 25; I taught school there for ten years; 3 of my children were born there, and many of my relations, including some of the nearest and dearest, are living there still. I could never be so placed in life that I should not have an abiding interest in the welfare of our people in the South.

The book was received by the public with respect, but not with any great enthusiasm. By the public I mean the great reading public whose opinion is reflected by the newspapers and magazines which reflect public opinion. It had a fair sale, but was criticized as being bitter. I did not intend it to be so. Nor do I think it was.[3] I would suggest to Miss Henderson, in her review of the book, that she eliminate anything that savors of rancor or bitterness. I have found by experience, that in writing on this subject, an attitude of fairness and impartiality is more likely to command attention than the partisan and personal view which it is so difficult to keep from taking.

Kindly give my regards to Mr. Henderson, and to your daughter, and believe me,
$\qquad$ Sincerely yours,

TCU: TNF

[1] The national network of relationships with African Americans that Chesnutt maintained, evidenced repeatedly in his correspondence, is nicely illustrated here. G. W. Henderson was the pastor of Straight University Church in New Orleans, and his surviving correspondence with Chesnutt dates from 28 February 1899, though it is obvious from that letter that they had long known each other—this suggesting that Henderson was originally from North Carolina. Another probable member of this same family (by marriage) is the recipient of the present letter, whose husband, attorney W. B. Henderson, was elected to the North Carolina Senate in 1896; he left Wilmington after the 1898 race riot, as Chesnutt notes below, and is referred to by Chesnutt as one familiar with his personal history. (Indeed, in an exchange of business letters in October 1916, it turns out that Henderson knew the "Frenchy" Tyson who distributed Chesnutt's books in the District of Columbia and was "an old acquaintance" of Chesnutt's wife.) Mrs. Henderson explained on 6 November 1905 that her daughter, Rose Agnes, was a high-school senior and had "chosen as her theme a review" of *Marrow*. Chesnutt's kindly reply answers the questions that she posed for her daughter.

[2] Dr. T. R. Mask was a Wilmington physician and a member of the African-American group to which a "Declaration of White Independence" was presented on 8 November 1898. It stated that whites should be given many of the jobs presently enjoyed by blacks; that the newspaper *The Record* must cease publication; that its printing press must be shipped from the city; and that its editor, Alex Manly, has to leave the city, forever. When Mask's and the others' response was not received by the deadline specified, Alfred M. Waddell led a crowd of whites to Manly's office. The building was burned as the riot began on the morning of 10 November.

[3] Chesnutt refers to Howells' review; see 30 December 1901 to Houghton, Mifflin, n. 6.

Houghton, Mifflin & Co.

◅◦▻

November 17, 1905.

Dear Sirs:—

I have been approached by the representative of a little magazine published in Indianapolis, which you probably never see or hear of, with reference to the publication in its columns, in serial form, of my novel, *The House Behind the Cedars*. There is no glory in it, and I imagine very little money, but of course I could not make any arrangement without consulting you. It may, however, help to bring my books to the attention of a class of readers who might be stimulated to buy some of them. Kindly let me know what your attitude will be in respect to such a proposition, after which I will be in position to make up my own mind about it.[1] Yours very truly,

TCU: TNF

[1] On 21 November, permission to reprint the novel serially in *The National Domestic* was granted, provided that the proper credit be given Houghton, Mifflin. Chesnutt wrote its editor, John L. Todd, on 1 December, to confirm "our conversation of Saturday," the terms being $60.00 in cash and $40.00 worth of advertisements. The issues of the magazine containing the serialization are not extant.

Richard R. Wright, Jr.

◅◦▻

December 11, 1905.

My dear Mr. Wright:—

Upon returning to the city after a week's absence, I find your letter of December 5th, which I hasten to acknowledge.[1]

The matter of the establishment of a center for social betterment, among the colored people here, is as yet somewhat in the air; but while no definite plans have been devised, there have come such offers of aid and comfort as to lead me to think that the matter may be taken up very soon and an effort made to get such an enterprise on foot.[2]

I am not altogether a stranger to your work and your accomplishments, and so far as my present information goes you would be just the sort of man needed to get such a work on foot. As soon as I can write you anything more definite, one way or the other, I shall be glad to do so. If you should make any change of address before you hear from me, I shall be obliged if you will let me know. Sincerely yours,

TCU: TNF

[1] Richard Robert Wright, Jr. (1878–1967) was a social worker and sociologist who would receive a Ph.D. from the University of Pennsylvania in 1911; the A.M.E. Book Concern published his

dissertation, *The Negro in Philadelphia*, in 1912. On 5 December, Wright related, "It has just come to me that you are interested in the establishment of a center for social betterment among the colored people of Cleveland." He offered his services in the organization and supervision of such a center. He then listed his credentials as the recipient of two degrees from the University of Chicago, as having been involved with several social-betterment movements in Chicago, and as a published writer on sociological topics now working on an "investigation of 'Negro Immigration to the North,' for the University of Pennsylvania." In his current position, he had "charge of the men's work at the 8th Ward Settlement" in Philadelphia. He referred Chesnutt to his "study of 'The Negroes of Xenia, Ohio' in the *U.S. Bulletin of Labor*, Sept. 1903."

[2] Chesnutt appears to have come to Wright's attention because of "Advocates New Social House," *Cleveland Journal* 3 (2 December 1905), 1, in which Chesnutt's remarks on the desirability of a settlement house for African Americans in Cleveland were reported. Chesnutt made no specific proposals for immediate implementation of his idea; he merely suggested that such a center on Central Avenue would be a very worthwhile project.

Walter Hines Page

༚

December 11, 1905.

My dear Mr. Page:—

I have your note of December 8th. I should have been glad to see you, but I did not get the word that I was to come in after leaving Marcosson; and I knew you were a busy man, and as I had really nothing of very great importance to say, I did not disturb you.[1] I assure you, however, that the loss was mine.

I enjoyed the Mark Twain dinner very much.[2] It was a great occasion and very inspiring—well worth the trip to New York and something to be long remembered. I spent the week in New York very pleasantly, not the least pleasant feature being the rather long interview which I did have with you.[3]

Sincerely yours,

TCU: TNF

[1] Chesnutt was in New York City on 7 December when he spoke with Marcosson. Page wrote on 8 December, expressing his regret that he was busy with "an insistent poet" and that Chesnutt did not wait to see him.

[2] On 5 December 1905 at the fashionable Delmonico's restaurant in New York City, a large throng of the American literati—including Chesnutt's one-time admirer William Dean Howells, one-time mentor George Washington Cable, and one-time nemesis Richard Watson Gilder—assembled to honor Mark Twain on his seventieth birthday. Chesnutt was the only African-American writer present. He was not one of those who delivered testimonials.

[3] Although Chesnutt met with him in New York, Page was not among the guests at the Twain fête listed in "Mark Twain's 70th Birthday," *Harper's Weekly* 49 (23 December 1905), 1884–1914.

INDEX

✧